JEAN A. PERKINS

THE CONCEPT OF
THE SELF IN THE FRENCH
ENLIGHTENMENT

GENÈVE
LIBRAIRIE DROZ
11, RUE MASSOT
—
1969

TO MY HUSBAND
Edward B. Perkins

ACKNOWLEDGMENTS

I would like to express my gratitude to three of my mentors, Edith Philips, Norman L. Torrey and Otis Fellows. These are the people who introduced me to the fascination of the eighteenth century and who encouraged me as to the feasibility of the current work. Edith Philips has been especially helpful, reading the manuscript before it went to the publisher and making many valuable suggestions.

I am also grateful to Swarthmore College, which granted me a leave of absence during which the bulk of the research and writing was done, and to the Old Dominion Foundation, whose generous grant to Swarthmore College made funds available for a trip to Paris and Geneva.

CONTENTS

Chapter I   Philosophical Concepts and Definitions   1

Chapter II   The Philosophical Background of Eighteenth Century
        Thought   11

        Aristotelian-Thomistic System   11
        Descartes and Cartesianism   12
        Malebranche and Occasionalism   16
        Leibniz   19
        Spinoza   22
        Locke   23
        Berkeley   27
        Hume   31
        Conclusion   37

Chapter III   The Eighteenth Century Concept of the Self   39

        Introduction   39
        Means of knowing the self   42
        The Nature of the self   59
        How the concept was used   69
        Self-concept   75

Chapter IV   Rousseau   85

        Dualism   85
        Savage and child   91
        Self-concept   97
        Le Sentiment de l'existence   106

Chapter V   Diderot   117

        The Developing Self   117
        Esthetics and Ethics   131
        Self-concept   136

Conclusion   145

Chapter I

PHILOSOPHICAL CONCEPTS AND DEFINITIONS

The concept of the self has been termed one of the persistent problems in philosophy[1]. Some of its complexity stems from the fact that it is an integral part of the whole mind-body problem, which embraces a major share of both metaphysics and epistemology. All sorts of interpretations of the self have been offered over the ages, each one of them dependent upon underlying assumptions, acknowledged or not, concerning the whole structure of the universe. Non-philosophers tend to think of the self as a separable and isolated problem, but in looking at these concepts carefully one can discern how they are dependent for their structure upon other beliefs.

A further element of confusion is introduced by the question of vocabulary. What do we actually mean in using such words as *the self, the ego, le moi, le soi, le je?* It is remarkable how much variation one can find in the use of these terms. Philosophers do not use them consistently, and when the psychologists are included, the problem is multiplied a hundred-fold. Of course we are dealing primarily with eighteenth century French concepts, but it is still worth-while to look closely at modern terminology before trying to untangle the question of eighteenth century usage.

A major source of confusion in terminology arises because of the basically ambiguous nature of the concept itself. When an individual speaks of his " self, " he may be referring to one of two separable ideas : either he is speaking of himself as an active agent or doer, or he is referring to his own attitude about himself, his self-concept. It has now become fairly standard in English psychological terminology to use the word *ego* to refer to the " group of psychological processes which govern behavior and adjustment, " and the word *self* to denote " what a person thinks of himself[2]. " Obviously the ego is conceived as an active, dynamic subject, whereas the self is viewed as an object in very much the same way as any other object, be it a thing or another person. However it is important to note, as do Hall and Lindzey, that " no modern theory holds that there is a psychic agent or ' inner manikin ' which regulates man's actions[3]. " Fortunately modern French psychological terminology is rather close to that of English : *le moi* is the generic term which includes within it the two meanings of *le je,* defined by Nuttin as " sujet ou agent de l'activité psychique " and *le soi* as " objet de connaissance ou de conscience[4] ".

Unfortunately, neither in English nor French are these distinctions made consistently even by psychologists, and when we turn to philosophy the neat pattern of self-as-process (ego) and self-as-object (self-concept) is completely obliterated. Since Gilbert Ryle's devastating attack on *The Concept of Mind* (1949), even the word *self* seems to have gone out of fashion among modern philosophers ; those few hardy souls who dare to enter this disreputable field use other more neutral terms such as *persons* or *individuals.* Of course the word *soul* has been out of favor with all but theologians for at least a century ; even Reinhold Niebuhr tends to avoid it in his *The Self and the Dramas of History.*

If we turn to Lalande's standard *Vocabulaire technique et critique de la philosophie* (7th ed., 1956), under the entry *Moi* we find three types of references : the psychological, the ontological, and the logical. The psychological meaning conforms to the self-concept as defined above, the ontological meaning confirms to the self-as-agent but includes the further particular of the self as a substance, whereas the logical meaning is one which is not used by psychologists. In the logical sense of the term, the *moi* is defined as follows : " Sujet pensant, en tant que son unité et son identité sont les conditions nécessaires, impliquées par la synthèse du divers donné dans l'intuition et par la liaison des représentations dans une conscience ". This is, of course, the transcendental subject, that which determines all our knowledge but which does not form part of that knowledge. It stands outside the limits of what we can conceive and yet is in itself the very limit of our conceptions. In some ways this meaning overlaps the ontological one, but neither one of them is sufficient unto itself. It is interesting to note also that Lalande uses quotations from Condillac to illustrate the psychological and ontological meanings of *moi,* and turns to Kant and Fichte for examples of *le moi transcendental.*

Littré's definition of *moi* as a philosophical term tends to combine all the various distinctions which we have been making : " Le moi, la personne humaine en tant qu'elle a conscience d'elle-même, et qu'elle est à la fois le sujet et l'objet de la pensée ". The examples given are from Pascal, Boulainvilliers, Buffon, and Bonnet : Pascal identifies *le moi* with " ma pensée " in an orthodox Cartesian way ; Boulainvilliers calls it " une substance unique, simple et absolument indivisible ", also a Cartesian concept ; Buffon refers to " la conscience de son existence " which includes both the present and the past ; Bonnet's definition is very much the same as Buffon's. In the latter two cases we see a shifting from the definition of *le moi* as an object, exposed to scrutiny, to a concept of the self as the subject of experience. But many *philosophes* did not make this distinction and tended to use the same term to refer to both concepts. As we shall see, there was a basic ambiguity in the philosophical approach of most of these writers, based primarily on their total confusion of the psychological or genetic with the logical approach. Both of these approaches were used to arrive at ontological positions despite the aspersions cast upon the makers of metaphysical systems.

The 1778 edition of the *Dictionnaire de l'Académie française* gives no definition of *je, moi* or *soi* which interests us. They are referred to simply as pronouns of the first and third person and the examples given serve to illustrate their grammatical distinctions. This should not surprise us since this work was primarily devoted to grammatical usage. The *Encyclopédie* also avoids these particular terms but discusses the concepts involved in various articles, notably in Turgot's " Existence " and in the unsigned " Identité " and " Individu ".

At least the eighteenth century writers in using these terms expected to be understood without the necessity of going into great detail, but this certainly no longer seems to be the case. So much analysis has been done in this and related areas that each author finds it necessary to define his own usage. In some ways this is confusing, but the process has uncovered a large number of very necessary distinctions which were not made by the *philosophes.*

The first distinction of real importance lies in the fact that when you describe the means of knowing the self you are not necessarily describing its nature or its status in the universe or even in the overall scheme of knowledge. Modern philosophical discourse is extremely careful not to confuse epistemological, ontological, and logical statements ; thus, after remarking that " before being able to have a personal relation to other human beings, I myself must first exist as an embodied person, " Strasser adds the following note : " Obviously, this ' before ' must not be taken in a genetico-psychological sense, but ontologically[5] ". A completely different set of priorities must be evoked in considering the method by which one reaches such decisions and the logical structure of the propositions which constitute them. The two series may at times overlap, but this is not always the case. Modern philosophy tends to speak in logical terms whereas the *philosophes,* following in the empirical tradition of Locke, put much more emphasis on the psychological genesis of ideas and assumed that this formed a logical sequence.

With a slightly different emphasis, the same distinction may be said to have existed between the *philosophes* and the Christian apologists of the eighteenth century. The latter, although certainly not a great deal more logical than their opponents, were working within the rational tradition which considered the soul to be an ontological entity in no way affected by its experiences in this life. As Robert Palmer has so succinctly noted :

The soul is the individual considered as pointed toward ends, not as arising from causes ; it is thus not developed during life, but exists entire from the moment of conception ... These ends toward which it is pointed are held to exist outside of time ... The empirical philosophy, of course, knew nothing of destiny or eternity, absolute values or goals not created by life itself ... Explaining the mind by sensation and experience, they wound up by identifying the soul with personality or consciousness[6].

Is it any wonder that these two groups had such difficulty convincing each other of their respective positions ? In any case, the empirical approach came to be more and more accepted as the only possible one to follow in the study of man, and this led to still further emphasis upon the origins and background of the self.

Even the psychological-genetic approach has been considerably sharpened by modern analysis. It is here that philosophy and psychology are still related, although in most other areas of inquiry they are poles apart. We need not go into the whole theory of perception, since we are only concerned with that area which concentrates on the inner being. If the self is considered as an object, it is assessed by the same set of criteria by which any other object is judged, and these are for the most part empirical and objectively determined. Your self-concept can be checked against what other people think of you, and against your behavior in response to certain stimuli. However, if the question is not so much *what* you think of yourself but *how* you think of yourself, the empirical psychologists tend to turn their back on the problem and go on treating the self-concept as if it were an object of knowledge just like any other piece of information. The Logical Positivists are not quite that cavalier, but they dismiss the evidence since it is self-defeating and not subject to proof.

The so-called " privileged access " theory of knowledge about the self has suffered badly in these analyses. The notion that the mind is constantly aware of what is going on within it (consciousness), and that it has in addition a type of perception about its own operations which it can use if it so pleases (introspection), does not stand up under the attacks of Wittgenstein and his school. In the first place it leads to an entirely solipsistic system, especially since there is no way of finding out what, if anything, is taking place within the minds of other people. Bergson is the best known of the modern philosophers to make an immediate and intuitive knowledge of the existence of the self the foundation of a system. But he tends to beg the question by assuming that everyone has the same intuitive reaction that he does, and what can one do in the face of the fact that other, equally perspicacious, philosophers have denied experiencing anything of the sort ? According to the Positivists, therefore, Bergson's system is good only for Bergson and as such cannot be given serious attention by the rest of mankind. A philosophical theory must have some relevance to knowledge in general and not just to a particular individual.

However, solipsism is not the only fault of the " privileged access " theory, although it certainly is the most damning. Introspection is supposed to give a superior quality of knowledge, one which is not subject to " illusion, confusion or doubt[7] ". If the person involved does not want to fall back on solipsism, how can he prove that this is so ? Obviously his only means of proof lies in the application of objective criteria, those criteria which govern our judgments of the rest of knowledge. There is no way of knowing whether the sensation a particular individual identifies as " pain " corresponds to the concept of " pain " in general except by observing his reactions and comparing his behavior with that of others in similar situations. Thus the private field of knowledge must become public in the end.

Wittgenstein himself pursued this line of investigation to show that the " privileged access " theory is self-destructive. As summarized by Malcolm, the argument runs as follows :

> one supposes that one inwardly picks out something as thinking or pain and thereafter identifies it whenever it presents itself in the soul. But the question to be pressed is, Does one make *correct* identifications ? The proponent of the " private " identifications has nothing to say here. He feels sure that he identifies correctly the occurrences in his soul ; but feeling sure is no guarantee of being right. Indeed he has no idea of what being *right* could mean. He does not know how to distinguish between actually making correct identifications and being under the impression that he does ... When we see that the ideas of correct and incorrect have no application to the supposed inner identification, the latter notion loses its appearance of sense. Its collapse brings down both solipsism and the argument from analogy[8].

All these objections rely on the criteria which must eventually be used in order to prove the truth about these statements based on some inner mode of perception.

Other objections have been raised, however, which strike at the operation itself rather than its results. Introspection involves a stepping aside in order to view one's own thoughts, feelings, and emotions ; each mental event can therefore be submitted to the scrutiny of an inner observer. This means that two things are going on in the mind at the same time, the mental event itself and the observation of this event. Eighteenth century psychologists objected to this idea, but modern criticism is directed, not so much at the synchronous aspects of introspection, but rather at the assumption that all mental events can be made subject to such an observation. Hume objected that there are some mental states which cannot be observed since the emotional state of the subject makes it impossible for him to step aside and observe himself during these periods. Another objection, raised by Ryle, is that there must be some mental processes which are unintrospectible since " there is some limit to the number of possible synchronous acts of attention[9] ". We are always left with an observer who needs to be observed if the theory of introspective knowledge is followed to its logical conclusions.

It is quite obvious that these objections will not satisfy a whole series of modern schools of philosophy, and in particular the phenomenological and existential groups. These thinkers claim that the critics of the introspective approach are asking the wrong questions ; for instance Strasser puts Ryle with the empirical psychologists and points to the fact that " what interests the psychologist evidently is not the contents of consciousness as such nor the psyche as such, but the course of a definite process of becoming conscious[10] ". According to Strasser we should pay more attention to what we do know rather than concentrating on how we come to know it and how we can prove that what we know is correct.

It is also pointed out that the objective method is totally inappropriate in this area, since what distinguishes the self from the rest of the universe is precisely its subjectivity. This argument leaves these critics in somewhat of a dilemma, since they insist that the analytic method can never lead to real self-knowledge and yet they are perforce bound to that same method in their own discussions. It may be the influence of Bergson which makes this particular approach more noticeable in French than in English philosophical argumentation today. An extreme form of this objection occurs in an otherwise useful work by Georges Gusdorf :

Ainsi la structure même de la conscience humaine empêche une analyse ... de jamais aboutir. L'analyse fausse la vie personnelle en l'objectivant ... elle dénature intrinsèquement ce qu'elle exprime ... En me racontant, je me mets devant les autres, je fais de moi-même un objet pour les autres et pour moi-même, je me mets sous le regard de tous, je me transforme en problème. Alors que je suis d'abord, et de moi à moi, un mystère[11].

Unfortunately a mystery is not normally accessible to analysis in any form, nor is it particularly appropriate to expression in ordinary language. This is where the element of literary ability comes in ; what cannot be explained may very well be expressed by a real master of prose such as Rousseau.

Another approach involves the identification of what are termed " primitive concepts, " concepts which are so closely embedded in our conceptual scheme as to be essentially unanalyzable. The self is said to be one of these concepts, a fundamental mental set, so to speak, which determines our outlook and knowledge. However just what constitutes the self is still a matter of debate. A modern Cartesian has revived the notion that the self is essentially a nonphysical entity which can be considered as distinct from its accompanying body[12]. On the other hand, Strawson considers a " person " to be the combination of mind and body, or rather of physical and mental aspects, since he does not accept Cartesian dualism, preferring to hold to a rather vague monism. But it really does not help very much to announce that a person is a combination of these two " aspects " if one then refuses to consider what they may be aspects of.

This leads us into another area of distinction which is now clear and distinct and which was anything but that in the eighteenth century : the twofold nature of the theory of substance. The most prevalent opinion of that time was that substance was to be defined as *substans accidentibus,* that in which accidents inhere. As we shall see, this was the definition which was attacked first of all by Locke and then by Berkeley and Hume. The other definition, *res per se subsistens,* which had played such a large part in the Cartesian metaphysical system, was used by Spinoza as the foundation of what was almost universally thought to be an atheistic, if non-materialistic, system. Modern transcendentalism is founded on two principles which embody these two definitions. In describing his concept of the " besouled body " Strasser resorts to them explicitly :

My *whole* being has a dynamic character. As a self-subsistent being *and* as an accidental one I am constantly modified. But this cannot be explained through the principle of self-subsistency but only through the principle of accidentality.

My *whole* being has a character of permanence. As a self-subsistent being *and* as an accidental being I am always the same. But this cannot be explained through the principle of accidentality but only through the principle of self-subsistency[13].

The transcendental explanation of the self is thus an attempt to arrive at a different kind of " primitive concept ", one which is primitive in a logical rather than a psychological sense. Using Strasser as an example, we can see that his division of the self into three parts, the social ego, the personal ego, and what he terms the originating ego, is an attempt to go beyond the objective knowledge of the self which was the subject of Ryle's attack. The originating ego is not a substance which you " have " ; it is rather something which you " are ". But what you are is only revealed through what you have, and so the contents of consciousness are pluralistic, whereas consciousness itself is monistic. The only way that we can possibly describe it is in terms of direction, of what it is trying to accomplish through its various mental states. It is this principle which gives unity to our diverse reactions and which constitutes the only real self. This appears to be satisfactory until one realizes that what is really being posited here, and in all phenomenological and transcendental systems is not the self as a unitary being but rather as a guiding principle. The very personal feeling of self-identity is automatically eliminated as being totally illusory ; what really counts is the whole structure of the universe which has become extremely idealistic and at the same time impersonal. This is obvious in the following remarks of Strasser :

> But as a transcendental " I ", I am not a *solus ipse,* a solitary " I ", for I and other egos constitute a transcendental intersubjectivity. Insofar as " we ", as a transcendental community, constitute or coconstitute in our intentional acts the " world ", we take part in the transcendental life of a creative " world foundation [14] ".

This may prove to be extremely attractive to some highly cerebral persons, but for the most part people do not have this in mind when they speak about the self. The word carries a connotation of intense personal warmth, which is surely lacking in a definition which makes of the self no more than a logical necessity. The eighteenth century writers were particularly disturbed by the universalistic aspects of Spinoza's system, and no definition which left out of account the highly individualistic quality of the self was given serious attention.

It is clear that in all of these approaches we are facing a major dichotomy, the necessity of establishing a principle of unity while at the same time allowing for considerable personal diversity. The age-old dilemma between a static and a dynamic interpretation of phenomena is at play, leading to widely divergent systems according to which one of these characteristics is given the most weight. The only major modern psychologist who has given much attention to the problem of the self is Gordon Allport, and he states quite adamantly that man is " not a homeostatic creature. He does not seek equilibrium within himself and with the environment. His restlessness is systematic [15]. " This unsupported point of view enables him to work out his theory of the ego as a dynamically developing system of " propriate striving ". However even Allport finds this definition lacking when it comes to the question of personal identity, and he then falls back on what he calls the " proprium ", the nucleus of personality, which appears to be a more slowly evolving version of the ego. This obviously begs the philosophical question, since it leaves unanswered the problem of identity. What makes a continually changing structure belong to one person rather than to a series of persons ? All the Gestalt theories of personality suffer from the same defect, since the *gestalt* itself is subject to change.

Today theories of personal identity are often discussed with no reference to the concept of the self at all. And yet it is surely demonstrable that they are intimately related. If one holds to a materialistic interpretation of the world, including the self, then bodily identity is going to be the major clue to personal identity. If one is an idealist, then mental activities will be the fundamental experience. And if one wishes to separate the self from the material world, then the *sentiment de l'existence,* the inner perception of one's identity, may be the appropriate criterium.   The criteria used are determined by the assumptions underlying the investigation.   We will find that most eighteenth century thinkers fall into one of three very broad categories : the dualistic (mind and body) and the monistic, either in the form of idealism (mind only) or materialism (body only).   But these categories are so broad as to be almost useless in discussions of individual interpretations, since the combinations possible within these general areas are almost unlimited. Some materialists are dynamic and organic, seeing the self as an open-ended system impossible to describe until after it has ceased to exist, whereas others will adhere to a rigidly closed system very close to the idealistic concept of an unchanging being which merely suffers existential mutability without being affected in any way.   These various combinations should be easier to grasp if we first investigate the philosophical background of the century.

Chapter II

THE PHILOSOPHICAL BACKGROUND
OF EIGHTEENTH CENTURY THOUGHT

For our purposes, the history of philosophy might be said to start with the famous *Cogito* of Descartes. This dictum was at the base of the " deep subjectivism[1] " which affected all eighteenth century thought, and this new attitude towards man swept away the long-established Aristotelian-Thomistic theories. However, since Aristotelianism remained the official philosophy at the Sorbonne until the condemnation of the thesis of the abbé de Prades in 1752 and since the vocabulary used in this particular account of the universe is somewhat at odds with that of the *philosophes*, it is worth-while to review this world-view briefly.

Aristotelian-Thomistic System

According to the Thomistic account, the universe is made up of matter and form. Matter itself exists in a completely undifferentiated manner, and it is only when matter is united to form that it begins to take on the features of substance. As a principle of organization, form exists only in conjunction with matter, except in one major exception. This unique entity is of course the human soul, whose attachment to the human body is merely accidental and not essential, as, for instance, is the union of vegetative form with its appropriate matter to make up vegetable substances.

One of the things which Descartes was most proud of was that his doctrine of substance finally provided a firm foundation for the belief in the immortality of the soul. The Scholastics did not consider the soul to be a substance, any more than they considered the body to be one. Only the combination of the two resulted in something which was self-sufficient. This led to considerable doubt about the possibility of the survival of the soul after its division from the body. As Gilson clearly notes : " l'Ecole, au contraire, qui lie l'âme au corps comme une substance incomplète à une autre substance incomplète, ne permet pas de concevoir comment une partie qui ne se suffit pas à elle-même peut cependant subsister à part. La substantialité complète de l'âme étant établie pour la première fois par les *Méditations métaphysiques,* Descartes devait nécessairement penser que sa philosophie rendait pour la première fois légitime l'assertion de notre immortalité[2] ". The Thomistic dilemma of the immortality of the soul when divorced from the body was solved by the belief in the ultimate resurrection of the body, which would enable the individual person to be reconstituted for eternity. In the interim the disembodied soul existed only in an incomplete and unsubstantial way[3].

According to the Scholastics, the human soul alone is not a sufficient explanation of what constitutes the self. As long as a person is alive in this world, the soul is joined to a particular body, and the knowledge it has of the world is siphoned through the senses before becoming part of the baggage of the soul. The well-known statement *Nihil est in intellectu quod non prius fuerit in sensu* is a clear indication of the intimate conjunction of these two facets of a human being. But the means by which the mind acquires ideas through the senses corresponds neither to the Cartesian account of perception, according to which ideas are modifications of the mind and have no real relationship to exterior objects, nor to post-Lockean materialism, according to which sensations are recorded in a material mind as representative images of exterior objects. Knowledge of material things, according to the Thomistic view, involves a participation on the part of the knower in the essential form of the known. It is this form which is transmitted in a rather mysterious way through the senses to the intellect. In any case, the real moving force in the universe is not a substance but a principle[4].

Eighteenth century writers sometimes used the Scholastic terms, *âme raisonnable, âme végétative, forme substantielle,* etc., but they were certainly not using them in the way in which the Scholastics did. Cartesian physics with its division of the universe into two substances had so permeated French thinking that by this period no one seriously advocated a return to the Thomistic point of view. Forms which gave being to matter were no longer an acceptable explanation of phenomena. However, the picture is somewhat confused, because, when the church adopted Cartesian dualism as its official doctrine, the more anti-Christian writers turned back to the vocabulary of the Scholastics in order to fight the Church with what had been her own weapons. Thus the dictum *Nihil est in intellectu...,* in the hands of such outspoken materialists as La Mettrie and d'Holbach took on a meaning which it had never had in the old days.

Descartes and Cartesianism

It is a cliché to state that Descartes is the father of modern philosophy, but no matter what the area of concentration almost all current discussion harks back to his remarkable achievement in the field of both metaphysics and epistemology. We may assure ourselves that his world-view is no longer adequate, that his physics is completely out-of-date, and yet his analysis of the universe is still basic to our attitudes and beliefs. For instance, without Descartes the whole development of individualism would have been unthinkable ; it was he who placed the individual human being at the very center of the universe and at the same time radically divorced this same figure from the rest of the world. As Marcel Raymond notes : " avec Descartes et au temps de Descartes, le *sujet* se pose en sa solitude, et la subjectivité vient au monde. Du même coup, ce monde, en son ensemble et en chacune de ses parties, devient *objet*[5] ".

The fundamental dichotomy between the knower and the known is somewhat concealed in the statement *Je pense, donc je suis*. In fact it is possible to interpret this statement as implying a unity of these two aspects of knowledge, and Descartes would seem to have believed that the one automatically involved the other. In the *Méditations* he is careful to point out that the existence of the knowing subject is implied in the awareness of the known object : " *Je suis, j'existe*, est nécessairement vraie, toutes les fois que je la prononce ou que je la conçois en mon esprit[6] ".

This particular ambiguity in the *Cogito* had been brought to Descartes' attention by both Gassendi and Hobbes in rather different ways. In his *Instances* (1642) Gassendi argued that the conclusion of the *Cogito* was dependent upon a syllogistic sequence which runs as follows : Everything that thinks exists ; I think ; therefore I exist. Descartes answered this objection by denying that his knowledge of his existence depends upon any logically prior principle but that it constitutes one of those clear and distinct ideas to which we instinctively give credence : " elle paraît si évidente à l'entendement, qu'il ne se saurait empêcher de la croire[7] ". The belief in one's own existence is therefore founded on a type of intuitive knowledge which admits of no analysis whatsoever. There cannot possibly be anything more primitive than this type of truth. However, Descartes did not consistently hold to this view ; in his ontological system he introduced the concept of God as logically prior to that of the self[8].

Hobbes' objection to the *Cogito* is not phrased in syllogistic terms, and, therefore, cannot be answered by falling back onto the intuitive nature of such a truth. Hobbes made the distinction between thought as such and an individual thinker, pointing out quite correctly that these two are identified in the *Cogito* : " I, myself, who think, am distinct from my thought, and although it is not separated from myself it is, nevertheless, different from me [9] ". Thus Hobbes shows that Descartes uses the *Cogito* as if it had established not only the existence of thought in general but also of a particular thinker. In order to build his system, Descartes needed both of these aspects of the self, the thinking subject and the thought object, combined into one simple substance.

As he makes very clear in numerous references, Descartes considered the self to be a finite, nonmaterial being whose essence is thought. This being serves as the base on which he constructs all the rest of his ontological structure. Epistemologically, it is the fact that an individual can totally and completely know his own self which allows Descartes to go on to establish the possibility of objective knowledge about the universe as a whole. The self must be both the known object of its own introspection and at the same time the principle which makes such knowledge possible. In addition to this, the self serves as the prime example of a substance, self-subsistent and in which accidents inhere.

In defining the self as " une chose qui pense ", Descartes assumes that all thought, which to him includes willing and feeling, is necessarily accompanied by a type of self-awareness which is directed both towards the operations of the mind and towards the mind itself. In the *Deuxième Méditation* he reverts to the stratagem of the all-powerful deceiver and then triumphantly declares : " Il n'y a donc point de doute que je suis, s'il me trompe ; et, qu'il me trompe tant qu'il voudra, il ne saura jamais faire que je ne sois rien tant que je penserai être quelque chose[10] ". Thus self-awareness accompanies every experience of the individual, and thought would not be possible without its presence. This immediate self-consciousness is the constant companion of our whole life experience and, indeed, constitutes the very foundation of all knowledge. Descartes would have been horrified at Hume's argument that mental events can exist by themselves, that ideas are as good as substances. This may be partly explained by Descartes' complete adherence to the substance-attribute doctrine, which clearly points to the necessity of some supporting and unchanging subject to which the ever-changing mental experiences can be attached, but the reasons for his belief in the substantiality of the self are even deeper than his beliefs in the doctrine of substance[11].

The whole structure of Descartes' system depends on the *Cogito* functioning in two directions : one inwardly and the other outwardly. The first type of thought must be going on all the time in order to establish any continuity whatsoever in the incredibly diverse series which characterizes our reactions to the outside world. Without the awareness of the self, a human being would not be able to have any knowledge at all. This conviction was even more ingrained than the belief in the substance doctrine, as is well expressed by Norman Kemp Smith :

Most probably what was ultimately decisive in his attitude was the conviction ... that there is no such thing as a mental experience existing singly ; that all such experiences are possible only in and for the abiding entity which we call the self—the self that has awareness of them. Not only—such is his unwavering contention—is the *existence* of the self necessary to the awareness of any feeling, the self's *awareness* of itself is equally indispensable. Descartes may, on occasion, seem to be suggesting that self-consciousness can exist in and by itself, i.e. can be an awareness that is an awareness of the self, of nothing save the self, but nowhere does he suggest that consciousness of an object, even if it be a feeling only or a passion, can be possible in the total absence of self-awareness [12].

Descartes does not use the term *sentiment de l'existence,* but it is easy to see the connection between his belief in self-consciousness and the eighteenth century one in self-awareness. However, one must realize that Descartes believed that self-consciousness led to real knowledge about the nature of the soul and not just about its existence.

However we should not overlook the fact that Descartes also defined the self as a *thing* that thinks. It is not only the mental operation which is posited but also a mental substance. Over against this type of substance he sets up a totally different kind of substance, matter. Problems arise when these two substances enter into a close relationship as they do in the case of individual human beings. Descartes' solution of the mind-body problem is to state that there is real interaction between the two in this particular instance. This leads him and his followers into many difficulties.

The relationship of the individual soul to God is also a thorny question. We have already noted that the *Cogito,* which established the existence of the self, does not serve as the logical support for Descartes' system. As long as it is aware of itself, the individual self exists, but there is a being who exists necessarily and eternally, God himself. We reach the idea of God through that of the self, which has been revealed to be both " finite and creaturely [13] ". This knowledge leads automatically into the concept of a type of being characterized as infinite and perfect. However, the idea of God necessarily carries with it the concept of existence, since his essence implies his existence. The soul, on the other hand, is a created substance, which is only known to exist while it is thinking of itself. Its immortality is completely dependent on the will and benevolence of God.

Once it is created, the individual soul has a certain amount of independence. It is of course ultimately dependent upon God, but through the will it is able to make a life of its own and be responsible for itself. In other words, the soul is free. This division of the soul into an active portion, the will, and a passive portion, the understanding, is another of the dichotomies in the Cartesian system which led to long and heated debate in the years to come. On the one hand, the soul is a unified whole, created by God, and contingently connected to matter which affects it through perceptions and feelings ; it remains unaffected in its essence by all these external events ; it is essentially passive. On the other hand, the soul, still a unified whole created by God, is an active center of force ; its will imposes itself upon the world and even effects changes in the essence of the soul itself, which is in a continual process of development.

It is surely not too far-fetched to see in Descartes' systematic dualism a formidable challenge to the Thomistic doctrine of Essences which exist *in* and *per se*. But his reaction to this strictly essentialistic interpretation of the universe carried him beyond dualism into a series of dichotomies which are hard to reconcile. In the Cartesian theory of perception there is no real interaction possible between the knower and the known, since they consist of totally unlike substances, mind and matter. This had not presented a problem to the Scholastics since each individual entity participated in both matter and form, and, therefore, there was no hard and fast break between the rational subject and the material object. In addition to this problem, Descartes had to face another type of dualism in his adherence to the age-old doctrine of substance and attribute. Whatever exists, whether it be ideas, things, persons, feelings, primary or secondary qualities, etc., must of necessity fall into one of these two categories. Attributes do not give us any real idea of the essence of substances, although one single attribute is sufficient to describe each of the two types of substance. Mind is characterized exclusively by thought and body by extension. According to a recent analysis by Richard A. Watson, the double dualism present in Cartesian ontology, first that of mind and matter, and second that of substance and accident, in combination with the causal and epistemological likeness principles according to which there must be a likeness between a cause and its effect and also between the representations and the object represented, led to *The Downfall of Cartesianism*[14]. As Watson so cogently points out, the abandonment of any one of these principles left the would-be Cartesian in an untenable position. If they gave up the likeness principle, " they could no longer explain how mental ideas could represent material objects, nor how a mind could causally interact with a body[15] ". If they gave up the substance-attribute distinction, they " could no longer explain how a mind could be directly acquainted with and thus know ideas[16] ". The thought of giving up the basic dualism of mind and matter was anathema, since it seemed to involve materialism on the one hand and idealism on the other.

The history of philosophy from Descartes to Kant can be read as an attempt to break away from this series of insoluble problems. Our concern is the narrower one of tracing the development in the concept of the self during this period.

Malebranche and Occasionalism

The first attempt to solve the Cartesian dilemma in the field of perception came with Malebranche who developed a system referred to as Occasionalism. According to him the soul is completely dependent upon God, not only for its creation, continuance, and salvation, but also for its experience and knowledge. Instead of ideas being modifications of the mind, as in Descartes, Malebranche insisted that all ideas are in God who controls access to them by human beings : " Pour l'idée qui se trouve jointe avec le sentiment, elle est en Dieu, et nous la voyons parce qu'il lui plaît de nous la découvrir[17] ". The dilemma of interaction between two fundamentally different substances, mind and matter, is avoided by recourse to God. Since He subsumes both mind and matter, there is no conflict with the causal likeness problem and the double substance doctrine can be continued although it is essentially by-passed by recourse to a higher type of substance. This attempt to introduce a third kind of entity, neither substance nor modification thereof, was difficult to understand at the time. The reaction of the Academician Simon Foucher is reported by Watson as follows : " When Foucher finally saw that Malebranche intended for ideas to be entities outside the Cartesian ontological framework, he decided that Malebranche was simply talking nonsense. Foucher dismissed the theory as an exhibition of religious enthusiasm[18] ".

But Occasionalism was an honest attempt to answer some of the fundamental dichotomies inherent in Cartesianism. This fact is also noticeable in Malebranche's approach to the problem of the soul. In the first place he denies that we have a clear and distinct idea of our soul and its constitution. On the contrary, we are reduced to a vague feeling about its existence, which does not give us any knowledge whatsoever of the essence of mind : " J'ai dit en quelques endroits ... que nous n'avons point d'idée claire de notre âme, mais seulement conscience ou sentiment intérieur ; qu'ainsi nous la connaissons beaucoup plus imparfaitement que nous ne faisons l'étendue[19] ". This is a far cry from Descartes' insistence on the fact that our self-awareness was so complete that it left no room for doubt about the essential quality of our soul.

However the fact that we do not have a clear and distinct idea of the soul should not blind us to the certainty which does accompany the *sentiment intérieur*. According to Malebranche, and this is a concept which will be constantly alluded to in eighteenth century discussions of the means of access to knowledge about the self, introspection is just about the surest method leading to true knowledge since " notre sentiment intérieur ne nous trompe jamais[20] ". What it does tell us may be limited in scope, but at least it is certain. Another point to be stressed in discussing Malebranche's *sentiment intérieur* is that to Malebranche this was not an easily acquired facility. On the contrary, as Beatrice Rome has pointed out : " Self discovery, like the discovery of God, is the achievement of a long, arduous, lived experience ... self-examination is an agonizing but continuous process of self-scrutinization[21] ". Everybody was theoretically capable of exercising this type of attention to the self, but not everyone does so or wants to do so. Introspection requires a forcible operation of the will, a prolonged desire to accomplish a very difficult task. This is a far cry from some of the later claims that the *sentiment intérieur de l'existence* is the most widespread and most accessible of all feelings.

Introspection, then, leads to an immediate awareness of one's own existence but tells one very little about one's own essence. To determine what actually constitutes the essence of the soul it is necessary to turn to other means of searching for the truth. Thus we apprehend the mind as thinking, willing, imagining, and sensing, but in order to be sure that these qualities are mental and not physical we must resort to rational analysis of body alone. This method will lead us to exclude these activities from the sphere of the physical[22]. We never actually grasp the essence of our being, in the way that Descartes had supposed we knew that thinking is the essence of the mind. Rather we grasp the existence of a mental entity, which is characterized by various activities, none of which is compatible with the essence of matter. Human beings are not perfect beings; this characteristic belongs to God alone and only in Him are existence and essence necessarily combined. Those beings created by God can only reach the conclusion that they exist by experiencing their existence through their powers of introspection : " Nous ne sçavons de nôtre ame, que ce que nous sentons se passer en nous[23] ". What does not exist cannot be apprehended, but only human souls have the power of self-apprehension necessary to found a true knowledge of existents.

What is revealed through the *sentiment intérieur* is therefore the content of existence and not of essence itself. This means that we know ourselves as active doers rather than as passive beings. Since he was a Christian writer, Malebranche could not deny that the individual was responsible for his own actions, and yet the soul's utter dependence on God would seem to point towards a denial of free-will. As far as ideas are concerned, the soul is passive and receptive, completely dependent upon God. But Malebranche continued the Cartesian split between the understanding and the will, and the latter faculty is what gives an individual his freedom. As Lester Crocker pointed out in speaking of Samuel Clarke : " the self is split between passive faculties of thinking and desiring, and an active will. The self is unable to confer value, or create it, but it can carry out or reject what it values, and in this lies its freedom[24] ". Unfortunately this interpretation would seem to introduce an inconsistency into Malebranche's system, an inconsistency which was derived from the necessity of making each individual responsible for his own actions. This fact is brought out clearly in a lucid discussion of Berkeley's concept of the self by Anita Fritz who shows Berkeley's dependence on Malebranche and his basically passive and receptive soul :

man is for the most part, if not wholly, determined to will as he does ... his will as well as the realization of his capacity to perceive, imagine, remember and reason are passive responses to the action of God. The finite soul neither produces, preserves nor commands ideas or actions ; according to its own unique capacity it receives. It differs from matter in this respect only in that it is a single focus whereby what is received is unified to become the experience of a single soul.   The minimal freedom which Malebranche allows to avoid making God responsible for sin seems granted only through countenancing inconsistency[25].

The attempt to build up the will at the expense of the understanding will be one of the most important elements in the eighteenth century drive to avoid determinism at all costs.   The essential passivity of the mind as revealed by Malebranche was even more fundamental to the post-Lockean developments in epistemology, as is clearly revealed in the doctrine that at birth the mind is a *tabula rasa*.   Before pursuing the developments which took place in consequence of Locke's empirical approach to the question, it would be wise to mention the contributions of two of the great rationalistic system makers of the seventeenth century.   Both Leibniz and Spinoza, reacting to and building on the Cartesian cosmology, developed their own very individual world views.

Leibniz

Leibniz' interpretation of the universe as a system of monads, created by God and all running smoothly according to a pre-established harmony, was early discarded by the *philosophes* as merely one more system by a " speculative metaphysician and theologian[26] ".   Barber has noted that French knowledge of Leibniz was severely limited by the fact that so little of his major work had been published during his lifetime :

> By 1720, then, the French public had the following works before them as a basis for judging Leibniz as a thinker : the *Système nouveau* (1695) and the various articles in the periodicals which we have already discussed ; the *Théodicée ;* and the Clarke correspondence.   Nothing more of significance was to appear in French until Raspe's publication of the *Nouveaux Essais* in 1765[27].

The *Monadologie* was not to appear in its orginial French until 1840 and none of Leibniz' logical views upon which his whole system is founded were available at all.   And so Leibniz' influence, while very large through the Wolffian school, was by no means as decisive as Locke's.   There was a renewed interest in Leibniz' thought during the latter part of the eighteenth century, due in part to the new organic and biological turn taken by the natural sciences.   To the *philosophes* of this period, the concept of a monad as a dynamic, spontaneous center of force which is essentially self-creative came to play a considerable role in their own approach to understanding the universe. But this reading of Leibniz required a divorce of the monad from the God-centered cosmos in which Leibniz placed it, and is really contrary to the very foundation of Leibniz' cosmology.

According to Leibniz, the universe is organized into a hierarchy of monads. Lowest on the ladder are the simple monads, which are characterized by the very minimum of perception and desire ; these are followed by souls, which add to these characteristics the additional ones of memory, feeling, and attention ; and finally the spirits or rational souls, which include apperception, the faculty of self-consciousness which enables them to have a kind of moral identity which results in their immortality. Actually all monads are eternally existent, but spirits have the additional attraction of always existing as conscious of themselves as individuals. Leibniz felt that his arrangement was superior to that of Descartes and closer to that of the Scholastics. This may have been one reason why his thought was in such disrepute in eighteenth century France, which disliked anything medieval.

In a world completely made up of monads, all of which have perceptions in some degree or other, since this is the very nature of a monad, how do we distinguish the self from all the other monads which go to make up an individual person ? Within the framework of this system, the monad which is more active than any of the others, the one which has the clearest perceptions, becomes the dominant monad, and it is the one which constitutes the self. The sum of the monads does not constitute the self ; on the contrary, there is a single substance to which this concept must be attached. As Leibniz puts it in the *Nouveaux Essais :* " As for the Self, it will be well to distinguish it from the *appearance of self* and from consciousness. The *Self* constitutes real and physical identity and the *appearance of self,* accompanied by truth, joins personal identity to it[28] ".

Leibniz asserts the existence of these individual substances on the basis of two proofs. The first proof is the appeal to consciousness itself ; in looking into oneself, one is immediately struck by the fact that an individual spirit exists : " The consciousness or feeling of the *Ego* proves a moral or personal identity[29] ". In commenting on the *Cogito* of Descartes Leibniz notes that there is no way to prove the fact that I exist, since it constitutes an " immediate truth[30] ". However he denies this statement the logical status of a necessary proposition : " You may, however, with some reason, exclude this proposition from among the Axioms, for it is a proposition of fact, founded on an immediate experience, and not a necessary proposition, whose necessity is seen in the immediate agreement (convenance) of the ideas. On the contrary, only God sees how these two terms, *I* and *Existence,* are connected, i.e. why I exist[31] ". We have here another instance of what will prove to be the most frequently used proof of the existence of a self, a kind of inner certainty which admits of no doubt :

" I believe that we have a clear but not a distinct idea of substance, which comes in my opinion from the fact that we have the internal feeling of it in ourselves, who are substances [32] ".

Nevertheless Leibniz does not rely completely on this kind of introspective proof of the existence of an individual and substantial self. He also uses a logical proof of the existence of individual substances, using the argument that the predicate is always found to exist in the subject :

> It is true that my internal experience has convinced me *a posteriori* of this identity, but there must also be an *a priori* reason. Now it is impossible to find any other, except that my attributes of the earlier time and state, as well as my attributes of the later time and state, are predicates of the same subject ... And since, from the moment that I began to be, it could truly be said of me that this or that would happen to me, we must admit that these predicates were laws contained in the subject, or in the complete notion of me, which makes what is called *I*, which is the foundation of the connection of all my different states, and which God knew perfectly from all eternity [33].

This kind of argument was to prove much less appealing to the French *philosophes*. In the first place the *a priori* kind of argument went out of favor ; everyone was looking for empirical proofs and not ones which relied on a series of highly abstract logical sequences. In the second place, this argument denied every vestige of free-will to the individual. God is the only being ultimately responsible for any action whatsoever, and the reduction of Leibnizian cosmology to the ridiculous refrain of Pangloss : " Tout est au mieux dans le meilleur des mondes possibles " clearly indicates what Voltaire thought of this theory as a way of explaining the existence of evil in the world. However if the monad could be considered as an independent entity, out of which unfolds the whole of its own existence, then the active force of the will could be regarded as the true center of responsibility. Leibniz argues against Locke and his *tabula rasa* in the *Nouveaux Essais* on many grounds, not the least of which is that each individual monad or mind is by no means the passive conductor assumed by Locke, but on the contrary the active mover, the one and only source of true knowledge which results in action.

Karl Barth uses Leibniz' monad as one of his illustrations of the typical eighteenth century idea of man : " Ne retrouve-t-on pas, d'ailleurs, l'homme de ce temps, dans la doctrine leibnizienne de la *Monade,* cette substance spirituelle simple et une, unique de son espèce, voire même unique absolument, donnée première de toute réalité, qui se suffit à elle-même, qui est une irradiation et un miroir de Dieu même, ce pour quoi elle ne rencontre de limites en aucun objet, mais seulement dans son propre être, qui est ' sans fenêtres ', et ne se modifie qu'en vertu de son propre principe et de sa propre tendance intime, mais qui ne peut ni se corrompre ni périr, étant immortellement comme le Dieu qui l'a créée "[34]? This outline of the eighteenth century concept of human nature can be drawn from Leibniz' monads only at the cost of ignoring the very center of his cosmology, the image and presence of God. This the *philosophes* were, for the most part, more than willing to do. Since it is really impossible to overlook the position of God in Spinoza's cosmology, this may help to explain why Spinoza had so little influence in this area.

Spinoza

Spinoza's systematic exposé of his metaphysical and ethical thought had been published posthumously in his *Ethica* in 1677. Even at that time he was known as an atheist and a destroyer of all possibility of morality on the basis of the publication of his *Tractatus theologico-politicus* in 1670. All critics agree in noting that Spinoza's influence on philosophical thinking was minimal until his discovery late in the eighteenth century by Lessing and Goethe [35]. His work was ignored even by those thinkers who were struggling with the same problems, and he was generally dismissed as immoral and pedantic. As Hampshire states : " His philosophy evoked no sympathetic echo in the eighteenth century, since his grand *a priori* method of argument repelled the sceptical, as his subversion of Christian theology repelled the devout [36] ".

Therefore we shall deal only very briefly with the salient point of Spinoza's doctrine of the self, primarily to note the divergence of his ideas from the mainstream of philosophic thought of his own and later periods. As is well known, Spinoza posits God or Nature as the one and only substance ; reality is constituted by a single type of being and all the varied phenomena are merely modes or modifications of this archetypal entity. Spinoza was not only a monist in distinction to Descartes' dualism, but he was also a singularist in distinction to the pluralistic attitude of all the other philosophers we shall be dealing with. They all posited the existence of numerous individual substances, be they material or mental or both, whereas Spinoza insisted that only one substance was conceivable in the universe.

Since Spinoza's primary interest was ethical he had therefore to speak of individual human beings acting in this world as if they were completely independent of God or Substance. In reality Spinoza notes that " the essence of man is constituted by certain modifications of attributes of God ... The latter is therefore something that is in God and which cannot exist or be conceived without God [37] ". But the self, or individual human mind, does exist as such ; it is an autonomous unit which is subject to error particularly since it refers all ideas and things to itself rather than to the infinite Nature of which it is only a part. This is the limiting factor which makes man into a slave of his emotions and passions rather than a free agent acting in accordance with his own inner destiny, conceived in rational terms as correlating to the whole of the universe. According to Spinoza, the mind can have no adequate knowledge of itself since it is finite and cannot see the whole infinite convergence of events which constitute reality[38].

Not only does Spinoza differ from the rest of these philosophers in denying the existence of individual substances, he also defines substances in terms of action, of drive. Leibniz had developed his monads along the same lines, but of course each and every monad is a separate entity. Thus Spinoza denies the differentiation within the human mind of the understanding and the will : " Will and intellect are one and the same thing[39] ". It is the whole self, rather than just a small part of it which is free to determine itself by liberating itself from the dominance of things. Self-determination according to the inner nature of one's own being, which in turn is a part of the infinite Substance which makes up the whole, is the ultimate goal of Spinoza's ethics. The mind is not a passive receptor, awaiting the arrival of ideas from outer space ; on the contrary it generates its own reactions and in this lies the true path to freedom for the individual.

We will conclude this highly schematic outline of Spinoza's concept of the self by noting yet another difference which sets him apart from the rest of the philosophers we are treating. The divorce between mind and body which had originated in Descartes was to become more and more pronounced as the British and French empirical philosophers developed the consequences of Locke's epistemology. But to Spinoza such a divorce is unthinkable ; mind and body are parts of the same, merely different ways of looking at the same thing. Therefore in defining a human mind in terms of its human rather than divine attributes, Spinoza notes that the mind is constituted by the idea of the body : " The object of the idea constituting the human mind is the body, or a certain mode of extension actually existing and nothing else[40] ". Is it any wonder that Spinoza was dismissed by one group as an atheist and by another as a pantheist ? If the mind is defined as both an idea of God and an idea of body, it is not hard to see how this appreciation of Spinoza's thought came about.

Neither of these concepts were to play a part in eighteenth century speculations about the nature of the self. To pursue the philosophical developments in this field let us now turn to John Locke.

Locke

Any attempt to discuss the philosophical concepts of the eighteenth century without reference to John Locke would prove immediately abortive. It is impossible to over-emphasize his immense influence on French thinkers especially during the first half of the century. Even before the first English edition of the *Essay Concerning Human Understanding,* the French public had access to an *Abrégé* published in the *Bibliothèque universelle et historique* in January 1688. The first English edition of the *Essay* dates from 1690, and this version was considerably revised in 1694. Pierre Coste first translated the *Essay* into French in 1700, and this translation had Locke's own personal blessing. By 1755 this translation was in its fifth edition and by 1774 in its ninth.

Modern critics are unusually harsh on Locke who managed to muddle a good many logical categories in his somewhat naïve presentation of how we know what we know. Typical of this attitude is Watson's remark : " From the rich debris of continental metaphysics, Locke cobbled his own version of the way of ideas [41] ". In some ways it was this very eclecticism which made Locke so useful to the *philosophes,* that and his empirical outlook [42]. Locke was not intent upon creating a self-sufficient system of philosophy, indeed he was very pessimistic about the possibility of doing this, and here the *philosophes* agreed with him completely. Obviously his doctrine was not accepted without criticism but accepted it was, and the future development of the concept of the self was indebted to Locke.

Locke was basically sceptical about the possibility of the human mind reaching any kind of absolute truth which could be certified as such. His critical empiricism laid the foundation for the future destruction of the major assumptions underlying the Cartesian system, the double substance theory, the substance-accident theory, and the dual principles of causal and epistemological likeness. All of these would be swept away in the course of much heated debate in the eighteenth century. And yet Locke himself did not draw the conclusions which seem perfectly evident to anyone looking back on the history of this development. He made suggestions which he never followed up, the best known being his question " whether any mere material being thinks or no [43] ". Even as he asks this question, which was to have such a fruitful career amongst the materialists, he denies that we could ever actually know the answer one way or the other. Since all our ideas are based on some form of experience, we are incapable of knowing the essence of either mind or matter. The direct experience of the thinking self does not lead to Descartes' edict that thinking is the very essence of mind, but rather to the more empirical position that thinking is merely a modification of substance and that we have no means of knowing substance itself. In reality, it could be anything at all.

What Locke concentrates on is the *idea* of substance as it exists in our minds. The origin of this idea is shown to be just as subject to interpretation as any other idea, and therefore just as fallible. It is his contention that this idea is of little use in philosophy, that we cannot penetrate into the inner being of substance, and so we might just as well ignore the problem : " it is but a supposed I know not what, to support those ideas we call accidents [44] ". But Locke is so wedded to the substance-accident theory that in the second edition of the *Essay* he adds the following passage :

> It is for want of reflection that we are apt to think that our senses show us nothing but material things. Every act of sensation, when duly considered, gives us an equal view of both parts of nature, the corporeal and spiritual. For whilst I know, by seeing or hearing, etc., that there is some corporeal being without me, the object of that sensation, I do more certainly know that there is some spiritual being within me that sees and hears. This I must be convinced cannot be the action of bare insensible matter, nor ever could be without an immaterial thinking being [45].

It is obvious that Locke was quite worried about the possibility of a materialistic system being erected upon his principles, and, of course, this is just what did happen in the eighteenth century. However, it is equally obvious that he could see no way out of this impasse except by reverting to the classical theory of substance. He only differs from Descartes in asserting that it is impossible adequately to describe this substance. This affinity with Descartes is acknowledged by Locke himself in a rough draft of the *Essay*, supposedly written in the summer of 1671 : " The Understanding knows undoubtedly that while it thinks reasons or imagins it is or hath existence, or that there is something that knows and understands which according to Cartes and I thinke in truth is the most certain and undoubted proposition that can be in the minde of a man [46] ".

The means by which we are made aware of the existence of such a thinking being is the faculty of reflection which Locke posits as a companion to sensation. There are two ways of getting knowledge according to Locke : knowledge of external objects is attained through sensation, and knowledge of the mind through reflection. This latter faculty, defined as " that notice which the mind takes of its own operations [47] ", makes of the mind an object similar to any other object. We have here, then, a statement of one-half of the *Cogito ;* what the mind perceives about its own operations is just as objectively recorded as are its ideas of the external world. In fact Locke is very insistent upon the true equality of these two spheres ; he will not allow the mind to be more accessible than matter, as Descartes had done. Introspection is no better, nor any worse, a source of knowledge than is sensation.

In the Fourth Book of the *Essay* which treats of " Knowledge and Probability " Locke distinguishes three types of knowledge about existence : " an intuitive knowledge of *our own existence,* and a demonstrative knowledge of the existence of a *God :* of the existence of *anything else,* we have no other but a sensitive knowledge [48] ". The first type closely resembles Descartes' belief in the intuitive truth inherent in the *Cogito ;* it leaves no ground for criticism since, according to Locke, " it neither needs nor is capable of any proof[49]". Locke even used the Cartesian example of a man doubting his existence to show that this is utterly impossible, but he does not use the *Cogito* itself as a logical proposition which will serve as a foundation for all other knowledge.

In one other sphere Locke follows Descartes very closely; he insists that all mental experiences must be conscious, that all our actions are automatically accompanied by self-awareness. He uses the example of a man sleeping and asks what the consequences would be if " the *soul* can, whilst the body is sleeping, have its thinking, enjoyments, and concerns, its pleasure or pain, apart, which the *man* is not conscious of, nor partakes in ". The answer is the self-contradictory statement that this would mean that two different persons make up one man : " If we take wholly away all consciousness of our actions and sensation ... it will be hard to know wherein to place personal identity.[50] " An important corollary to this is that the mind is not always thinking, as Descartes suggested. On the contrary, according to Locke, there must be gaps in the thinking process, or we must all be made up of a number of selves. Thus it is consciousness which serves as the empirical basis for personal identity, a problem of such importance that Locke added a whole chapter on the subject in the second edition of the *Essay*.

Personal identity cannot be treated in the same terms as other types of identity which Locke carefully defines in terms of space and time. The identity of a person is not determined solely by his bodily characteristics ; to this type of identity Locke reserves the term " man ". As a generic type man is defined in the same way as an animal : " a participation of the same continued life, by constantly fleeting particles of matter, in succession vitally united to the same organized body[51] ". Locke uses the term " person " to refer to what we have been calling " self " and his definition is clarity itself : " a thinking intellligent being, that has reason and reflection, and can consider itself as itself, the same thinking being, in different times and places ; which it does only by that consciousness which is inseparable from thinking[52]. " Thus it is the empirically verifiable fact of self-consciousness which permits a person to identify himself through the changes which take place in time. In the next section, Locke is careful to note that this definition does not serve as a basis for a belief in a unitary unchanging substance. Many substances could conceivably be united by a single consciousness and thus come to form a " self ", although Locke does not come right out and say so. This discussion of personal identity will have fruitful results for the concept of the self later on. It introduces multiplicity into the previously simplified concept of the self as an identical, unchanging substance. The only criterium which Locke allows here is that of consciousness of self ; if a person has the same consciousness of past events that he has of present ones, then he is the same person. As a principle of identity, self-consciousness was to receive many and varied interpretations. It is not as clear and distinct as the single substance theory since, as an empirical principle, it was subject to analysis and criticism.

And so we can summarize Locke's views of the self as falling into two distinct parts. On the one hand, he continues the definition in terms of a simple substance characterized by thought. On the other hand, he introduces the modern concept of personal identity, dependent on a continual stream of consciousness. His ideas thus serve as a kind of half-way house between the two extremes of Descartes and Hume.

Berkeley

With Locke we reach the end of the seventeenth century formulations and Berkeley carries us into the eighteenth. The major portion of Berkeley's work was published in the 1730's and translated into French in 1734 (*Essay Toward a New Theory of Vision* and *Alciphron : or the Minute Philosopher*) and 1750 (*Three Dialogues Between Hylas and Philonous*). However Voltaire had given a good outline of Berkeley's thought in his *Eléments de la philosophie de Newton* (1738), so the French writers were well acquainted with his system. They were troubled by his extreme idealism, worried about the fact that no one seemed to be able to disprove such a far-fetched thesis, one that was so far removed from common sense.

Actually the French *philosophes* were very little influenced by the developments of British empiricism. Berkeley's immaterialism was considered scandalous and Hume's radical speculations in the field of epistemology were overlooked. Only those conclusions which could be used in the fight against superstition and Christianity appealed to the *philosophes*[53]. What the *philosophes* took from Berkeley was not his whole cosmology, in which God plays such a central and necessary part ; this aspect of Berkeley is very much like Malebranche and suited the anti-Christian *philosophes* not at all. What they did find to their liking was Berkeley's hostility towards abstract general ideas and his critical attack upon the doctrine of substance. His concept of the self, involved as it was with the doctrine of spiritual substance, seemed to be, and actually is, less radical than some other parts of his system.

Berkeley's cosmology is monistic in that it denies the existence of matter as a substance, but his world is made up of numerous individualized minds, each existing separately from the others. Berkeley uses the distinction that Locke had made popular between primary and secondary qualities and shows that there is no more reason to assign the primary qualities to an external object than the secondary ones. All that we can know are ideas and so, since we cannot know matter, it cannot exist. Objects are no more than " the various sensations or ideas imprinted on the Sense, however blended or combined together[54] ".   One may wonder why this type of associational explanation is not also sufficient to describe the nature of the mind which assimilates these ideas and sensations.   The publication of Berkeley's *Philosophical Commentaries,* written in 1707-1708, but not published until 1871, shows clearly that in his first thoughts about his new system Berkeley was much closer to Hume than is evident in his later writings.   A few quotations will serve to elucidate this starting point of his thought :

478. certainly if there were no sensible ideas there could be no soul, no perception, remembrance, love, fear, etc. no faculty could be exerted.

478a. The soul is the will properly speaking & as it is distinct from Ideas.

577. The very existence of Ideas constitutes the soul.

578. Consciousness, perception, existence of Ideas seem to be all one[55].

580. Mind is a congeries of Perceptions. Take away Perceptions & you take away the Mind put the Perceptions & you put the mind.

This kind of analysis of the self is fully in accord with Berkeley's own logical and epistemological principles, but his need to establish the existence of individual entities overrode his critical sense of building only from principles which were impervious to criticism.   The majesty of God and the responsibility of the individual for his own conduct were more pressing than his critical principles.   As Anita Fritz points out, both Malebranche and Berkeley were intent upon giving some kind of " a positive characterization of the self to support the thesis common to both philosophies that man is a substance other than and apart from God[56] ".   Neither wished to fall into the universalistic trap of Spinoza's monistic system.   Therefore, the first section of the *Principles* is devoted to the assertion that the only objects of human knowledge are ideas, but the second section categorically insists upon the existence of a " perceiving, active being " known variously as " *mind, spirit, soul, or myself* ".

On what grounds does Berkeley posit the existence of mind ?   He goes about proving its existence in two ways.   The first is logical ; ideas are passive and so cannot be the cause of each other ; therefore, according to the causal likeness theory, it is legitimate to infer the existence of an active being which can serve as the cause of these inactive ideas. This may be very satisfying logically, but it is not enough really to prove the existence of individual souls.   This is accomplished by appealing to our " intuitive " knowledge of the existence of our own soul.   In the *Dialogues* Philonous answers Hylas' question about how an inactive idea can possibly convey any knowledge of mind or of God by the following remark :

I do nevertheless know that I, who am a spirit or thinking substance, exist as certainly as I know my ideas exist. Farther, I know what I mean by the terms *I* and *myself ;* and I know this immediately or intuitively, though I do not perceive it as I perceive a triangle, a colour, or a sound. The Mind, Spirit, or Soul is that indivisible unextended thing which thinks, acts, and perceives[57].

The appeal to an intuitive perception of the existence of the self allows of no criticism whatsoever ; it is presented as self-evident, if not axiomatic. Hume was the first to publish doubts about this type of evidence, and even he did so primarily by appealing to the fact that he did not personally experience this supposedly universal perception of the existence of the self.

Berkeley does not claim that we actually receive any knowledge about the nature of the self through this intuitive process, only that we know that it exists. How we can possibly know what mind is like is a real difficulty for Berkeley ; he comes back to it again and again and finally introduces a new type of knowledge, " notion ", to account for it. Ideas or sensations cannot serve here since they are defined as *being perceived,* whereas the essence of mind is the active faculty of *perceiving.* But we do know both our own minds and those of other people and so in Watson's résumé : " he introduced notions which are *in* the mind or *had* by the mind without being modifications of the mind[58]. " These notions also serve to alert the mind to the existence of relations. The resemblance to Malebranche's theory of ideas and the vision of God is striking, and when we turn to Berkeley's concept of the nature of the self we shall see even more of Malebranche's influence.

Berkeley retains the old Cartesian concept of the self as a substantial being characterized by thought. This point of view is vigorously defended in the 1734 edition of the *Dialogues* by Philonous who is goaded by Hylas as follows :

Hylas—it should follow that you are only a system of floating ideas, without any substance to support them...
Philonous.—How often must I repeat, that I know or am conscious of my own being ; and that *I myself* am not my ideas, but somewhat else, a thinking, active principle that perceives, knows, wills, and operates about ideas[59].

In the *Alciphron* a person is defined as " that individual thinking thing[60] ". This leads us to believe that the self was for Berkeley, as for Descartes, a simple, undivided substance, whose essential characteristic is thought. Nevertheless the problem is considerably complicated by the fact that thought is dependent on the existence of ideas, that ideas are completely passive, and that, therefore, the mind itself, since it exists only in and through its experiences, must also be passive. This Berkeley vigorously denies, insisting instead upon the active nature of spirits who do the perceiving. A still further complication arises when we realize that in the fully developed version of Berkeley's cosmology, perceptions originate in God. The dilemma for Berkeley is the same as that faced by Malebranche, and Berkeley's solution follows that of his French precursor.

Although the activity of the self as it perceives ideas suffices to establish a distinction between a perceiving subject and a perceived object, it is not sufficient grounds to substantiate the claim that the self is an active entity, since Berkeley admits that we do not control our perceptions. In fact he uses this argument to prove the existence of God, and, if it is God who is ultimately responsible for the perceiving activity of the mind, then the soul is not an independent entity, responsible for its own actions. Both Berkeley and Malebranche turn to another aspect of the self since the understanding or perceiving part of the mind proves to be inadequate to the task. Following Descartes, Malebranche had split the soul into the twin operations of understanding and willing ; Berkeley is vaguer in his terminology, but it seems that the mind's independence is ultimately reduced to how it feels about what it perceives. As Mrs. Fritz phrases it :

> the individual is held to contribute nothing to his experience of the so-called outer or natural world. The self is seen to be passive in relation to that series of events which constitutes the basis of its history. As for the inner, introspectively apprehended, accompaniment of this history, the emotional, imaginative, reflective and volitional life of the individual, it is found by both Malebranche and Berkeley to be the principal range of whatever in the way of activity may be attributed to self [61].

This leads to the interesting position that only the inner apperception is free and active, which involves the corollary that while the inner being is independent and active, its experience is dependent and passive. What happens to the soul merely serves as the occasion for its individualized and internalized reaction thereto ; on the other hand, this reaction has no real relation to the experiential aspect of the soul.

This divorce of essence from existence is one way of solving the dilemma of the freedom of the self, but not one which many of the *philosophes* were willing to accept. Berkeley was to be much admired and much misunderstood by the *philosophes* who saw in his system the best developed and most coherent statement of the extreme case of idealism, which eventuates in solipsism. His arguments to prove the existence of God and the soul's dependence thereon were not given the same attention as his critical attack on the concept of material substance. Therefore his ideas on the nature of the self may be taken more as symptomatic of the general dilemma facing the age, rather than as influential among the *philosophes*.

Hume

Hume's position vis-à-vis the *philosophes* is much more complicated than that of Berkeley, who represented such an exaggerated form of idealism that very few of them were willing to follow his thinking through to its logical conclusions. Hume's ideas were much more acceptable, partly because he was considered to be in the family, so to speak. The personal contacts between Hume and the major French writers are too well known to be repeated ; suffice it to say that he was friendly with many of them. How well known his philosophical works were is a somewhat harder question to answer. Hume published the first two books of *A Treatise of Human Nature* in 1739 and the third book in 1740. The reception given to this work was far from overwhelming ; as Hume remarks in his autobiography : " Never literary Attempt was more unfortunate than my Treatise of Human Nature. It fell *dead-born from the Press :* without reaching such distinction as even to excite a Murmur among the Zealots [62]. "

Mossner has studied the Continental press to see if there were any more reaction there than in England and has been able to locate only three reviews in French periodicals and two in German ones. The *Bibliothèque britanique,* the *Bibliothèque raisonnée* and the *Nouvelle bibliothèque* gave it some space but the *Treatise* was not even mentioned in the *Journal des savants,* the *Mercure de France, Le Pour et contre,* the *Mémoires de Trévoux,* or the *Observations sur les écrits modernes.* Mossner notes that in these few reviews Hume's " scepticism was stressed at the expense of his constructive system [63] ".

The question of the distribution of the *Treatise* in France is a particularly important one for this study since it is only in the *Treatise* that Hume makes his now famous attack on the self as a " bundle or collection of different perceptions [64] ". As he rewrote the *Treatise* over the next twenty years, publishing the first part as the *Enquiry Concerning Human Understanding* (1748), the third part as *An Enquiry Concerning the Principles of Morals* (1751), and the second part as *Of the Passions* (1757), he deliberately omitted all reference to the problem of the self. That he was not satisfied with his results in the *Treatise* can easily be seen in the passage in the *Appendix* in which he withdraws from the controversy with the following words : " For my part, I must plead the privilege of a sceptic, and confess that this difficulty is too hard for my understanding. "

The *Enquiry Concerning Human Understanding* was translated into French in 1758 by J.B. Mérian, and this edition included a critical preface by J.H.S. Formey. Hard as it may be to believe, the *Treatise* was not translated into French until 1878, and then only Part I was translated [65]. Of course this does not mean that the *Treatise* was unknown to the *philosophes ;* many of them could read English, but it does indicate a certain lack of interest in Hume's most critical work, and, as far as the concept of the self is concerned, it points to a certain lack of clarity about the whole issue of the introduction and dissemination of the " composition " theory of the self. Obviously Condillac had no direct access to Hume's thought on this matter since Condillac did not read English [66]. Actually it has been fairly well established that Hume's reputation was almost non-existent in Europe until the mid-1750's, witness the remark of Maupertuis in a letter of February 28, 1755, written to the Abbé Le Blanc who had translated Humes's *Political Discourses* : " Comment est-il possible qu'un tel homme ne soit pas plus connu ici et ne soit pas l'admiration de l'Europe ? [67] "

This is not to deny the spread of the " composition " theory, but merely to emphasize that, in this respect at least, while Hume may have been the first to enunciate it carefully he was by no means the only one thinking along these lines. It was really the next logical step in the disso-lution of the substance theory, and Hume may be considered to be sympto-matic of the mid-eighteenth century dilemma in this field of inquiry. Once the unchanging Cartesian mind-substance disappeared, the philoso-phers found it difficult to delineate a new principle of unity which would serve to explain the permanence and unity of the self. Furthermore, as we shall see, Hume's own position was by no means as clear-cut as is often thought. His own dissatisfaction with the results of his empirical inquiry into the nature of the self becomes more interesting when one realizes that he continued to use the self as the basis of a large part of his psychological and moral philosophy although he admitted to having des-troyed all rational grounds for belief in such a concept.

Let us first examine Hume's analysis of the self as it occurs in Book I of the *Treatise,* an analysis which Isaiah Berlin has termed " the most characteristically devastating application of his empirical method [68] ". Hume begins by questioning what is meant by the term " substance ", and shows that we are incapable of knowing anything at all about it since all our knowledge is dependent upon ideas which are in turn derived from impressions. Relying upon the epistemological likeness principle, according to which resemblance between ideas and " things " is the only true ground for belief in our knowledge of the world in general, Hume proves that it is absolutely impossible for us to have any knowledge about substance. This, of course, was the way in which Berkeley had attacked the concept of material substance, but Hume extends the argument to the mind as well. He denies that we can have any better knowledge of mental sub-stance than we have of material substance. Berkeley had found it neces-sary to posit the existence of " notions " to explain how we get knowledge of the soul ; Hume will admit into his system nothing but impressions and ideas derived therefrom. This first step in Hume's refutation of the self is a logical one and results in the conclusion that such a concept is not only unnecessary but also contradictory. Impressions are all that can exist in the mental world, and they can exist by themselves. Each impression functions in such a way that it " fulfils for itself the alleged requirement of a substance[69] ". The idea of substance is absurd since substance " is supposed to be a simple, uncompounded and indivisible essence, while its modifications or actions retain their multiplicity and diversity[70] ".

After this initial logical thrust, Hume turns to an empirical approach. He makes an appeal to his own experience in order to prove that no such entity exists. After stating the position of the philosophers who believe in the existence of a self-substance as follows : " There are some philosophers who imagine we are every moment intimately conscious of what we call our *self ;* that we feel its existence and its continuance in existence ; and are certain, beyond the evidence of a demonstration, both of its perfect identity and simplicity ", Hume goes on to show that " all these positive assertions are contrary to that very experience which is pleaded for them ", since no impression can be " constant and invariable ". The final blow falls with his famous appeal to introspection :

> For my part, when I enter most intimately into what I call *myself,* I always stumble on some particular perception or other ... I never can catch *myself* at any time without a perception, and never can observe any thing but the perception ... I may venture to affirm of the rest of mankind that they are nothing but a bundle or collection of different perceptions, which succeed each other with an inconceivable rapidity, and are in a perpetual flux and movement[71].

There is no substance in which these perceptions inhere, nor is there any behind the perceptions themselves ; they are the only units of being known to man ; thus they alone must form the basis of all knowledge. However, Hume does not deny that we do have some idea of personal identity, and he goes on to inquire how such a " fictitious " idea comes about.

Hume denied the introspective approach to the proof of the existence of the self, primarily by saying that he does not experience this type of insight himself. The belief in personal identity is, however, part and parcel not only of other people's but also of Hume's philosophical baggage. How could such an idea have come about ? The answer to this question seems to be clear-cut : memory.

> To begin with *resemblance ;* suppose we could see clearly into the breast of another, and observe that succession of perceptions which constitutes his mind or thinking principle, and suppose that he always preserve the memory of a considerable part of past perceptions ; it is evident that nothing could more contribute to the bestowing a relation on this succession amidst all its variations ... the memory not only

discovers the identity, but also contributes to its production, by producing the relation of resemblance among the perceptions. The case
is the same, whether we consider ourselves or others[72].

First of all we must notice that Hume was very reluctant to use the
argument from personal experience any more than was absolutely necessary ; he wanted to find an objective method of positing the belief in the
self. Secondly, he has difficulty in deciding whether memory serves to
produce personal identity or merely to *discover* it. The first interpretation
would dovetail with his critical approach to the concept of the self : there
is nothing there but what is going on at that very moment in the flow of
perceptions, including those which are characterized as having to do
with past impressions. The second interpretation coincides with another
strain in Hume : there is something there which can be found if properly
attended to.

Although Hume liked to think he was merely outlining the scope of
human knowledge, he was more tied to the previous philosophical trends
than he was willing to admit. Isaiah Berlin states his dilemma in modern
terms : " Whether or not some memory relation between the discrete
impressions and ideas constitutes the meaning or part of the meaning of
the expression ' the same as ' as applied to persons, or whether, rather
it is by means of memory that we find out that several discrete impressions and ideas ' belong ' to the history of the ' same ' person[73]. " Unfortunately Hume does not stay within the rather narrow field of the definition of terms ; on the contrary, he extends his inquiry into the whole
nature of human knowledge, its genesis, development, and ontological
status. As Berlin points out, " Hume supposes that he is overthrowing the
metaphysics of substance in favor of the (equally indemonstrable) metaphysics of sense data[74] ", and to do so he uses the epistemological likeness
theory, which in turn makes it impossible for him to reach a viable concept
of the self. Hume points the way to both Transcendentalism and Logical
Positivism, but he fits into neither of these categories. His thought
was transitional, and as such contradictory and full of tensions ; it is for
this reason that he is such an outstanding example of Enlightenment
thought.

The dual aspect of Hume's doctrine of the self is clearly spelled out
in Norman Kemp Smith's indispensable *The Philosophy of David Hume,*
and the following presentation follows his rather closely . It is fairly easy
for even a layman to see that Hume's famous statement about not being
able to discover anything corresponding to the concept of the self when
making an introspective examination of himself suffers from a serious
logical defect. The opening sentence, " For my part, when I enter most
intimately into what I call *myself,* I always stumble on some particular
perception ", uses the word *I* in a most ambiguous way, especially if one
keeps in mind the fact that the very identity of this *I* is going to be chal-

lenged in the following sentence. There seems to be present an observer who is doing all the introspecting and yet is unable to turn his attention on himself. This *I* stands on the threshold of knowledge, serves as the organizing principle which permits the mind to assimilate and use the varied sense data, but is not itself subject to analysis as an object. According to Smith, the source of this silent observer is to be found in Hutcheson, who posited a double function for the mind, the first as a reactor to stimuli and the second as an observer of these reactions[75]. Hume tends to ignore this second function of self-as-observer in Book I of the *Treatise* but to fall back on it in the second and third books which deal with the passions and ethics. But even in Book I it is never entirely absent, and it is clear that Hume needed this concept of the self-as-observer in order to arrive at any kind of an understanding of human knowledge. When he turns to the question of what makes us believe in the existence of a self, or of any kind of causal relation amongst what he posits as discrete existences, he falls back on just this attitude of mind. There is within the individual mind itself a principle of unity which serves as a basis for our belief in causal sequences and in moral values. Impressions are in themselves totally neutral, and it is only what we bring to them which gives them any kind of association[76].

To return to Hume's delineation of his concept of the self, we can now observe that he does not actually deny its existence, but only denies the existence of a simple, unitary, and permanent substance. Actually he gives to the self a new kind of definition, comparing it to a " republic or commonwealth, in which the several members are united by the reciprocal ties of government and subordination, and give rise to the other persons who propagate the same republic in the incessant changes of its parts[77] ". There is therefore some reason for belief in the self as a referent for all perceptions, a principle of connection which gives unity to the multi-faceted and always changing perceptions themselves. This Hume terms " human nature " and posits as a basic concept to all our beliefs, thus avoiding the logical dilemma in which he finds himself. The famous passage in the *Appendix* fully illustrates both this dilemma and its solution :

If perceptions are distinct existences, they form a whole only by being connected together. But no connexions among distinct existences are ever discoverable by human understanding. We only feel a connexion or determination of the thought to pass from one object to another. It follows, therefore, that the thought alone finds personal identity, when reflecting on the train of past perceptions that compose a mind ; the ideas of them are felt to be connected together, and naturally introduce each other ... But all my hopes vanish when I come to explain the principles that united our successive perceptions in our thought or consciousness. I cannot discover any theory which gives me satisfaction on this head.

In short, there are two principles, which I cannot render consistent ; nor is it in my power to renounce either of them ; viz., *that all our distinct perceptions are distinct existences,* and *that the mind never perceives any real connexion among distinct perceptions*[78].

It is perfectly obvious that there is no real inconsistency between the two principles enunciated by Hume ; contradiction only arises if one admits a unitary principle, that of personal identity. As soon as one posits a principle of unity in seeming complexity, one is faced with the difficulty of explaining how such an odd idea got started. Hume does not deny that we experience the feeling of a unitary self ; he only denies that there is any way of explaining it.

One of the problems involved in the belief in personal identity is that not only is the idea of the self a complex one, it is apprehended as such. Here we see the basic trouble of the " composition " theory as a whole. Since this world-view assumed that simple entities are in some ways more " real " than complex ones, it is obviously assumed that a total enumeration of the individual parts of a whole would be sufficient to account for it. That this is by no means true is obvious in Hume's dissatisfaction with his own theory of the self as a " bundle of perceptions ", but the fault is basic to many other philosophical problems which the eighteenth century found impossible to handle adequately, such as time, space, causal relations, and judgments. As long as the assumption that an enumeration of the parts suffices to describe the whole remained dominant, no composition theory of the self was going to prove to be any more satisfactory than Hume's. As Smith points out, Hume did have another explanation to fall back on, though he does not admit it in *Book I* or in the *Appendix*[79]. Elsewhere Hume assumes the existence of a unitary principle of feeling, an emotive addition to the given facts of perceptions, which serves to explain all causal relations. It is to " human nature " itself that Hume turns in order to elucidate human understanding, and human nature includes a great deal more than the purely rational.

We are again witnessing the old pattern of the split between the understanding and the " will ", the passive and the active functions of the self, this time dressed up in terms of " perceptions " and " feeling ". On the one hand, the soul is completely subject to suggestion from the exterior ; it has no control over its ingredients ; in fact, it does not exist apart from those ingredients. On the other hand, the soul controls its own destiny ; it subjects these ingredients to a kind of internal form which determines their value to that inner being whose existence is denied in the first thesis. This becomes very clear in Hume's doctrine of the passions, especially his description of pride and humility, and of love and hatred. In these discussions the self is the " object " to which the passions lead the mind and is described as follows : " self, or that identical person of whose thoughts, actions, and sensations we are intimately conscious[80] ". It is even more obvious in his moral philosophy which explicitly posits the existence of the self as the basis of the doctrine of sympathy. The self is always there, even though it may not be accessible through introspection and reflection. It does not become an object of knowledge, but remains on the outskirts of human understanding as an observer, which paradoxically enough, is more active than the seemingly ebullient series of perceptions which it observes.

Conclusion

With Hume we reach the end of the philosophical background of the French Enlightenment as it concerns the problem of the self. But the transcendentalist solution is already fairly clearly indicated in certain of Hume's contentions, as is that of the Logical Positivists. However let us not jump from Hume to the twentieth century, but rather close this lengthy section by examining briefly certain developments of Hume's thought in the works of Thomas Reid, Johann Hamann, and Immanuel Kant.

Reid's investigation of the human mind reviews all the various explanations of the self and of personal identity, concentrating on Descartes, Locke and Hume. His conclusion is that the concept of personal identity is such a primitive one that it is logically and genetically prior to all other forms of thought. It is so intimate a part of our experience that " all languages have it interwoven in their original construction ... this opinion preceded all reasoning, and experience, and instruction[81] ". It is due to the constitution of human nature itself that we believe in the existence of an identical self and as such this concept must be termed one of the " judgments of nature ".

The German philosopher Hamann's major contribution to the history of philosophy lies in his discovery of the fact that thought processes do not exist in splendid isolation but are intimately connected with language. As noted by Berlin, Hamann antedates Wittgenstein in this respect : " philosophers who think that they are studying concepts or ideas or categories of reality are in fact studying means of human expression—language—which is at once the vehicle of man's views of the universe and of themselves, and part and parcel of that world itself, which is not something separable from the ways in which it is experienced or thought about[82]. "

But it is Kant who really gives to modern philosophy a whole new way of looking at reality ; his distinction between the phenomenal and the real world, his attempt to analyze all our concepts and categories in rela-tion to the kinds of evidence used to prove them, changed the very way in which philosophers look at the cosmos.   In the field of the self, Kant was the first to clearly distinguish the two aspects of the self, the *I* and the *me* which Descartes had so conveniently merged in his *Cogito*. Kant gave to these two aspects of the self the names of the transcendental and the empirical self.   Very briefly, the transcendental or " real " self is contrasted to the empirical or " phenomenal " self in three ways : first, it is an identical rather than a momentary self ; second, it is a thinking, catego-rizing, active self rather than a conscious, passive self ; third, it has the power of universalizing, of discovering the " things-in-themselves " rather than the mere phenomena of existents.

The transcendental self is not, and never can be, an object of know-ledge ; by its very nature it remains outside the scope of what can be known ; it is the knower and as such cannot partake of the known. Another way of looking at this distinction is to realize that only the world of appearances is known, and to this phenomenal world belongs that part of the self which can be grasped by the intellect.   But the principle which enables the intellect to know anything at all belongs to the transcendental world, the world of ultimate reality.   The transcendental self is on a par with the things-in-themselves and, like them, must remain unknown.   In more logical terms, as Strasser notes :   " that which gives our thought objective validity cannot be identical with any object of this thought[83]. " The transcendental subject determines the limits of knowledge while at the same time taking its place within the limits of the real, non-pheno-menal world.

One final characteristic of the transcendental self needs to be mention-ed.   Kant transforms the old dichotomy between the understanding and the will, the passive and the active functions of the self, into a new kind of dynamic relationship between these two factors.   Man does not come into the world full-blown ; on the contrary he forms himself, creating his essence out of his existence.   In his *Anthropology,* Kant states :   " The primary characteristic of the human species is the power as rational beings to acquire a character as such[84]. " In the words of Lester Crocker, whose main concern is with Kant's ethical philosophy :   " The self is not merely a given nature, a potentiality awaiting only to be fulfilled.   Through the will, each man must himself create the structure of his existence[85]. "

The French *philosophes* and their Christian adversaries were not, for the most part, arguing as philosophers when they discussed the nature and existence of the self.   This was an important consideration to them because it underlay so many of their pronouncements on how man should conduct himself in this world.   The basic constitution of human nature itself was the major issue of the age, and the self serves as a nucleus or focus for their various interpretations.

Chapter III

THE EIGHTEENTH CENTURY
CONCEPT OF THE SELF

General developments

The French *philosophes* and their adversaries never actually attacked the philosophic problem of the self in a systematic way, but it kept finding its way into a great many of their discussions. If we accept the thesis that the major interest of the age was to determine the nature of man and his place in the universe, it is easy to see that the question of the existence and nature of the self could hardly fail to arise. There is a certain development throughout the whole century in terms of this particular concept but, except towards the end, the general lines of argument did not change radically. For this reason we shall treat their ideas in a systematic rather than a chronological way, reserving the two key figures of Diderot and Rousseau for special treatment. These two writers developed certain tendencies which can be discerned in other minor figures, but their thought is so original in this sphere that they deserve individual treatment.

In a review of Jean Ehrard's *L'Idée de nature en France* Jacques Roger notes three major periods which distinguish the development of that concept : " le temps des grands rationalismes théocentriques, le temps de la nature sensible et multiple, le temps de la nature autonome et toute puissante[1]. " If we substitute *l'homme* for *la nature* in this critique we should not be far from the mark. The very early period was still dominated by the thought of Descartes and Malebranche, both of whom related man to God in a logical, rational fashion. Then came the flood of Lockean ideas, which liberated man from his complete dependence on God but at the same time loosened the bonds which made him into a recognizable entity. And finally we reach a period in which man really comes into his own ; he is considered as part of a greater society of men, able to determine his own and his fellow men's destiny.

The Cartesian concept of the self as a single substance underlying all thought had provided a rational explanation of the abstract essence of the human condition, a unitary substance to which all fleeting experiences are attached. The Lockean *tabula rasa* reduced man to a series of sensations, each existing in isolation and producing a sense of personal identity through mechanical relationships. The idea of an organic structure gradually replaced this atomic concept as the biological sciences and the wave of *sensibilité* pervaded French thought after 1750. On the one hand man was considered to be a creature of sentiment, and it was, therefore, possible to concentrate on his inner being, his state of feelings, in isolation so to speak. This interest in the life of the individualized and isolated self led to what Roland Mortier terms the "fascinante expérience de la solitude[2]".

However it was also possible to look at man as an active member of society, what might be termed an existential being in action, and in this case man's nature can by no means be determined solely by attention to his inner states of being. What really counts in this latter approach is the way in which the individual is related to and reacts to the society. And it is in this area that the self as self-concept, the image of the self, comes to the fore. In this instance, it is the means by which one projects one's self image to others that are important rather than the means by which one finds out about oneself. *Amour-propre* and its devious ways are just as important to the late eighteenth century as to the seventeenth, but the feeling had become rather more socialized and certainly much less condemned. The basic human need for both self-respect and esteem was judged to be over-riding in its sway, and various authors, particularly the novelists, studied the ways in which men and women managed to produce these feelings.

Even though the individual, in this last analysis, was considered to be an integral part of society, it was the individual as such which really counted by the end of the century. The concept of the self had passed from that of a static substance, through that of a fluid, non-organized entity, to that of an active formative structure. In this process the individual had been submitted to a series of dependencies, first of all on God, then on external stimuli, in order to emerge finally into a state of inner development activated by individual experiences. At the same time, the balance of certitude had swung from the early dependence on rational logic, represented by "Je pense", through empirical sensationalism, represented by "Je sens", to come to rest, temporarily at least, in the rather peculiar certainty of existential being, represented by "Je suis". Lockean terminology continued to hold sway through the whole century, as did a certain undercurrent of Cartesianism, but by the latter part of the century when either Rousseau or Diderot announce "Je sens, donc je suis", one can just as easily understand "Je suis, donc je sens".

The pervasiveness of this type of argument can be appreciated when one realizes that it infected even the pro-Christian writers. In his *Examen du matérialisme* (1754) Denesle starts from the Cartesian *Cogito* and concludes : "L'ame dit : je pense, donc je suis ; elle peut dire également : je suis, donc je pense. Si elle ne sentoit pas son existence, comment pourroit-elle l'affirmer ? Et qui pourra sentir à sa place, ce qu'elle ne sent pas ?

Donc penser & exister, n'est qu'une seule & même essence de l'ame humaine[3]. "

Neither rational thought nor empirical sensations had proved to be satisfactory in the pursuit of the truth about human nature. Some writers sought certainty in the so-called " sentiment de l'existence " which was interpreted in different ways, whereas others stressed the ever-developing organic center of force which constituted the new version of the self. Neither rationalism nor empiricism were denied a place in this new scheme, but they were not given control over human destiny and thought. Man was recognized as an extremely complex being who could not be adequately described either by abstracting his essence or by describing his fleeting experiences. Both facets needed to be synthesized in order to do away with cold pronouncements which do not correspond to the warm and active nature of man.

This line of development is of course complicated by a number of factors, not the least of which is the situation which existed in France in the eighteenth century between the *philosophes* and their Christian adversaries. No compromise could be effected between the ideas of these two groups ; nothing but radical solutions were acceptable. In terms of the self this tended to become a dilemma for those *philosophes* who were not willing to accept the Cartesian, and eventually Christian, idea of a unified, separate substance, usually identified with the soul, as the true self, and yet were unhappy at the ultimate consequences of empirical sensationalism which led to the denial of the existence of the self. It seemed to be a case of all or nothing, but new approaches were finally worked out which permitted an organic concept to emerge sufficiently different to meet the objections of both groups. This development in the direction of a center of dynamic force and an open system of the self came extremely slowly and with many returns to previous approaches. It was certainly delayed by the fact that the denial of the existence of the self was assumed to involve the denial of the existence of the soul. Very few *philosophes* were willing to argue in favor of the soul, and so, perhaps, pushed their denial of the self beyond what they ordinarily would have done. In any case, the desire for some grounds of certainty became more and more pronounced, leading to the development of intuitive ways of knowing which had no relation to either reason or sensation, but which were in some subtle way more clear and distinct than either of these two. Descartes' methodical doubt and Locke's genuine uncertainty were pushed aside by this new epistemology which allowed of no doubt whatsoever and was therefore much more satisfactory.

We shall now proceed in our discussion not chronologically but analytically, but these general developments should be kept in mind. We will first analyze the various means of knowing the self, then approach the nature of the self thus revealed to the individual, then discuss how this concept was used, and finally turn to the self-concept, its formation and projection.

Means of knowing the self

The Cartesian dictum " Je pense, donc je suis " continued to attract adherents throughout the eighteenth century. An early example may be found in Fontenelle who remarked in his *Connoissance de l'esprit :* " Toute la nature de l'esprit est de penser, et nous ne considérons l'Esprit humain que selon ses idées[4]. " If the nature of the mind, which is here identified with the inner being or self, is thought alone, it follows logically that we know this inner being through a rational process, that we learn about its existence through reason. Its existence is the clearest and most distinct idea available to mankind and serves as a kind of model for all other knowledge. For instance, the Christian apologist Denesle takes into account the then fashionable reliance on sensations as the only true source of knowledge but rapidly turns the statement " Je sens, donc je suis " into a version of Cartesian rationalism by insisting on the fact that feeling involves thinking : " Car qu'est-ce que sentir, si ce n'est pas du moins connoître implicitement que l'on existe ? Et qu'est-ce que connoître, si ce n'est pas penser ?[5] " This association of sensations with a conscious type of knowledge about them is found even in Condillac who is for the most part one of the best representatives of the composition theory of the self in French thought. Condillac distinguishes " la connoissance " from simple sensations and insists that it accompanies all of them : " nous avons toujours conscience des impressions qui se font dans l'ame[6]. " We will return to this type of self-awareness at a later stage, but it has certain obvious affinities with the Cartesian proof of the existence of the self.

Other writers, both Christian apologists and *philosophes,* used a rational approach although they did not necessarily say that knowledge of the self involved a clear and distinct idea in the Cartesian sense. In his *Recherches philosophiques* (1743) St. Hyacinthe notes that thought necessarily implies existence since " Dire je pense, c'est dire je suis un être pensant[7] ", and it is contradictory to believe or state both terms of being and non-being at the same time. This confused reasoning leads him to posit the rather redundant result : " Je sens, que je sens que j'existe[8]. " Ilharat de la Chambre, another Christian apologist, wishing to go behind the current " sentiment intime de l'existence " tries to prove its veracity by appealing to a syllogistic argument which in sum states that what seems to be " vraisemblable " cannot emanate from nothing and that therefore these thoughts and feelings must have a " sujet d'inhésion réellement existant, puisque le néant n'est susceptible d'aucun mode, ni d'aucune qualité[9] ".

A far more subtle rational proof of the existence of the self is given in Quesnay's article " Evidence " which was published in the *Encyclopédie* in 1756. Quesnay's main interest lies in establishing the validity of our belief in the existence of the outside world, but in order to accomplish this aim he ties it in with our belief in our own personal existence, stating that the one is as sure as the other since neither of them exist separately. It is only through the exterior world acting upon our senses that we come to have any knowledge whatsoever of our self, which otherwise would exist *in vacuo* beyond the limits of human knowledge. In addition he resorts to the argument that a knowledge of personal identity over a period of time is completely dependent on memory and that it is only through the continuous repetition of certain sensations that we have any reason to believe in what he terms " la fidélité de notre mémoire[10] ". His thoughts on the role of memory in personal identity are not particularly original, but he is an excellent representative of that group of thinkers who still wanted rational proof for the existence of the self.

In general it is fair to say that these rationalists were a distinct minority ; most thinkers were not satisfied with an abstract proof of the type offered by Quesnay and wanted something more personal and individualized. In the wake of Malebranche this group was willing to concede that the vague feeling to which they appealed might not give any real idea of the nature of the self, but at least it gave, in their eyes, irrefutable proof of its existence. These thinkers can be divided into two groups, the first relying on sensations, the *sentiment intime* as a kind of sixth sense, and the other relying much more on emotional tone, *le sentiment de l'existence* detached, as it were, from all ties to the senses. Sensationalism and emotionalism often occur in tandem, but one can usually determine which element is foremost in the mind of a particular author.

Although the *Dictionnaire de l'Académie* (1778) ignores this particular definition, both the *Dictionnaire de Trévoux* (1771) and the *Encyclopédie* give separate entries to " Sentiment intime " as a metaphysical term. The *Dictionnaire de Trévoux* is fairly circumspect in its definition, merely stating that it is the means by which we get to know all the things which take place within ourselves. However it adds that there is sometimes a secondary meaning attached to this term : " Ce mot désigne quelquefois une persuasion que nous sentons intérieurement, sans qu'on en puisse rendre raison aux autres ni les en convaincre ", going on to stress the marked difference between this type of knowledge to that gained by the rational process which proceeds step by step and is accessible to all. The article in the *Encyclopédie* is longer but not much more conclusive ; John Lough points out that most of it is taken from Père Buffier's *Traité des premières vérités*[11]. A large part of the unsigned article, presumably the work of the Chevalier de Jaucourt, is devoted to contradicting the statement that the *sentiment intime* produces the only completely true and sure evidence of anything. This is disproved by showing the ridiculous consequences of such a position ; first of all, we could have no knowledge of the external world at all, second no knowledge of the past since this feeling is always in the present, and third no knowledge of other intelligent beings. The principle of truth embodied in the *sentiment intime* is therefore rendered " bisarre, ridicule & absurde ", and the reader is referred to the articles " Evidence " and " Sens commun " for further enlightenment.

A number of other articles in the *Encyclopédie* touch upon this particular topic but for the most part only " Délicieux " by Diderot and " Existence " by Turgot consciously apply the terms *sentiment intime* and *sentiment de l'existence*. Diderot's article will be discussed at length in the chapter devoted to his ideas, but his *sentiment de l'existence* falls into the emotional category, having very little to do with either the senses or the rational faculty, whereas Turgot most definitely conceives of it as a type of sensation. The latter actually uses the term *sixième sens* to refer to the whole series of internal sensations of which we are not consciously aware, but which are nonetheless constantly present :

> Il ne faut pas omettre un autre ordre de sensations plus pénétrantes, pour ainsi dire, qui rapportées à l'intérieur de notre corps, en occupant même quelquefois toute l'habitude, semblent remplir les trois dimensions de l'espace, & porter immédiatement avec elle l'idée de l'étendue solide. Je ferai de ces sensations une classe particuliere, sous le nom de *tact intérieur* ou *sixieme sens*... cette multitude de sensations confuses qui ne nous abandonnent jamais, qui nous circonscrivent en quelque sorte notre corps, qui nous le rendent toujours présent, & que par cette raison, quelques métaphysiciens ont appelées *sens de la coexistence de notre corps*[12].

This sense of bodily identity is the basic foundation of any knowledge of the self. It is no more than a conscious appreciation of these habitually unconscious feelings. The fact that these particular sensations persist in time and are subject to variation in intensity makes us become aware of them and identify them as belonging to a particular object, the self. However Turgot's main interest lies in proving the existence of the material world and of other intelligent beings, and so his discussion of the self goes no further than this bare outline. It is noticeable however that he relies almost entirely on Lockean sensationalism to prove both the existence of the inner self and then from that the existence of other beings[13].

Another Encyclopedist, d'Alembert, also discussed the problem of the proof of existing beings in his *Eclaircissemens*, published in 1767 as a supplement to his *Essai sur les éléments de philosophie* (1759). D'Alembert is interested in explaining how we come to form the abstract idea of existence and states bluntly that " la notion abstraite d'existence se forme d'abord en nous par le sentiment du *moi* qui résulte de nos sensations & de nos pensées[14] ". This combination of sensations and rational thought is not an unusual one for the age, but as a mathematician d'Alembert is perhaps a little more inclined to appeal to rational, logical proof wherever possible. He argues that since we can separate the " subject " of the idea of the self from the idea itself, we form an abstract idea of our own existence and by analogy extend this idea to the existence of other beings. Here we have a separation of the two functions of the self, the *I* as initiator and ultimate being and the *me* as a collection of sensations. Since d'Alembert's interest lay in the exterior world of physics rather than the internal world of the self, he never pursued this division which might have led him on to interesting conclusions. However it is possible that he would merely have ended up in the Cartesian distinction between the thinker as independent substance and thought as its modes. As Grimsley has noted, d'Alembert's philosophical thought is basically Cartesian with an overlay of Lockean sensationalism[15].

The appeal to sensations as the basis for the self was not confined to the *philosophes*; many of the Catholic apologists adopted a similar position although they used it to prove the existence of a soul rather than that of a self. One example is the abbé Para du Phanjas in his *Principes de la saine philosophie conciliés avec ceux de la religion* (1774). He refers to the *sentiment intime* as the source of all our knowledge about ourselves and our existence, states that it is the means by which the soul is apprized of all its sensations, sentiments and ideas, and concludes that it gives us an absolutely sure means of arriving at the truth about ourselves[16]. Another apologist, Jean Formey, in his *Mélanges philosophiques* (1754) discussed the means of knowing the self and concluded that " le sentiment, la réflexion, l'expérience intérieure sont les moyens que nous avons de découvrir la nature de l'âme[17] ". He went on to state, rather than prove, that this knowledge is much more sure and certain than any knowledge we can ever hope to attain about the external world, agreeing explicitly with Descartes that " il est plus aisé de connoître l'esprit humain que le corps[18] ". However, according to Formey, a conscious idea of the self is ultimately dependent on memory, since it involves the identification of a whole series of individual *sentiments intimes* as belonging to one and the same subject[19].

Formey stated one of the main arguments against that concept of the self which relied upon the senses, or a particular one, as the means of knowing it. The standard contention of those opposed to this idea was that a sensation is merely a momentary, fleeting feeling which could not, because of its very nature, lead to any knowledge about a simple and unified being such as the self. This dichotomy between a philosophy of being and one of existence is endemic to eighteenth century thought in general and becomes particularly noticeable in those spheres of thought which involve the nature of man. Ethical ideas also suffered from the same kind of difficulty, and it seemed impossible for any solution to be presented which would effectively avoid the twin roadblocks of relativism and absolutism. The concept of transcendental values was slow in forming and even when formulated was not understood for the most part. Numerous authors found themselves forced to choose between relativism and absolutism although most of them saw something of value in both. The appeal to memory as a kind of independent faculty within the nature of man can be seen as an attempt to have the best of both worlds, the relative as reported by the senses and the absolute as made accessible through memory.

This correlation is shown quite clearly in the introductory remarks of the Benedictine Pernety in his monumental work on physiognomy, *La Connoissance de l'homme moral par celle de l'homme physique* (1776). Using the rather shop-worn example of the caterpillar, Pernety observes that its various metamorphoses do nothing to the essential being which has remained fundamentally the same through the whole series of changes. He enlarges upon this theme in his second book devoted to the same topic, *Observations sur les maladies de l'âme* (1777) : " Rien n'est constant dans l'univers que l'univers, considéré dans son tout, & non dans ses parties. Le désordre qui regne en apparence parmi celles-ci est ce qui fait l'ordre de celui-là[20]. " Man is one of those creatures most subject to change, and it is only thanks to memory that any man is able to conceive of himself as a single being. He refers to memory as the consciousness of having already been through certain situations and insists that without this " compagne inséparable de toutes les opérations de l'entendement " no one would be able to conceive of himself at all. A fall or an illness which affects the memory also affects one's self, since a new existent entity would appear at the moment that past memories are wiped out[21]. However, judging by the analogy of the caterpillar, this existent entity would be merely another phase of the unitary being which underlies all these metamorphoses. Nevertheless the underlying being does not seem to be accessible except to a superior intelligence linked to the unchanging absolute universe.

The appeal to an outside agent as being the ultimate source of certainty in questions of identity also occurs in Bonnet. Again using the familiar example of the caterpillar, Bonnet makes a distinction between personality and person. The first is ephemeral and disappears when memory is disrupted. The second never changes regardless of the numerous metamorphoses to which the personality may be subject. To an outside agent only those changes which appertain to this particular person are attached to it : " Mais, l'intelligence qui connoît à fond cet Etre & qui le contemple, lui rapporte & ne rapporte qu'à lui toutes les modifications qu'elle y découvre. Elles composent pour cette Intelligence une suite dont toutes les parties se lient dans son Entendement & concourent à former cette sorte d'unité qu'on nomme le *Sujet* ou la *Personne*[22]. " The capital letters betray Bonnet's ultimate resort to God as the only guarantor of individuality.

This appeal to the divine in order to uphold the human is also noticeable in another Protestant writer, Le Guay de Prémontval who distinguished between the personality and the soul on the same grounds. Prémontval extended the caterpillar image even further to include life after death ; though a man may not remember his earthly life he remains the same being in the eyes of God, and it therefore behooves each person to pay attention to what happens in his day-to-day life since each and every circumstance of existence adheres to his essential being. The individual might lose track of himself but a higher intelligence sees and knows all[23].

To these thinkers, all of them Christian, memory does not seem to be strong enough to bear the burden of the self. It is subject to too many interruptions and dislocations and ultimately must be supplemented by something outside the human sphere. It is obvious that no self-respecting *philosophe* would be willing to make such an admission, and when we examine such a representative work as Helvétius' *De l'esprit* the importance of memory cannot be overstated. To Helvétius there are only two causes of ideas, " deux puissances passives ", the first, known as " sensibilité physique " permits us to receive impressions from the outside world, and the second, memory, permits us to keep these same impressions[24]. Helvétius specifically refuses to follow his train of thought into the area of metaphysics, stating that an empirical investigation such as his is incapable of arriving at metaphysical pronouncements about the existence of the soul. In *De l'homme,* published posthumously and therefore more free in its pronouncements, Helvétius identifies the soul with the faculty of sensing, but without memory the soul is incapable of self-consciousness. The role of memory is thus fundamental in any discussion of the means of knowing the self, since Helvétius assumes, as do most eighteenth century thinkers, that thought is *ipso facto* conscious.

In a more physical explanation, d'Holbach also has recourse to the faculty of memory as the ultimate base of the self. In his *Système de la nature* d'Holbach introduces a sixth sense, one which permits a man to be aware of what is going on inside himself[25]. In combination with memory this interior sense leads to all forms of thought : " le corps est une machine sensible, qui a nécessairement la conscience momentanée dans l'instant qu'elle reçoit une impression, et qui a la conscience du *moi* par la mémoire des impressions successivement éprouvées ; mémoire qui, ressuscitant une impression antérieurement reçue, ou arrêtant comme fixe, ou faisant durer une impression qu'on reçoit, tandis qu'on y en associe une autre, puis une troisième, etc., donne tout le mécanisme du raisonnement[26]. " La Mettrie provides another good example of the importance given to the faculty of memory by the more outspoken materialists. In his eyes a man is not a man at all unless he can refer back to his previous experiences : " Enfin un homme qui perdroit toute mémoire, seroit un atome pensant, si on peut penser sans elle ; inconnu à lui-même, il ignoreroit ce qui lui arriveroit, & ne s'en rappelleroit rien[27]. "

Voltaire is an especially useful indicator of the problems inherent in reliance upon memory as the foundation of the self. In the early *Traité de métaphysique* (1734) Voltaire announces unequivocally that memory alone leads to personal identity ; loss of memory during an illness is glossed over by the remark that it is usually restored at a later date and that, therefore, the fictitious Jacques is still the same person[28]. By 1766 Voltaire is less willing to gloss over major problems ; he states that it is not only illness or a fall which interrupts the functioning of memory and, therefore, of the formation of the self ; the fact of the matter is that all individuals have the same problem at some point in their lives. even if it only involves those childhood experiences which took place so early that they never did have a place in consciousness. This leads to the conclusion that a new identity comes into being with each lapse of memory, at which Voltaire exclaims : "et de là quelles singulières conséquences ![29] " In the *Questions sur l'Encyclopédie* (1771) Voltaire repeats this argument and adds the example of a river whose waters are never the same but which remains the same river nonetheless. However the river has no physical identity as such, and, in applying the analogy to man, Voltaire lapses into uncertainty about the self. He cannot allow the fact that personal experiences have no connection whatsoever with the self, nor can he assume that the only real entities are those fleeting experiences themselves. As usual he declares that such questions are beyond the scope of human intelligence and retreats ironically behind the final authority of faith.

Buffon makes knowledge of the self, based on memory, the main distinction between man and the animals : " La conscience de son existence, ce sentiment intérieur qui constitue le *moi*, est composé chez nous de la sensation de notre existence actuelle, & du souvenir de notre existence passée[30]. " This is expanded into the rather unexpected conclusion that the more ideas one has the surer one is of one's own existence ; not only that, but the more intelligent one is, the more one exists, and this certainly puts all animals on a vastly inferior plane to man. Without the ability to recollect their past experiences animals have few ideas and are therefore deprived of " la conscience d'existence ". It is obvious that only human beings can attain the dignity of possessing a self ; animals are reduced to a series of personality changes with no principle of organization. This result, which Buffon confines to the animal sphere, was seen to be threatening humanity as well by a large number of apologists and *philosophes* alike. Memory appeared to be a very weak link indeed, and a self which was formed of nothing more than sensations plus the memory of past sensations seemed to be in danger of total disintegration. Other means of access to this elusive element became more and more desirable as the ultimate consequences of reliance on empirical data alone were made clear.

Those writers who derived knowledge of the self from a sentimental rather than a sensationalistic base did not have to face the problem of how a series of sensations could possibly form a unified concept. The appeal to the *sentiment de l'existence* simply by-passes this particular problem and states that what is garnered by this mode of knowledge is the whole existent being of an individual, and not just a single momentary state of its being. This distinction between the appeal to sensations and the appeal to emotions is an important one. Sensations can only be cumulative and must eventually depend on some other principle of unification, such as memory, causal relationships of various kinds, or rational explanations such as that offered by Quesnay.

By declaring that the *sentiment de l'existence* was another mode of knowledge, authors as diverse as Rivarol, Rousseau and the abbé Lelarge de Lignac introduced a different kind of epistemological principle, although few of them would have been willing to give up the sensationalistic epistemology on which they assumed all knowledge rested. What they actually did was to take the word *sentiment* in one of its meanings, the one which refers to emotions, and use it as if it were referring to its other definition, the one which the *Dictionnaire de l'Académie* (1778) defines as " Perception que l'ame a des objets, par le moyen des organes des sens ". By this sleight of hand these authors managed to prove the existence of a continuing self which did not need to be supported by memory or any other faculty. Its existence was intimately known in an utterly irrefutable manner to each individual who was willing to allow this particular feeling to penetrate his conscious mind. Certain writers see this feeling as a substratum of all existence, while others insist on the conscious application of it. We shall rather arbitrarily call the first *le sentiment de l'existence* and the second *la conscience de l'existence*.

The appeal to the *sentiment intérieur* as a vague feeling tone is directly traceable to the influence of Malebranche as most of the authors were willing to admit. This new mode of knowledge was particularly attractive to the Christian apologists who were anxious to prove without the question of a doubt the existence of an immortal soul. Denesle states this in its clearest form : " L'ame humaine est créée avec le sentiment intime de son existence " and " il est contre l'essence de l'ame d'exister, & de ne pas sentir qu'elle existe[31]. " Other Church writers are more subtle ; for instance Ilharat de la Chambre notes the immediacy and absolute certainty of the propositions suggested to the mind by this faculty and stresses its affective affinities in his *Abrégé de philosophie* : " Les vérités du *sentiment intérieur*, sont celles qui ont pour objet des choses qui se connaissent immédiatement, c'est-à-dire, sans aucune discussion, & par le simple sentiment intime qu'on en a. Les propositions *je suis, je pense, j'ai de la joye, je souffre* expriment des vérités de cette espéce[32]. " But Ilharat is aware of the fact that the certainty of this mode of knowledge has very definite limitations since it is only convincing to the person actually experiencing it and cannot be communicated to others. He therefore renounces it as the only indicator of truth and refers to " sens commun, autorité & raisonnement " as the true guides in this pursuit[33].

In his widely read *De l'homme* Rivarol insists on the priority in time of *sentiment* over *sensation*. Rivarol objects that if sensations preceded sentiments there would be a multiplicity of the latter and that this is not the case : " nous avons des sensations différentes, mais nous n'avons pour toutes qu'un sentiment. Cette faculté première a tout précédé dans nous, et n'y a été précédée par rien, pas même par l'existence[34]. " It is to the *unicité du sentiment* that we must look to find an explanation for the fact that man is not merely a series of sensations or even a combination of two impulses, one originating in the body and the other in the mind or soul, but rather a single unified whole. Both Cartesian dualism and Lockean pluralism are the target of Rivarol's criticism, and this attitude is not an unusual one in the late eighteenth century when most thinkers were striving towards some form of monism.

By far the most interesting Catholic writer to appeal to the *sentiment de l'existence* was the abbé Lelarge de Lignac whom Palmer calls " probably the most considerable metaphysician among defenders of the church[35] ". His whole philosophy is based on the principle that this feeling is the simplest, most fundamental mode of knowledge known to man. He developed this theme through a number of books, none of them widely read as he rather plaintively notes in his last work, *Le Témoignage du sens intime* (1760)[36]. According to Lignac no person is without a fundamental certainty about his own existence, and any philosopher who doubts it is merely deceiving himself. This feeling is so very basic to human nature that it is absolutely impossible to be uncertain about one's existence. In normal eighteenth century fashion Lignac goes back to infancy to establish the genetic priority of this feeling and assumes that this also establishes its logical priority : " le sentiment de l'existence est en nous antérieur à toute connoissance et à tout raisonnement. Dans un enfant d'un jour, incapable de raisonner, l'ame se sent exister[37]. " While this feeling is completely natural, it becomes submerged in the press of everyday life, and an adult must be willing to withdraw into himself in order to be able to appreciate the importance of it. Only when we rid our minds of all external impressions, when we reduce the exterior stimuli to zero, are we able to fully comprehend this deep-seated and penetrating feeling. He notes that this condition is popularly known as " rêver à la Suisse " but insists that this is not a state of pure inertia but rather one in which the soul is in direct contact with itself[38]. He even goes so far as to point out that Descartes was mistaken in his dictum " Je pense, donc je suis " since all that he needed to say was " Je ". The use of the first person pronoun assumes all that is supposedly proved by the forthcoming statement [39].

Not only does this feeling give the individual irrefutable proof of his current existence, according to Lignac, it extends itself to all phases of his existence, past, present and future. It is what gives a person the ability to compare and to judge since it is the only unchanging facet of our multiform existence : " Cette conscience de mon identité, je la trouve comme le fond de toutes mes pensées, de toutes mes sensations, de toutes mes affections [40]. " By this he means more than Locke's idea of the mind always perceiving itself perceiving, for Lignac sees this feeling as the sure proof of his individual identity reaching back all the way into childhood, whereas Locke had introduced the principle of self-consciousness to prove his theory of personal identity. Lignac tries to show how radically his principle differs from any which have been proposed in the past by contrasting it with the ideas of Descartes, Locke, Condillac and Buffon. All of these philosophers, according to Lignac, ultimately had recourse to some other faculty : Descartes to reason, Locke to self-consciousness, Condillac to memory and Buffon to a sense of bodily identity. Lignac insists that his principle is anterior both genetically and logically to any and all of these other modes of knowledge.

Lignac asserts that without *le sentiment de l'existence* no kind of knowledge could exist at all ; it is the only immediately accessible way of penetrating to the interior of an entity. Only the self can be known in this way ; all bodily objects, including other people, are known through the senses which only approach them from the outside, and abstract ideas as conceived by reason are even less directly known. This intuitive knowledge of the self about itself is therefore extremely precious : " Notre ame se voit, pour ainsi dire, de dedans en dedans, il n'y a qu'elle qui puisse voir de cette manière [41]. " Our knowledge of our own bodies does not approach this intensity since we can view them objectively. In this case our knowledge is projected from the inside but appears on the outside in contrast to our view of our soul which is entirely internalized. The self combines these two modes of knowledge, and is known by a combination of the internally generated *sentiment de l'existence* and the externally controlled *sens de la coexistence de notre corps* [42]. But in the final analysis it is only the *sentiment de l'existence* which counts ; it is so primitive in human nature that Lignac takes the unusual step of identifying it with existence itself : " le sujet qui se sent identique en moi sous une infinité de sensations accidentelles, est absolument un, & simple ... Son existence & le sens de son existence ne sont pas deux êtres distincts, ne sont pas même distingués, comme le mode l'est du sujet [43]. "

Because an individual person is made up of a combination of a particular soul in a particular body, the two means of access are necessary to form an idea of the self. The *sentiment de l'existence* can be distinguished from the *sens de la coexistence de notre corps* although they usually occur together ; it takes a special effort on the part of the individual to feel his way into the unusual experience of relying entirely on the former in order to penetrate his inner being. Lignac is quite clear that this represents a totally different means of access to knowledge about one element of human nature. He heaps scorn on those authors who try to get at the self through a process of thought which is entirely externalized, whether through sensations or reason itself. He insists on the fact that if the *sentiment de l'existence* did not give access to an unchanging self there would be no grounds whatsoever for comparisons or judgments ; it follows therefore that this principle is anterior to memory, that memory actually relies on " le sens fondamental de mon individualité " rather than forming it.

Lignac's *Suite des Lettres à un Américain* (1756) adds criticism of Condillac to his earlier criticism of Buffon. In the *Traité des sensations* (1754) Condillac developed the image of a statue coming to life by being endowed with the use of a single sense organ at a time. However this work was by no means either the first or the last to use this metaphor to explore the nature of man. As early as 1741 Boureau-Deslandes in his *Pygmalion ou la Statue animée* had used the same image to prove the radical thesis that matter might be able to think. He insisted on the importance of movement in the development of the ability to think, and his statue passes from inanimate matter to animate and thinking person rather abruptly. Thought arrives on the scene " comme un trait de lumière qui éclate dans une nuit obscure ", and the statue, no longer a statue, begins to question itself in philosophic terms about its nature and reason for being. The only certain answer at this point is the fact of existence itself : " Tout ce que j'apperçois, tout ce qu'il m'est permis de connoître, c'est que j'existe & que je sens que j'existe [44]. " After this promising beginning Boureau-Deslandes develops an apostrophe to " la pensée " which he seems to confuse with the ability to realize one's existence. This is a far cry from Condillac's carefully worked out scheme of bringing a statue to complete self-realization through the accretion of individual sensations.

Although Condillac's treatise was, and is even today, almost always held to be the most carefully worked out system of complete sensationalism, upon close examination it turns out to have many other elements in it which are not compatible with an exclusively sensationalist epistemology. These elements were of course ignored by such contemporary critics as Lignac who tended to take Condillac's vocabulary at face value. In the first place Condillac was a great deal more influenced by Cartesian rationalism than would appear on a superficial examination of his work. It is easy to be misled since Condillac himself stressed the empirical aspect of his thought and, according to his avowed intentions, wished only to elucidate the generation of ideas in a human mind. At times he admits to other aims, notably in an interesting chapter of his work on *La Logique* (1780) in which he reduces the whole field of epistemology to algebra, showing that every question, including the one he had already treated about the origin of human thought, must of necessity include within it the necessary elements which permit it to be answered in the same way that an equation is solved, that is by the simple process of substituting certain known factors for unknown ones[45]. This " logical radicalism " as Herbert Dieckmann terms it, is characteristic of Condillac's thought even at the times when it appears to be most closely aligned with pure empiricism[46].

Even if one overlooks the logical basis and intention of Condillac's thought, it is clear that one has to be very wary of his use of the term *sensation*. As Lenoir notes in his study of Condillac, this term has three distinct connotations : " les conditions physiologiques de la sensation, l'aspect affectif et l'aspect représentatif de la perception[47]. " The physiological conditions which make sensations possible are not very heavily stressed in Condillac's theory ; for the most part the word *sensation* can be taken to mean either the perception in the mind which is occasioned by external stimuli or the reaction of the individual to such a perception. There is an attempt to differentiate these two meanings by using *perception* for the first and *sensation* for the second, but Condillac is not very consistent in his use of these terms and, since his avowed aim is to reduce all human thought to *sensation,* it is obviously more useful to have this one term cover a number of concepts.

In addition to this fairly frequent ambiguity in the use of this term, there also exists a much more radical philosophical ambiguity. In a brief but penetrating article Carré has carefully analyzed Condillac's use of the word *sensation* and has shown conclusively that in a great many instances it involves not just the impression produced by external stimuli but also a type of self-consciousness against which all these perceptions are in some degree measured[48]. This helps us to appreciate Concillac's annoyance at the criticism which was so often levelled against his system, namely that it reduces man to a completely passive entity at the mercy of outside forces. In a letter of 1779 to Comte Potocki, Condillac vehemently denies this : " quoique nos sensations soient passives, il ne s'ensuit pas que tout ce qui vient des sensations soit passif également[49]. " He insists on the fact that our ideas are of our own making, not only that, but that our ability to have ideas is also of our own making and plaintively asks how this could possibly be interpreted as a denial of activity to the mind. The impressions which the mind receives through its physiological organization are turned into something quite different by the very fact of being received in that mind. They are turned back on themselves before being admitted into the company of all the other sensations, past and present, which make up the self. It is this process of self-consciously relating the new perceptions to those which are already present which constitutes the essential characteristic of the human mind. To Condillac *conscience* is implicit in *sensation* ; the former is both genetically and logically prior to the latter. The thought of any kind of sense impression existing without a conscious mind to receive it was inconceivable to Condillac.

If we follow the growth of Condillac's statue in the *Traité des sensations* we will be able to note some of these assumptions. The first sense impression which the statue receives is that of the odor of a rose ; at the very first odor the statue becomes that odor ; it identifies itself entirely with the sense impression. But this is the only moment at which such a simplistic theory of personal identity is ever possible. At that particular moment the self of the statue could actually be said to be nothing more than the sensation which it has received. As soon as other sense impressions, which Condillac limits to odors in this first section, impinge upon the statue's sense organs and thence on its mind, the statue develops the faculty of memory which enables it to compare the newly received sensations with those which have come before. This leads to a new type of self, one which is very close to the idea of personality discussed earlier. According to Condillac the word *moi* involves more than a series of sensations : " Ce qu'on entend par ce mot, ne me paroît convenir qu'à un être qui remarque que, dans le moment présent, il n'est plus ce qu'il a été. Tant qu'il ne change point, il existe sans aucun retour sur lui-même : mais aussitôt qu'il change, il juge qu'il est le même qui a été auparavant de telle manière, et il dit *moi*[50]. " Condillac would therefore deny that the statue at the moment it receives its very first sensation has a self at all in the sense in which he is using the term. A self involves the possibility of self-consciousness ; " un retour sur lui-même " becomes the fundamental principle to which Condillac will turn every time he discusses the self. It is not, therefore, an entirely empirical process nor an entirely phenomenal being which is assumed to exist.

The chapters on the sense of touch elaborate this theme by pointing out that every person, here allegorized into the statue, is conscious of his own existence through what Condillac terms " le sentiment fondamental ", the feeling which surrounds our every movement and which is best exemplified by respiration itself. This is an internalized sense of touch which accompanies us at every moment and which leads on to the idea of the self as a unit. This *sentiment fondamental* develops into what Condillac terms either " le sentiment de mon être " or " la conscience de mon existence ". The first is a more rationalized version of the *sentiment de l'existence,* the feeling tone which accompanies all our thoughts and actions according to the numerous followers of Malebranche. But Condillac goes beyond this reliance on emotions as a basis for the self ; he uses the emotive reactions of an individual to a sense impression only to indicate that what really counts is the reaction and not the impression itself. Thus any externally stimulated impression, even one generated within one's own body, only takes on relevancy when it is turned into a part of one's self-consciousness. A mere collection of sensations in the ordinary sense of the word will not do for Condillac ; these sensations are fused into an individual's existence by a process which he often assumes to be part of the sensation itself, that is the relating of it to all the other sensations which have preceded it in that particular individual. The last section of the *Traité des sensations* effectively dispels any grounds for the belief that Condillac was in favor of an empirical self, one which could be completely described by a mere listing of the contents of the mind :

> Mais ce *moi,* qui prend de la couleur à mes yeux, de la solidité sous mes mains, se connoit-il mieux pour regarder aujourd'hui comme à lui toutes les parties de ce corps auxquelles il s'intéresse, et dans lesquelles il croit exister ? Je sais qu'elles sont à moi, sans pouvoir le comprendre : je me vois, je me touche, en un mot, je me sens, mais je ne sais ce que je suis ; et, si j'ai cru être son, saveur, couleur, odeur, actuellement je ne sais plus ce que je dois me croire[51].

The dissatisfaction of the author with the theory he has outlined is clear ; sensations, even ones which are so intimately involved with consciousness, are not sufficient to attain any knowledge about the true self, the self which exists behind the mere content of the self. There seems to be no way for a man to penetrate beneath the surface of his identity ; he is limited to what can be analyzed and listed and this is not what is meant by the word *moi.* Is it surprising that Lignac was so insistent that what Condillac needed was a new epistemological principle, one which assured not only the existence of the self but the knowledge of that existence ?

Condillac did give a rational proof of the existence of the self, one which was by no means original to him. He states that unity of consciousness itself is sufficient grounds on which to posit the existence of an individual self, one to which all the various sensations and feelings could be attached[52]. But this logical statement does not come anywhere near satisfying his need not only to prove its existence abstractly but also to demonstrate it in terms of everyday life. His reliance on *la conscience* is noticeable in his *Dictionnaire de synonymes* where it is defined as " sentiment intérieur. Nous connoissons notre ame par *conscience*[53] ". It is most unfortunate that the notebooks containing the entries from " Science " to " Signe " are no longer available ; the definition of " Sensation " and " Sentiment " would have been most enlightening. A very brief entry under " Perception " gives a definition of no great originality : " l'action de l'esprit qui saisit les idées " and refers the reader to the now non-existent entry " Sensations ". On the other hand it is interesting to note that Condillac felt no need to give any definition whatsoever of *moi* or *soi* ; these concepts are covered in the entries " Ame " and " Esprit " which reminds us that Condillac, while writing in a philosophic vein, never broke with Church doctrine. " Le bon abbé " always had the metaphysical concept of the soul to fall back on when his epistemological theories failed to provide a basis for a belief in the self. The soul exists as an independent entity, unified and comprehensive, to which all the passing perceptions, emotions and ideas could be attached.

The best known definition of the self in Condillac, the one which was constantly picked out for criticism by his contemporary critics, reads like a paraphrase of Hume, although we know that Condillac did not read English and that Hume's *Treatise* was not translated into French until the nineteenth century. We have already noted that Hume's philosophical work was almost unknown in continental Europe until the mid-1750's. What little interest there was in his work at that time was directed more towards his political and religious thought. It is therefore extremely unlikely that Condillac knew of Hume's speculations concerning the self at the time he wrote the *Traité des sensations* (1754). Describing the statue limited to the sense of smell, Condillac gives the following definition : " Son *moi* n'est que la collection des sensations qu'elle éprouve, et de celles que la mémoire lui rappelle. " But this succinct definition has a footnote appended to it in which it is clear that it is merely the empirical self which is accessible through the senses and that standing behind it is another, more solid kind of self. Commenting on a paragraph from Pascal which purports to prove that one can only like or dislike qualities and not an individual person, Condillac remarks :

> Ce n'est pas l'assemblage des qualités qui fait la personne ; car le même homme, jeune ou vieux, beau ou laid, sage ou fou, seroit autant de personnes distinctes ; et pour quelques qualités qu'on m'aime, c'est toujours moi qu'on aime ; car les qualités ne sont que moi modifié différemment.

He goes on to show that in the sense of Pascal's definition of *moi,* God alone would be able to apply this term to himself[54].

Another author who used the statue analogy is Bonnet who claims that he had written thirteen sections of his *Essai analytique sur les facultés de l'âme* before being informed of the publication of the *Traité des sensations.* Rather than abandon his own project he continued to develop his own theory of the statue while introducing into his presentation criticism of Condillac's approach. Bonnet reproached Condillac with being altogether too analytical in his description of the nature of man ; a naturalist himself, Bonnet stressed the organic concept of growth, using examples such as the chain and a series in a certain pattern, rather than Condillac's algebraic formulation. The simplistic reduction of all man's thought

processes and emotional and volitional reactions to the crude base of sensations was not satisfactory to Bonnet, who insisted more openly than
Condillac had done on the important role of consciousness and most
especially self-consciousness in the formation of the personality.

In the preface to his *Essai analytique* Bonnet takes pains to point out
that his discussion of the nature of man is confined to his physical and
psychological characteristics leaving completely out of the picture his
metaphysical status. Yet Bonnet constantly uses the word *âme* and
accepts with very little questioning the dualistic interpretation of human
nature which is accompanied by a belief in the interaction of the two
spheres. He states that he is recording nothing but facts, but his aim is
to determine exactly how ideas are formed in the mind through the
agency of the senses. He is unsure whether there is any parallel between
sensations and things but says it really does not matter since he is only
going to study the effects which things have on the mind. No one can
tell what matter is really like; all that one can discuss and analyze is the
effect that it has on individual minds. Bonnet is also willing to admit that
no one has any idea of what mind is like either, and that all that one can
analyze are the effects of its interaction with the effects of matter[55]. After
these preliminary qualifications, Bonnet goes on in the main part of his
work to discuss ideas as if they were actual representations of material
things and the mind or soul as if it were being directly affected by these
same things. But Bonnet is obviously troubled by the problem which
had already defeated Condillac; if the only means of access to knowledge
of any kind is through the data furnished by sensations, these being intimately allied to the material organs through which they are channeled, how
can one arrive at any knowledge whatsoever of an immaterial entity such
as the self? Again and again Bonnet stresses the fact that he is really
only talking about the effects which occur when sense impressions penetrate into the mind, and his definition of perceptions is illuminating:
" je conçois qu'en conséquence de l'action des fibres nerveuses, il se passe
dans l'Ame quelque chose qui répond à cette action : l'Ame réagit à sa
maniere, & *l'effet* de cette réaction est ce que nous nommons *perception*
ou *sensation*[56]. " And yet he is capable of coming out with such a
blatantly unprovable remark as the following : " La supposition que l'Ame
existe n'est cependant pas gratuite : elle est fondée sur l'opposition qui est
entre la simplicité du sentiment & la composition de la Matiere[57]. " In the
first place he cannot assume that what he terms elsewhere " l'unicité du
moi" has anything to do with the spiritual substance which underlies it, nor
that the " multiplicité " of matter as recorded by sensations has any more
validity. The fact is that very few eighteenth century authors were willing
to admit that empirical data cannot lead to ontological truths. Most of
them just assumed that the two spheres of thought, like the genetic and the
logical levels already mentioned, existed as parallel elements in some

overall structure and that describing one series automatically accounts for the other.

If we follow Bonnet's statue in its development from inanimate matter to thinking human being we can easily see how his thought differs from that of Condillac at certain strategic points. When Bonnet's statue smells a rose as its very first sense impression, Bonnet slips into the vocabulary of substance and modification to elucidate his thought : " J'approche donc une *rose* du Nez de la Statue : au même instant elle devient un *Etre sentant*. Son Ame est modifiée pour la première fois : elle est modifiée en odeur de rose ; elle devient une odeur de rose ; elle se représente une odeur de rose[58]. " Obviously we are dealing with an independently existing entity which is only waiting for sense impressions in order to make itself known. However at this point, Bonnet would deny to the statue any true self, in fact any true personality whatsoever. The latter term he reserves for what we have termed the empirical self, that collection of sensations, ideas and emotions which are linked by memory into a series which forms a whole. This kind of personality Bonnet is willing to grant to animals but he posits for man a far higher form of personality, one which is termed *le moi,* and which is dependent for its development on self-consciousness and on the ability to articulate and communicate this idea to others.

The evolutionary nature of Bonnet's thought is perhaps more in evidence in his *Contemplation de la nature,* but it is discernible here in a graded series of possible selves which emerge as one goes further up the ladder of complexity. The point at which the true self comes into being is only reached when the mind has acquired sufficient experience to be able to stand back and contemplate itself. In so doing it begins to separate itself from what it is contemplating : " elle sépare de la perception le sujet qui apperçoit[59]. " This alone constitutes the true self, the self which lies behind the ephemeral perceptions which seem to constitute its being. However Bonnet is still not content to allow to the statue the ability to call what it thus perceives a self. In addition it must be able to reflect on its discovery, and reflection automatically involves language[60]. Since the statue is as yet incapable of speech it is also incapable of entertaining such a complex idea as the self. The idea of the self is an abstraction, but one which must be mastered before the true self can be said to exist in any individual.

These qualities of self-awareness and of the ability to communicate the idea of such a feeling to others are therefore the principal means by which any human being gains access to his true self, not just to his ephemeral one. The role of reflexion or self-analysis cannot be slighted according to Bonnet. *La conscience de l'existence* is related to a whole series of reflexive reactions on the part of the mind ; it only comes into being at the moment the individual is capable of abstracting from his experience the subject to which these experiences adhere. In order to have a self, one has to be able to conceive of it in the abstract ; in order to do this, one has to be able to identify it, and the identification of the self by an individual is ultimately dependent upon his ability to distinguish the subjective aspect of the self from its objective content. We are a long way indeed from the emotional *sentiment de l'existence* of Lignac or Rousseau, and yet there are some affinities, most noticeably the insistence on self-consciousness as the central principle of any knowledge about the self. We see here another example of that desire to turn in on oneself which characterizes so much of late eighteenth century thought. Societal man can only be understood in terms of the inner being which constitutes each and every man.

The Nature of the self

Many writers, among them some of those whom we have already noted, felt that the nature of the self was so obscure that it could never be penetrated by any means and that all one could hope to prove was the fact of personal identity. In his *Système de la nature* (1770) d'Holbach specifically states that it is impossible to see oneself, but at the same time insists that the only reality is a material one and that the soul or self is merely matter organized in a certain way. His analogy is that of the harp capable of playing itself, which reacts to certain external stimuli but has no internalized spiritual entity to control its reactions. Man cannot get outside of himself in order to determine what makes him act the way he does ; therefore the external observer is in a better position to describe the self than is the individual himself[61]. However, in another passage, d'Holbach questions whether anyone could deny the fact of his own existence, so it would seem that the theory of " privileged access " is relied on even though it can do no more than prove the existence of a particular individual to that individual alone[62].

This position was taken by many writers who, following in the footsteps of Locke, stated that the self was unknown by its very nature, that the human understanding was not capable of penetrating beneath those activities which occupy its various faculties. D'Alembert is rather a good example, because he states that the nature of the self is unknown, only to go on to point out what constitutes personal identity. His denial of our ability to analyze the self is forthright : " La connoissance de la nature de l'ame ne peut servir à la résoudre, puisque cette connoissance nous manque[63]. " And yet he uses the sense of touch to determine just what does belong to a particular individual as distinguished from other similar beings. It is by the difference which we note between touching foreign bodies and our own that we form the notion of " mine[64] ". This is sufficient to act as a base for a sense of personal identity although we have already seen that d'Alembert relied on a very internalized sense impression, *le sentiment intime,* to give access to the idea of existence as such. But neither the abstract idea of existence nor the actual experience of it is sufficient to permit anyone to arrive at any kind of knowledge about what constitutes the self. This remains an unknown quantity, and the best that can be said for it is that we know it exists.

In most cases however, even if the authors profess that the nature of the self, or the mind, or the soul is unknown and can never be known, it is still possible to discern certain underlying assumptions which enable us to categorize these writers into groups. The French writers of the eighteenth century may have professed ignorance about many fields of inquiry but actually few of them were convinced of the impossibility of the human mind to reach true knowledge about almost anything. Genuine uncertainty was not in very great demand during those times ; what the *philosophes* wanted were pronouncements which would enable man to live a fuller, happier life. As Vartanian has shown in his critical edition of *L'Homme machine,* La Mettrie is one of the few authors who saw the possibilities in the area of scientific hypotheses. But however much La Mettrie may have been impressed with the usefulness of a hypothesis which cannot be proved to be true or false except insofar as it works out in practice, very few eighteenth century authors would have agreed with him. As a matter of fact his man-machine hypothesis was not so understood by his contemporaries, and even today a good case can be made out in favor of the thesis that La Mettrie was not that much different from the rest of the materialists of the age.

In any case the example of La Mettrie can be used to emphasize once again the need for a radical solution which was pressed upon French writers of the eighteenth century partly if not wholly because of the peculiar societal conditions under which they operated. No compromise seemed to be either possible or desirable to those thinkers who lined up on one side or the other of the great debate between Christian and non-Christian thinkers. Most of the former saw the self as a closed system, a simple subject to which the various sensations, emotions and ideas merely attached themselves in passing ; most of the latter inclined towards an open system, an unformed self which creates itself as it goes through a series of experiences.

According to the Christian apologists the self, very frequently assimilated to the soul, has a kind of static identity which never changes no matter what the circumstances may be. The argument most frequently advanced in favor of this concept of the self cites the unifying influence of the mind in assimilating all the various emotions and sensations. A good example of this occurs in the article " Ame " of the *Encyclopédie* in which the abbé Yvon writes : " L'*ame* n'a donc point de parties, elle compare divers sentimens qu'elle éprouve. Or, pour juger que l'un est douloureux, & l'autre agréable, il faut qu'elle ressente tous les deux : & par conséquent qu'elle soit une même substance très-simple[65]. " The fact that the abbé Yvon is merely copying a section of another work goes to show how widespread this particular argument was[66].

A great many of these writers followed the Cartesian line in insisting on the primacy of the thinking faculty, *l'esprit,* in the make-up of the self. Gerdil's remarks may be taken as typical of such authors as Para du Phanjas, Hayer, Ilharat de la Chambre, and Denesle :

> Je conviens sans peine avec M. Locke, que l'esprit est un Etre aussi réel que le corps ... Or en considérant la pensée en elle-même, & non selon ses différens rapports aux différens objets qui la terminent, de ce que M. Locke soutient quelque part qu'il est essentiel à tout Etre pensant de se sentir, j'en pouvois conclure avec assez de probabilité contre lui-même, que la pensée est le fond même de la substance de l'esprit, puisque l'esprit ne sent rien en lui-même de plus intime que la pensée[67].

It is amusing to note the same arguments being used in favor of an illuministic interpretation of the universe in Dupont de Nemours' *Philosophie de l'univers* (1792). He insists that the real self is made up of intelligence alone and that the body is merely an adjunct which we use to advance our individual being on the road to ultimate perfection ; for Dupont was convinced that after the death of the body, the self of an individual went on to inhabit some higher type of being, unknown to us in our current position of dependence on the body.

But the Cartesian identification of the self with the thinking and perceiving powers of the mind is by no means confined to the Christian apologists. Many *philosophes* from beginning to end of the century used this concept. It is not surprising to find Bayle giving a definition of the self as " une substance qui pense[68] ", but Buffon seems rather out of place in this particular group. However his statement that " L'existence de notre ame nous est démontrée, ou plutôt nous ne faisons qu'un, cette existence et nous : être et penser sont pour nous la même chose[69] ", leaves no doubt as to the source of his thinking on this subject. It is thought alone which forms the very essence of the self, and Buffon even questions whether thinking is not possible without the aid of externally stimulated perceptions : " ne viendra-t-on pas à penser que cette présence des objets n'est pas nécessaire à l'existence de ces sensations, & que par conséquent notre ame & nous, pouvons exister tout seuls & indépendamment de ces objets ?[70] " The existence of the exterior world cannot be demonstrated in the same way as that of thought itself which needs no proof to the individual experiencing it.

Bonnet also uses the argument of the simplicity and unitary quality of the mind to identify it with the self. He points out that all the various

operations of the mind are subsumed under this singular point of view and
that the self is always the same although all its contents may change completely[71]. Bonnet uses this definition to point out the difference between
mind and matter since, according to him, it is perfectly obvious that no
combination of matter could possibly lead to this type of psychological
unity. The adjective that recurs frequently in all these discussions is
identique, and the definition of identity is such that no change of form
can be admitted at all. Since the Lockean concept of a different kind of
definition for personal identity does not appear in these discussions at
all, the self is seen as a fixed, an almost static entity, one which is never
affected by any of the myriad vicissitudes to which the body is subject or
to which even the mind is submitted. Buffon again provides one of the
best examples of this concept of the self as a closed system : " Cependant
inaltérable dans sa substance, impassable par son essence, elle est toujours
la même[72]. "

To the Christian apologists intent upon proving the existence of a
God-given soul, the definition of the self as an independent being came
quite naturally. Nothing that happens to a person in the course of his
life has any real bearing on the ultimate nature of the self. Of course
this led to certain moral problems, primarily the question of whether what
one does in this life has any bearing on one's ultimate destiny. As Palmer
points out, only the Jansenists were willing to take the radical position
that nothing but the grace of God has any bearing on the decision about
the individual's eternal life[73]. For the most part the other Christian
writers tended to skirt this problem, assuming that the essence of the soul
was a God-given entity which remains the same throughout an individual's
earthly life in order to enter into eternity in the very form in which it
entered its temporal existence. The essential quality of the self is unrelat-
ed to its existential mode of being ; many of the writers make the distinction between a substance and its modes even though they may claim not
to be able to tell what a substance really is.

One of the major obstacles which these writers had to overcome was
the argument from childhood experiences which would appear to have no
real relationship to the adult and yet obviously belonged to the same
person. The usual response was that the self only manifested itself through
experiences but that this does not mean that it was not present during
childhood or even infancy. Denesle summarizes this point of view in his
Examen du matérialisme :

> *Je vois,* que si cette substance, que nous appelons l'ame humaine,
> paroit faible dans l'enfance, ce n'est pas que, de sa nature, elle puisse
> subir quelque altération dans son essence ; mais que c'est uniquement
> parce que les organes n'étant pas développés, ni assez analogues, faute
> d'usage, aux impressions des corps extérieurs, les sensations conséquem-

ment qu'ils occasionnent dans l'ame sont indécises, obscures, implexes, ou embarrassées : & cela par une suite de la loi d'union [74].

This leads us back to the dual nature of man, a being made up of a combination of mind and matter whose interaction can never be clearly explained or even understood. Individual souls are felt to be totally unlike bodies which are in a constant state of flux and yet, since mind is always conjoined with a body, it is hard to distinguish the quality of fixedness which characterizes the mind from that of fluidity which characterizes matter.

The favorite analogy is that of a river which is always changing but nevertheless remains the same river. That this type of identity would not long satisfy an eighteenth century writer can be deduced from Rivarol's use of the metaphor : " Nous sommes comme des fleuves qui ... portent toujours le même nom et ne roulent jamais les mêms eaux : la fixité du nom représente le *moi*, et la mobilité des flots celles de nos idées [75]. " Nominalism may have satisfied the scholastic forebears of Descartes, but even Descartes had felt it necessary to give more than merely nominalistic identity to the self.

The other example used by this particular group of writers was that of the caterpillar and the moth. Even though there may seem to be no real connection between these two forms of being, the underlying individual has not changed at all. This particular example had been used for centuries by Christian writers to symbolize the change in form from this life to that of eternity, but during the eighteenth century, while still being used as an example of what happened to the soul upon the decease of the body, it was transmuted into an argument about the very nature of the self. Despite the fact that the moth may have no recollection of its existence as a caterpillar, there is no denying that these two forms of the individual are intimately related, and, according to the Christian apologists, the inner being had undergone no change whatsoever. All that changes is the external shell, the ephemeral existential form which effectively covers up the solid internal self. A child may not seem to have any relationship to an adult, and yet the self of that particular individual has remained fixed within the changing form, and it is only the self which determines the ultimate destiny of that person.

An interesting case can be made in favor of the essentialism of Marivaux, especially in *La Vie de Marianne* (1731) in which Marianne distinguishes between her life and herself :

L'objet qui m'occupa d'abord, vous allez croire que ce fut la malheureuse situation où je me restais ; non, cette situation ne regardait que *ma vie* ; ce qui m'occupait regardait *moi*. Vous direz que je rêve de distinguer cela : point du tout, *notre vie, pour ainsi dire, nous est moins chère que nous, que nos passions.* A voir quelquefois ce qui se passe dans notre instinct là-dessus on dirait que pour *être,* il n'est pas nécessaire de *vivre,* que ce n'est que *par accident* que nous vivons ; mais que c'est *naturellement* que nous *sommes*[76].

The distinction between *être* and *exister,* as later writers will term it, is made here as clearly as can be found anywhere in eighteenth century literature. The balance which had lain with the essential quality of the self slowly was changed until the self was identified with its existential way of life rather than with its essential unity and sameness.

Another interesting illustration is in the works of Lelarge de Lignac who was struggling towards an open concept of the self and who found himself more tied to his Cartesian background than we might expect. In his attempt to give the self a very special place at the center of his philosophical thought, Lignac developed it into a self-moving self-ordering unit which grows with its existence. It is only through *le sentiment de l'existence* that we have access to the self, and these two are so closely related that Lignac almost reaches the conclusion that the self is a system of existential events which is controlled and developed by a central source of energy, the mind itself. Arguing against Buffon Lignac states : " L'existence est une chose positive & non relative, & le sens intime que l'on en a, est indépendant de tous les autres Etres[77]. " If he had followed this lead Lignac might have opened up a genuinely new field of investigation, one which Diderot was to develop in his own clandestine writings. But Lignac never did go all the way in stressing what he terms the absolute value of existence as such. In the last analysis his determination to disprove the materialistic thesis that the self could be identified with some part of the body, either the brain or the stomach, led him back into the Cartesian fold.

Thus Lignac's concept of the self, while much more open to the influence of experience and existence, remained that of a closed system, predetermined in some way and unchanging regardless of the various trials to which it was subject in this life : " Ce fond d'être fixe que je sens en moi le même individu sous tant de modifications, qui n'a été sujet à aucune variation depuis que j'existe sous la succession d'un nombre infini de modes, étant rapporté à la cause suprême, devient le tipe de toutes les substances[78]. " The dependence of the self on a supernatural order is evident, as is the underlying doctrine of a substance and its attributes. In another passage Lignac notes that no matter what happens to him in his lifetime, his inner being is not affected in any way. In fact he notes that he could have been pirated away to Turkey as a child and still have remained exactly the same individual with the very same self he now possesses[79].

It would be unfair to Lignac to dismiss his thoughts on the nature of the soul without showing some of the interesting developments which he

sketched out before he found himself confused by the prevailing Cartesianism of the Church. Unlike most of the other Christian apologists
who relied on innate ideas at least insofar as the idea of God was concerned, Lignac absolutely denied the existence of any such ideas. God may be
the ultimate source of the individual soul, but he does not reveal himself
directly to man. Lignac argues just as vehemently against Malebranche
and Descartes as he does against Buffon and the *Lettre à Thrasibule.* As
he outlines his system in the *Témoignage du sens intime,* he notes that
all knowledge is ultimately dependent on the *sentiment de l'existence,*
even knowledge of God's existence :

> Mon ouvrage est divisé en trois Parties. Dans la première, j'oppose
> le Témoignage du Sens intime & de l'expérience à la foi ridicule des
> Fatalistes, en faveur de la liberté humaine. Dans la seconde, je me
> sers du même témoignage pour établir la présence de Dieu sentie en
> nous par son efficacité, & dans tous les effets de la nature. Dans la
> troisième, j'emploie encore contre eux le même témoignage, pour leur
> démontrer la liberté divine [80].

It is easy to see that Lignac has reversed the usual scale of values ;
instead of man's liberty being dependent on God's he proposes that God
must be free since man is obviously self-motivated.

The inner proof to which Lignac has recourse is only accessible to
an individual willing to undergo a rather special process of turning inward.
He mentions with approval the *Encyclopédie* article " Délicieux " and its
description of the experience known as *rêver à la Suisse.* As we know,
this article was by Diderot, and it shows how closely Lignac's thought
parallelled his famous contemporary's. Lignac refuses to term the mind
a *tabula rasa* during this process : " mais c'est *tabula rasa sui conscia,*
c'est une toile qui se sent exister sans aucune maniére d'être acciden-
telle [81]. " And it is this very self-consciousness which makes it possible
for an individual to identify himself as an individual, which enables him
to reach any conclusions whatsoever about himself or the universe :
" Que ce sens vous ait été enlevé, que reste-t-il ? nul individu ; rien où
vous puissiez supposer les maniéres d'être existantes dont nous venons de
parler. Votre moi disparoît ; vous n'avez plus que l'idée de l'être abstrait,
de l'être en général [82]. " Abstractions are useless in forming ideas about
living, thinking, acting beings such as man who exercises his volition at all
moments of his existence and thereby helps create his own destiny as well
as that of the rest of the world. However, as we have already seen, when
confronted with the necessity of disproving the materialistic thesis that
the self was merely a certain portion of matter, or even the associationist
thesis that the self was merely a collection of perceptions, Lignac found no
better answer than that of the familiar substance-modification argument
which immediately made of his self-forming self an already formed and

pre-determined substance ultimately dependent for its very being on a supernatural power.

Lelarge de Lignac was not the only eighteenth century thinker who found it difficult to accept the ultimate consequences of a purely sensationalistic epistemology. Carried to its logical conclusions this point of view leads only to Hume's " bundle of perceptions " ; the content of the mind is the only reality to be found when one actually observes the mind at work. Condillac avoided the disintegration of the personality inherent in such a stand by postulating the existence of a self-substance which stands behind all the various modifications of existence and which gives unity to them all : " L'unité de personne suppose nécessairement l'unité de l'être sentant ; elle suppose une seule substance simple, modifiée différemment à l'occasion des impressions qui se font dans les parties du corps [83]. " Once again the influence of Descartes is decisive in the final analysis.

Although Helvétius says very little about the self as such, it is clear from his principles that such an entity could be no more than an accumulation of various experiences and not something which accompanies these experiences. According to his system, the mind is a complete blank at birth and each person is equally capable of development as any other person. All that determines his future are the various educational experiences to which he finds himself exposed even before the moment of parturition : " L'Esprit n'est que l'assemblage de nos idées. Nos idées, dit Locke, nous viennent par les sens ; & de ce principe, comme des miens, l'on peut conclure que l'esprit n'est en nous qu'une acquisition [84]. " All of which seems to point in the direction of an open-ended self which develops as the mind gains perceptions. But Helvétius also postulates the existence of what he terms *l'âme*, the principle which enables man to have sensations. This factor does not develop during the course of one's lifetime ; on the contrary, Helvétius declares : " L'ame existe en entier dans l'enfant comme dans l'adolescent. L'enfant est, comme l'homme sensible au plaisir & à la douleur physique : mais il n'a, ni autant d'idées, ni par conséquent autant d'esprit que l'adulte [85]. " Which of these factors, *l'âme* or *l'esprit* does he equate with the self ? Helvétius never actually chooses between the two but insists on both of them as equal partners in this strange new kind of dualism. The nuclear center of the self is an unchanging unit which always remains distinct from the external world. Regardless of the stimuli brought to bear upon it, it remains constant while the mind is in a constant state of flux.

The attraction of a stable, absolute center of life itself is very strong for most eighteenth century writers. This can be seen rather clearly in the two favorite images used by the *philosophes* in their discussion of the constitution of human nature : the spider's web and the self-activated clavecin. Georges Poulet has analyzed the first image rather extensively [86], so we need do no more than point out the rather obvious fact that the spider in the center of the web corresponds to the nuclear self while the web represents the means by which this inner being is affected by external stimuli.

Montesquieu is one of the first to use the spider-and-web image in his unpublished *Essai sur les causes qui peuvent affecter les esprits et les caractères*. In his analysis Montesquieu makes a great deal more out of the influences which reach the spider through the web than the central nucleus itself. According to Montesquieu, an individual is merely what he terms " une suite d'idées " and if these impressions are interrupted in any way, the annihilation of the individual is the automatic result[87]. As Mauzi has pointed out, Montesquieu's concept of human nature involves a constant state of flux as not only normal but desirable. If the self is not agitated in some way it tends to disappear, and one of the best sources of pleasure lies in the active appreciation of " le sentiment de notre existence[88]. " Montesquieu specifically denies the necessity of any kind of retreat from society in order to gain access to this feeling : " Il ne faut point beaucoup de philosophie pour être heureux : il n'y a qu'à prendre des idées un peu saines. Une minute d'attention par jour suffit, et il ne faut point entrer pour cela dans un cabinet, pour se recueillir : ces choses s'apprennent dans le tumulte du monde mieux que dans un cabinet[89]. " Thus Montesquieu would seem to deny any real structure to the personality ; the spider is completely determined by the external stimuli and only exists insofar as it is acted upon by them. But Montesquieu's thought is hard to judge in this area since he did not work it out systematically, only jotting down single ideas in a somewhat haphazard way.

Other writers using the spider-and-web image tended to make more of the spider itself, the inner unit which reacts to the external stimuli. Diderot comes immediately to mind in this connection and of course he was also to use the image of the self-activated clavecin. Both Diderot and d'Holbach assumed that the basic construction of the whole universe involved movement and that such an intricate part of it as the human being must also be in a constant state of flux. According to d'Holbach this movement is inherent in the very nature of matter itself, and since in his eyes man is merely a certain combination of matter, human nature is also a self-motivated open-ended system[90]. This leads d'Holbach on to very much the same position vis-à-vis the self that Montesquieu had upheld : there is no stable center. On the contrary the nature of the self automatically involves change. Each person can become conscious of his own existence and is happiest when this feeling is most intense : " L'Homme veut toujours être averti de son existence le plus vivement qu'il est possible, tant qu'il peut l'être sans douleur[91]. " Inaction leads to boredom and, what is worse, lethargy, which is only relieved by the rush of new needs and desires[92].

D'Holbach and Diderot, for we know that Diderot collaborated with his friend on the *Système de la nature,* were struggling towards the formulation of a new concept of human nature, one in which man would really be freed of his dependence on extra-natural forces and one in which man would have some degree of control over his own development. This last phase is more noticeable in Diderot's private writings than it is in d'Holbach's rather cold presentation of the individual as merely a small part of the whole universe, subject to laws over which he has no control whatsoever. Diderot's thought is much more man-centered than is d'Holbach's.

More typical of eighteenth century thought is that of Bonnet who carefully distinguishes between the self and the soul. The first is identified with all the ideas and feelings which the latter accumulates during its earthly existence. But Bonnet had to have recourse to an impartial observer to guarantee the integrity of the individual personality which might otherwise disappear entirely as memory and/or self-consciousness fails[93]. The self expands with each new sensation and emotion, and the individual is happier as he becomes conscious of these variations. But it is not true that his very being is changing ; it is only that these various experiences offer him different ways of becoming conscious of his inner being : " Nous avons étendu son Etre. Son Moi s'étant approprié toutes les sensations, s'est, en quelque sorte, multiplié avec elles. Elle a goûté l'existence par un plus grand nombre d'organes. Plus ses manieres d'être ont varié, plus elle a senti qu'elle étoit. Par rapport à lui-même un Etre sentant n'existe qu'autant qu'il sent : il existe donc d'autant plus qu'il sent davantage[94]. " That Bonnet is hedging is obvious from his very wording : *en quelque sorte, par rapport à lui-même,* are parenthetical additions which serve to qualify what might otherwise be a straightforward account of a dynamic concept of the self. The very next section serves to clear up this ambiguity : " L'existence n'est donc point en soi un bien : elle n'est que la conscience de ce que l'on sent ou de ce que l'on fait[95]. " The verb which is so noticeably absent is of course *être* ; being and existing are placed in two separate compartments which have no real interconnection.

Out of this mass of opinion on the nature of the self, three main currents can be discerned : first the predominantly apologetic point of view that the self is a simple substance which is not affected in any way by the changes which take place in the mind or emotional center of an individual ; second the composition theory according to which these changes in perception, ideation, and emotive tone are the only content of the self, which is, therefore, an ever-changing group of impressions related to each other only through some principle such as memory or self-consciousness ; and third the organic, developmental view that the self is a center of dynamic force, not a static nucleus but one which is itself in a state of development and which does not just passively become what happens to it. This last theory was barely conceived in the eighteenth century but bears certain similarities to modern psychological ideas on the nature of the ego processes. Gestalt psychology posits the existence of a frame of reference which the individual uses to control the myriad sense impressions with which he is constantly being assaulted. This can be viewed as an active projection of something which is unique to that particular individual; no *philosophe* used exactly these terms but certainly Lignac, d'Holbach and Diderot had something of this kind in mind when they refer to the self as a self-generating organism which both develops according to what happens to it and at the same time determines what happens to itself.

How the concept was used

The two main schools of thought on the self were divided fairly clearly on the burning ethical issue of the age : whether man was passive or active, determined or free. Since this area of investigation has been treated at length elsewhere, we will merely sketch in the position of some of the major figures who have already been discussed. The Christian writers obviously emphasized the freedom of man, his ability to control his own destiny and his responsibility for what he does. The Cartesians among them played up the role of the will in this process. The understanding may be a completely passive activity of the mind ; this they were willing to concede to the Lockean sensationalists. However they insisted that this by no means exhausted the mind's capacities and that the urge towards action as expressed in the act of willing is just as distinguishing a feature of the self as is the ability to absorb sense impressions. Even Lelarge de Lignac falls back on this distinction in his *Témoignage du sens intime :* " vous ne sçavez ce que c'est que la liberté ; consultez-vous vous-même, vous le sçaurez[96]. " This was such a commonplace that the *Mémoires de Trévoux,* commenting on one of Lignac's books, cites a whole series of works which distinguish four fundamental characteristics in human nature : " On extrait de la nature de l'ame quatre propriétés universelles, la sensibilité, l'intelligence, la volonté, la mémoire[97]. "

The proponents of the doctrine of sensationalism denied any independent activity to the mind. According to them it is merely the accumulation of impressions which impinge upon it. Helvétius is the most extreme example of this point of view. According to him, complete control of the environmental factors would lead to complete control of the development of the personality. Nothing counts at all except the external stimuli which slowly build up the internal processes which control the behavior pattern of the individual. D'Holbach's moral theories laid more

stress on the physical characteristics of the person involved ; the actual
structure of the brain cells determines the ability of that particular person.
Environmental factors also enter into the picture but the limits are set by
one's physical organization.   In any case nothing can be done by the
individual to control either his hereditary or his environmental factors.
He is subject to a strict type of determinism, one which governs the whole
of the universe and which makes no exception even for man himself.

These ethical speculations were tied closely to the metaphysical
question of whether man has a soul, and if so whether this soul is
immortal or not.   Some writers approached this question through the
concept of the self.   For instance Condillac uses the argument of unity of
consciousness to prove rationally the existence of a spiritual soul.   He
gives this definition of *âme* :   " Substance qui sent, qui pense.   Parce que
cette substance est le principe qui nous fait agir et mouvoir, on dit qu'un
homme est l'*ame* d'une entreprise, lorsqu'il en est le principal instru-
ment[98]. "   It is the soul which imparts movement to man and which is
responsible for his ability to make decisions and to act upon them.   This
in turn justifies the concept of immortality with its attendant punishment
or reward as the case may be.   Dupont de Nemours reverses the usual
pattern and proves the existence of an individual soul on the basis of his
concept of the whole universe.   His cosmos resembles a monarchy with
God as the king who disburses justice according to the merits of individual beings.   Therefore it is clear to him that these individual entities must
have souls which are ultimately responsible for the conduct of that particular person.   The thesis that the true self involves only intelligence seems
to him to conform better to this concept of the universe than the materialistic thesis of the self being identified with the body :   " j'espère vous
montrer avant de finir cet Ecrit, qu'elle est celle qui s'accorde le mieux
avec les loix générales, avec l'ordre équitable et plein de raison qui règne
dans l'Univers[99]. "

To the *philosophes* who denied the existence of God, the existence of
an individual soul seemed to be just as foolish and unnecessary a doctrine.
Immortality is a pleasant day-dream but not one which should be taken too
seriously.   From an ethical standpoint, since man is determined by either
environmental factors or his heredity, there is no justification for the existence of an immortal soul which might be called upon to suffer retribution
during eternity for acts over which it really has no control.   On the
contrary it would be unjust to postulate an immortal soul under these
circumstances.

The question of the existence or non-existence of the soul also led
to speculation about the location of the soul or the self within the body.
Descartes had started all this discussion when in his physiological speculations he had maintained that the pineal gland was the true seat of the soul.
As the man-machine thesis evolved during the late seventeenth and

eighteenth century, this idea of a single point within the human frame which serves as a *sensorium commune* took on more and more importance. As long as the self was identified with the rational faculty of thought, a location somewhere in the brain seemed to be called for. What was needed was a central place in which all the external stimuli and internal reactions could take place. La Mettrie makes a great deal of this concept and continues to stress the importance of the brain in this process.

To later *philosophes* who were more influenced by the idea that what they needed to find was not so much the place in which ideas are formed but rather the source of sensibility, attention shifted from the general area of the head to that of the torso. Buffon refers to the diaphragm as " le centre du sentiment[100] ", and specifically denies to the brain any power of sensibility. Here we see not only a shift from the pure *res cogitans* of Descartes to the *res sensitans* of Locke, but a further development towards reliance on man's emotive reactions as his most distinguishing feature. Many animals have brains which closely resemble those of man but none of them has the same reactions to their thought processes. Thus that element of man's physical organization which leads him into joy or sorrow is much more important in determining his very essence than the brain which does not have the power of instigating activity.

In his refutation of Buffon, Lelarge de Lignac completely misses this particular point. Arguing against the thesis that matter organized in a certain way is capable of becoming conscious of itself, Lignac notes in a mere footnote that Buffon is speaking not of the organization of the brain but of the diaphragm[101]. He continues to discuss the place in which *le sens intime de l'existence* might be said to exist assuming that by this everyone means the same thing that he does, namely a principle of conscious unity which serves as the base for all other sensations and ideas. That Buffon is referring to another kind of sensibility does not occur to him.

Bonnet is particularly interesting as an example of the lengths to which some thinkers were willing to go in order to pinpoint the existence of a substantial self which could be identified with an immortal soul. His definition of the self as dependent on self-conscious reflexion and the ability to identify what is thus apprehended by means of speech leads him into a rather curious position of positing the existence of what he terms " une petite machine éthérée ", a minute, extremely subtle material substance which serves as the *sensorium commune* and at the same time is " le véritable siege de l'Ame[102] ". In typical Cartesian fashion this little material entity is placed in the brain, and it is formed of such a rarefied kind of matter that it can survive the death of the rest of the body. What Bonnet is really doing is postulating the existence of a material, immortal soul which can assure the continued existence of the personality of a particular individual. Therefore what one does in one's earthly existence, by which means one forms one's own personality, is also important to one's eternal destiny. Bonnet also felt that this doctrine answered many questions of a theological nature particularly about the resurrection of the body. If the soul itself were material, then the continued existence of it alone would be sufficient to fulfil this particular Christian doctrine.

Involved in all this discussion of the existence of an individual soul was the whole controversy over the relationship between man and the animals. We have already noted that Buffon sees the distinction in the fact that animals have no real self since they are not able to apply consciousness of past events to their current activities :

> Si je me suis bien expliqué, on doit avoir déjà vû que bien loin de tout ôter aux animaux, je leur accorde tout, à l'exception de la pensée & et de la réflexion ; ils ont le sentiment, ils l'ont même à un plus haut degré que nous ne l'avons ; ils ont aussi la conscience de leur existence actuelle, mais ils n'ont pas celle de leur existence passée ; ils ont des sensations, mais il leur manque la faculté de les comparer, c'est-à-dire, la puissance qui produit des idées ; car les idées ne sont que des sensations comparées, ou, pour mieux dire, des associations de sensations [103].

To the animals Buffon also assimilates imbeciles and infants, who lack the ability to make the necessary comparisons which lead to the creation of an individual self. He notes that the neonate neither laughs nor sheds tears until the sixth week and, since these are the truly distinguishing human emotions, the ones which involve comparison and thought, he denies that these very tiny infants are actually human [104]. The mature man is constantly looking back on past activities and planning for the future on the basis of these reflections while the animal lives wholly in the present, reacting to external stimuli purely on the basis of habit and immediate need. Since animals have no principle of individuation, they are much more adept than man in copying each other and perfecting means of coping with the ever-recurring problems of that particular species :

> Les animaux, au contraire, qui n'ont point d'ame n'ont point le *moi* qui est le principe de la différence, la cause qui constitue la personne, ils doivent donc, lorsqu'ils se ressemblent par l'organisation ou qu'ils sont de la même espèce, se copier tous, faire tous les mêmes choses & et de la même façon, s'imiter en un mot beaucoup plus parfaitement que les hommes ne peuvent s'imiter les uns les autres [105].

Therefore to Buffon the line of demarcation between man and animal is a sharp one, one which no amount of change in the behavior pattern of any individual animal could possibly hope to change. The distinction is made on the basis of the fact that man has a self of which he is conscious ; Buffon speaks of man as *homo duplex,* a being composed of two principles, one material and the other spiritual, but this Cartesian dualism is not his only grounds for dividing the human and the non-human so sharply. It is possible that Buffon was careful to include the Cartesian doctrine of a spiritual soul merely in order to protect his works and himself from persecution. The fact of the matter is that even without this supposedly spiritual soul, man in the eyes of Buffon is radically different from any animal purely on the basis of his ability to reach a sophisticated degree of self-consciousness.

Buffon's position is parallelled by his Protestant counterpart, Bonnet, although it is a little easier to accept the sincerity of Bonnet's belief in the existence of a soul substance than it is in the case of Buffon. Bonnet was actually willing to concede the possibility that animals might have souls since they perform most of the same activities as men, but there is one ability which man possesses and which no animal has ever or will ever possess. This is the power of speech, and, as we have already noted, it is this power which gives to man the ability to identify his own self and therefore to really have such an entity. Without the ability to speak of the self, to communicate one's sense of self-hood to others, no real self exists. It seems a little strange to contemplate the possibility of animals having souls but not selves but this is certainly what Bonnet means when he insists that although both man and animals are " Etres mixtes ", animals cannot actually do any judging since they are unable to generalize their ideas : " ils n'ont que des notions particulieres, parce qu'ils ne sont point doués de la Parole ; & c'est là ce qui paroît les distinguer essentiellement de l'Homme[106] ". The type of memory that animals show is radically different from that of man who is always conscious of having existed as the same person over the span of time represented by these memories. Animals do not feel this sense of identity but react purely on the basis of present stimuli and certain habit patterns[107].

Still another type of distinction between man and the animals on the basis of a concept of the self is that of Denesle. According to him animals are not machines *à la Descartes* but this does not mean that they are the equal of man. In the same way as Buffon and Bonnet, Denesle denies to animals any true sense of past or future, but he also goes on to point out a difference in their *sentiment de l'existence.* This is a feeling common to both man and the animals but the latter have no means of using this feeling : " L'ame humaine s'entretient continuellement de son existence ; la bête n'a aucune notion de la sienne ; elle sent qu'elle existe, mais elle ne le sçait pas[108]. " Thus the reflective power of man's mind, which in turn leads him on to concentrate on his own existence, is the main factor which distinguishes him from the animals.

An author like Rivarol moves slightly away from this very clear-cut distinction between these two forms of living beings. He speaks of *le moi* as existing in both man and the animals ; the distinction does not lie in the knowledge that you exist but is to be found in the moral sensibility which is man's alone :

On distingue deux sortes de conscience dans l'homme : la *conscience du sentiment* qu'on appelle *conscience du moi,* conviction fixe dont la nature a pourvu tous les animaux, tant ceux qui réfléchissent sur leur *moi,* que ceux qui agissent en vertu de ce *moi,* sans reflexion : et la *conscience morale* qui, toute fondée qu'elle est sur la justesse et la sensibilité naturelle de l'homme, ne germe pas chez les uns et dépérit chez les autres, si l'éducation ne vient à son secours [109].

It is not quite clear whether this *conscience morale* is a principle common to all men or if it is one which is a result of social conditioning. In any case it seems obvious that animals, even under carefully controlled conditions, would be incapable of developing this principle. It also seems that some men never develop it either, perhaps because they are not exposed to the correct influences during the educative process. In another passage Rivarol notes that animals are not very good at making comparisons, that they are incapable of forming abstract ideas, particularly in the realm of time sequences and that they are therefore less capable than man of directing their activities [110]. But all this is merely quantitative ; Rivarol allows to animals a great many human qualities but to an exceedingly small degree. Only the *conscience morale* is clearly the possession of man alone and even this is not evident in all men.

The controversy which raged over the *bête machine* thesis and the relations between man and the animals is much too complicated to even attempt to delineate here. Obviously the various concepts of the self played a part in the discussions since such a concept would be basic to any definition of human nature. Whether man is an active or a passive being, whether he is free or determined, whether he is conceived of as an abstract being or as an existential entity, whether his natural state was assumed to be one of quiet calm or of frenetic movement, each and all of these suppositions has a bearing on the whole problem of man's nature and of his position in the overall scheme of the universe.

The philosophical basis of these various considerations has been followed in some detail and we shall now turn our attention to the more psychological aspect of the very same questions. It is clear that these two areas of thought were much more closely related in the eighteenth century than they are today. In any case the latter considerations are ultimately dependent upon the former ; a person's image of himself is determined by his image of the nature of man. If he believes in a closed and unchanging inner self it is unlikely that he would see himself in terms of a constantly changing individual, ready to assume new responsibilities as they present themselves in experience. In addition, his ideal self-image would be affected by these philosophical assumptions, and the degree to which he could expect adherence to these standards would vary according to whether he thought each person to be an active or a passive being.

Self-concept

Very few authors of the eighteenth century made a clear distinction between the self in its aspect of the moving driving center which controls the reactions of man to his environment and that of the idea which a person has of his own personality. Lelarge de Lignac is one of the few who harped on this point, primarily because he was anxious to establish a whole philosophical system on the basis of the existence of the first of these concepts. Thus he points out the difference which any reflective person would notice between those passing phases of his being and the ultimately unified and identical being to which these characteristics adhere : " Celui qui pense actuellement à la nature de l'ame, celui qui vous communique ses pensées par l'écriture, celui qui voit le papier, qui suit les traccs que la plume y laisse, celui que le bruit distrait, celui qui sent du froid en écrivant, n'est que le même être ; ce ne sont point six ou sept personnes réunies, & différentes numériquement[111]. " All these passing sensations, thoughts, and emotions adhere in a single person and are only modifications of this primal unity. His proof, as we have already seen, rests on the privileged access theory of *le sentiment de l'existence*, what Lignac terms " mon sens intime ". It is interesting to note, however, that he reinforces this proof by an appeal to *amour-propre :* " Assurément l'amour de l'être est inné dans le sens de l'existence. Mais de quel être l'ame a-t-elle l'amour inné ? de l'être en général ? il y auroit du ridicule à le soutenir : c'est du sien propre, c'est de son individu ; cela n'est pas douteux. Et j'en conclus ... qu'elle sent le fond de son être, puisqu'elle l'aime[112]. " This concept of self-love will be the central issue in our discussion of the self-concept.

The first question which eighteenth century thinkers felt called on to ask is how *amour-propre* gains entrance to an individual human being. Is it indeed so natural to any human being that it could be considered to be innate ? Or, on the other hand, is it too determined by environmental factors ? Does an individual automatically have an image of himself to which he attaches a certain degree of approbation or disapproval or is this image a product of the opinions of other men, who in fact dictate to him what he should think about his own self ? As in most of these issues, the eighteenth century writers are to be found on both sides on this problem. Rousseau at least tried to distinguish between *amour de soi,* the natural function, and *amour-propre,* the societal one, but most authors used the term *amour-propre* indiscriminately, which results in a somewhat confused situation.

One area in which this question can be seen most clearly is in the fascination exerted throughout the whole period by the question of what happens to a man if he is raised far from the influence of other men, particularly those cases of children who had been brought up by animals in the forests. Condillac for one denies that such children would be human since they would not have developed their thinking powers through the use of arbitrary signs[113]. Authors as diverse as Boudier and Pernety will join Condillac in denying the perquisites of humanity to these unfortunate people : " l'homme reste dans l'état de brute s'il est séparé de la société[114] ", and " Exister isolé, ce n'est pas sentir son existence ; *vae soli !* Il faut exister heureux ... l'homme est donc fait pour la société[115] ". But even these few examples show the confusion which reigned in this sphere. Boudier is talking about how a child becomes a man, whereas Pernety is talking about how a man achieves happiness in this world.

Other writers, notably Diderot, will approach the same problem from a slightly different angle, making the forces which isolate the individual from society those of internal deficiencies rather than of external circumstances. Both his *Lettre sur les aveugles* and *sur les sourds et muets* use physical disabilities as the basis of the isolation from society. Diderot's biological interests may have determined this choice, but it is also obvious that he wants to reduce the number of factors involved so as to be able to answer with some degree of directness the question about the source of one's self-concept. In *Le Neveu de Rameau* Diderot deals with still another facet of this problem, the degree to which role-playing will determine personality and one's own reaction to oneself. Can one detach oneself from what one does or is one in some way determined by one's acts ? The anguish of Lui seems to stem from the fact that he would like to answer that what he *is* has nothing to do with what he *does* but that he realizes that he now considers himself to be the kind of parasite which he despises.

The question of role-playing and the formation of personality concepts is also fundamental to the work of such novelists as Marivaux and Laclos. Marianne is surprisingly alert to the effects which her words and actions have on other people, but for the most part she acts " naturally ", that is in accordance with her " bon cœur ". This is not to say that she is not capable of playing a role if necessary, only that these roles are taken on consciously, are analyzed as such and are then put aside as not being worthy of incorporation into her inner being. The split between the outer and inner world of a character such as Marianne is marked, and the external does not really impinge upon the internal.

In the case of Laclos the virtuous role-playing of Mme de Merteuil and Valmont are purely and simply masks which they assume in order to keep the position in society which they need to support their *libertin* activities. Beneath this surface, however, there is the suggestion that indeed the distinction between the natural personality and the assumed one is more complicated than it may seem. For instance, Mme de Merteuil explains at some length how she trained herself in the arts of seduction at a very early age[116]. It is therefore permissible to presume that the " real " Merteuil, the one which occurred before the assumption of the *libertin* mask, is still lurking at the center of her personality. She projects to Valmont only one aspect of her self-concept, but at times the reader gets the impression that she would like to be loved for what she really is ; she would like to be able to give herself up entirely in her love for Valmont and not have to be constantly considering the question whether she remains in control of the situation. The jealousy she feels of Mme de Tourvel is in part motivated by the fact that the latter plays from the heart and not the head and that Valmont seems to prefer this kind of a life-long companion. Mme de Merteuil sees Mme de Tourvel as a threat to her own self-concept, one which she has spent many years in building up within herself. If this image of herself is no longer successful in the area in which she has chosen to operate, love and sex, then she begins to have doubts not only about its utility but also about its veracity. Is there a chance for her to go back to the young, innocent, lovely and totally natural creature which lies at the base of her self-created personality ? The answer would seem to be no, since Laclos never permits her to step out of the personality which she has assumed as her own, at least in relation to Valmont. There is only the one letter in which she speaks of her formation of herself and then follow the actions which she takes in order to re-establish control over Valmont, the erring lover.

Central to these considerations of the formation of the self-concept through societal influences and deliberate role-playing therein are the actual characteristics which are assigned to such a concept. It is possible to create an ideal self-concept to which one is constantly trying to live up. This rather heroic ideal does not play too large a part in eighteenth century discussions. They concentrated instead on the question of approbation by society and of self-esteem. The cynical attitude of La Rochefoucauld, that *amour-propre* is the only source of any thought, feeling or action, was basic to eighteenth century psychology. No one really doubted that this passion is what makes people act the way they do ; the argument centered rather on whether this was in any way reprehensible. For the most part, the consensus was that *amour-propre* cannot be condemned since it is a natural component of human nature.

Leaving aside for the moment the ethical consequences of such a belief, let us look at some individual author's pronouncements in the psychological sphere. Marivaux presents Marianne in a totally sympathetic light, and yet she is by no means the ideal heroine of earlier fiction. Her every move is determined by her desire to find a way of life commensurate with what she feels to be her worth. Marianne cannot be at home in

Mme Dutour's shop, not because she does not find Mme Dutour likeable, but because her own sensibilities are on a higher plane than that of her mistress. In this way, one can say that she has a certain image of herself which guides her towards rejection of the advances made by M. de Climal but acceptance of the offers of Mme de Miran. The idea of being a kept woman, even if no physical intimacy is involved, does not suit her idea of what Marianne ought to be in life. Her entrance into the convent under the tutelage of Mme de Miran is closer to this ideal, but, since it involves a retreat from the hustle and bustle of the Parisian world to which Marianne had already responded positively, let alone a retreat from the delicious prospects offered her by the idea of marriage to such a worthy suitor as Valville, even this conduct does not entirely satisfy her. We know from the opening pages that Marianne achieved her goals in life, that she can look back with a certain degree of satisfaction over what she managed to make of herself. But this ideal Marianne, which she is always striving to emulate, is at the same time the real Marianne ; it represents the best part of her nature, and it therefore excuses certain rather egotistical decisions which she makes of necessity in the course of her life. During the pathetic scene in which Mme de Miran learns that it is Marianne who stands in the way of her son's marriage, Marianne controls herself at the opportune moment since a reiteration of her previous announcement of her intention to withdraw permanently into the religious life would go against the prospect opened up by Mme de Miran's sympathy : " Cet excès de désintéressement de ma part n'aurait pas été ni naturel ni raisonnable [117]. "

Other authors point to the fact that self-esteem determines to some degree one's relations with others. In his biography of Helvétius, Saint Lambert remarks : " Chaque homme a de soi la plus haute idée, et n'estime dans les autres que son image, ou ce qui peut lui être utile [118]. " This looks like a criticism of man's character but is merely a statement of fact about how individuals operate. No reprobation attaches itself to *amour-propre* as such in eighteenth century thought, unless it leads to total illusion or the assertion of one's own ego at the expense of others.

Voltaire even gives a certain dignity to this aspect of man's condition, by pointing out that it is only through his power of self-analysis and self-awareness that man is able to be the measure of the world, in however small a degree this may occur. The Lockean philosopher in *Micromégas* represents both the weakness and the strength of mankind ; unable to rise above his own limitations, he is at least able to apply these limitations to determine certain general principles about the universe as a whole. But Voltaire was not optimistic about man's ability to solve any of the major questions, and the fact of the matter is that Voltaire preferred to keep himself to himself. As Henri Peyre has noted, no author has revealed less of his own personality in his writings than Voltaire :

" Repeatedly he entertained the project of memoirs, but they soon turned into the villification of alienated friends ... or they became pseudo-memoirs attributed to Wagnière or some other person ; they never touched upon his own inner life ... he did not choose to translate his own experience directly into his literary works. He did not wish the man and the author to be one, and he mischievously concealed his personality and even his identity under masks or in borrowed characters[119]. " This helps to explain the shock which swept the scholarly world when Voltaire's letters to his niece M[me] Denis were published a few years ago. No one had imagined that the patriarch of Ferney could possibly have been carrying on such a passionate affaire over such a long period of his life. In his imaginative works, his characters very seldom take on the three-dimensionality which we think appropriate to fiction, but remain for the most part expertly contrived and even quite complex organisms which are motivated by other than psychological considerations. One could almost say that Voltaire, and his characters with him, preferred to isolate himself from the normal sphere of human motivation and that this results in a covert refusal to project his ego in any way at all. The only thing that counted for Voltaire himself was the result which was obtained, and he did not have to rely on his own personality to accomplish this in the way that Rousseau did.

Montesquieu is another author who reveals very little of himself even in the so-called " Mes pensées ". These tend to be a series of jottings about various subjects which caught his attention, but as soon as he approaches anything resembling self-analysis, he tends to turn aside in the direction of factual accounts about his family or other generalized statements about humanity in general. It is Montesquieu's contention that self-analysis is not only an illusory activity since everything is automatically deformed by *amour-propre*[120], but that indeed any such attempt is itself an indication of the degree to which individuals are determined by their vanity : " Il y a de la vanité à parler de soi, lors même qu'on en parle avec modestie : c'est un art de s'attirer l'attention des autres. On découvre tout son amour-propre lorsqu'on paroît ingénieux à le cacher[121]. " He goes on to point out that pride is a necessary component of any self-analysis and indeed it is this element of self-esteem which gives piquancy to this activity : " L'orgueil est un miroir toujours favorable ; il diminue nos défauts, augmente nos vertus ; c'est un nouveau sens de l'âme, qui lui donne à tous les instants des satisfactions nouvelles[122]. " It is therefore not surprising that Montesquieu should have chosen not to partake in this type of analysis, concentrating instead on broader societal issues which could be approached in a more impartial way. He makes one other comment of interest about self-concept when he points out that there is no need to allow other people's judgments to determine the way in which you look at yourself. This argues for a certain degree of self-satisfaction and certainly for a rather sure appreciation of his own worth which fits in very well with the portrait of him given in Shackleton's biography.

Ego-assertion and projection is one of the major themes of eighteenth century fiction. Whether the hero is trying to create for himself a place in a rather closed society (i.e. Marianne and Jacob in Marivaux' novels) or is merely trying to occupy that place which is due him because of his birth-right (Meilcour in Crébillon fils' *Les Egaremens du cœur*), each and every one of these characters is strongly motivated by a desire to impose their view of themselves on society. Crébillon is most interesting because he takes Meilcour at a stage in his career when he is not really sure what he is or how he ought to go about assuring his position in society. The necessity of introducing such secondary characters as Versac to serve as mentors for the hero is also noticeable in other *libertin* novels. This is more than a mere convention in the novel ; it is even more than the moral warning which these authors so dearly loved to draw from these portraits ; it really involves the problem of how one thinks of oneself in society. Meilcour is determined to be a success and he needs an ideal figure on which to pattern himself. Versac appears just as the whole novel seems to be grinding to a stand-still and in his long conversation with the young hero manages to instill in Meilcour a new image of himself, that of a daring, successful lady-killer who uses love as a means of advancement in society and also as a means of self-gratification.

The ultimate development of such a view of human personality may very well be the cynicism of Laclos, Rétif de la Bretonne and Sade, as Lester Crocker asserts[123], but it had been identified and clearly stated by such an early writer as Deschamps : " L'ambition de dominer est primitivement de l'état sauvage ; c'est d'elle que vient notre état social, où elle n'a fait que s'accroître de plus en plus " to which he added a very penetrating foot-note : " L'ambitieux, qu'on y fasse attention, n'a pas pour premier objet d'avoir de la supériorité sur ses semblables ; mais de n'avoir aucun de ses semblables qui aie de la superiorité et de l'avantage sur lui[124]. " The late eighteenth century novelists would appear to have forgotten this distinction : to them the desire to dominate takes over a person's motivation to such an extent that he is willing to forego his own personal pleasure in order to assure his domination over others. Laclos' M[me] de Merteuil is an excellent example of this misguided psychology ; realizing full well the risk which she was taking in requiring Valmont to break with M[me] de Tourvel, she is still compelled to go ahead and ask this of him in order to prove to herself that she is still the dominant member of the couple.

The only feeling strong enough to stand up in the face of this necessity of ego-assertion is that of passionate love, and very few of the characters in late eighteenth century novels seem to have any idea of what this is all about. In the course of the development of the *libertin* novel into a some-what moral tract, the hero's conversion was normally accomplished by the effect of true love on his character. It is obvious that Meilcour's love for Hortense will eventually redeem him from his life of wasteful *libertinage*; Valmont comes very close to this same kind of redemption through Mme de Tourvel but at the last moment is deflected by the necessity of proving his superiority to Mme de Merteuil. With Sade we have passed out of the range of normal human reactions into a rarefied and abstract realm which does not allow such human foibles as love to operate. By stripping eighteenth century psychology of all its nuances and ambiguities, Sade was able to portray men and women entirely in the grip of the necessity to project their ego at the expense of others. The apotheosis of evil into the guiding rule comes quite naturally after this initial step, but it is by no means the only possible outcome of such a psychology.

But the fact that this kind of a moral or immoral system could indeed be developed out of the basic psychological principle of *amour-propre* led most eighteenth century writers into infinitely convoluted ways of proving that this was not the only nor even the logical development of their principles. Nothing is more central to eighteenth century concerns than the fear that the new morality would not stand up in the face of such cynical criticism. Even Marivaux, whose central characters do not partake in the ruthless activities so characteristic of most *arrivistes,* noted the distinction which must be made between pride and virtue, the first being innate and the second acquired :

> le plus pressé pour nous, c'est nous-même, c'est-à-dire, notre orgueil ; car notre orgueil et nous, ce n'est qu'un, au lieu que nous et notre vertu, c'est deux ... Cette vertu, il faut qu'on nous la donne ; c'est en partie une affaire d'acquisition. Cet orgueil, on ne nous le donne pas, nous l'apportons en naissant ; nous l'avons tant, qu'on ne saurait nous l'ôter ; et comme il est le premier en date, il est, dans l'occasion, le premier servi. C'est la nature qui a le pas sur l'édu-cation [125].

Fortunately Marivaux' characters are possessed of " un bon cœur " which keeps them on the path of virtue without too much damage to their pride.

The question immediately arises as to what happens in a society which is not made up of men and women guided by a certain instinct towards the good. Obviously this is not the place to outline all the various ethical systems proposed by eighteenth century writers on this thorny subject, but a few examples will serve to show its relationship with the problem of the self. For the most part there was universal acceptance of the fact that human beings are motivated by a desire to promote their own individual good ; as Boudier states it : " Le premier acte de la volonté de l'homme, est un retour sur lui, par lequel il souhaite son bien : ce sentiment, inséparable d'un être intelligent, est le principe de toute son action [126]. " We have already seen that this " retour sur lui " is fundamental in most of the psychological systems of the day ; for instance, Condillac's statue does just this as soon as it experiences more than a single sensation and is immediately subject to *amour-propre* [127]. But this is not sufficient in Condillac's eyes to explain all the varied reactions of a real man. Therefore he distinguishes between " le moi d'habitude " and " le moi de réflexion ", the first of which governs all the animal functions of the body and the second of which guides his psychological and moral actions : " Il s'occupe du soin d'ajouter à notre bonheur. Ses succès multiplient ses désirs, ses méprises les renouvellent avec plus de force : les obstacles sont autant d'aiguillons : la curiosité le meut sans cesse : l'industrie fait son caractère [128]. " It is easy to see how far Condillac was from a belief in a passive, composite self ; his *moi de réflexion* is on the contrary in a constant state of striving, and each and every decision is based upon a desire to increase the well-being of the self.

Helvétius, despite his lip service to the passivity of human personality, presents his essential man in the grips of the same desire :

D.   En qualité de sensible, que doit faire l'homme ?
R.   Fuir la douleur, chercher le plaisir. C'est à cette recherche, c'est à cette fuite constante qu'on donne le nom d'amour de soi [129].

It is this fundamental quality of self-love which drives man on to acquire knowledge in the hope of increasing thereby his own personal happiness. But simply aiming at happiness through egotistic concentration on the desires of the individual is not sufficient grounds for the establishment of true happiness. All the *philosophes* are united in their attempt to provide some justifiable base for altruistic actions as well as egotistical ones. Many of them appealed to the concept of enlightened self-interest. By this term they meant to convey the idea that the narrowly individualistic and hedonistic ethic, as represented to their horrified eyes in La Mettrie, could lead only to unhappiness. For true self-interest must involve a concern for others since man lives in a larger society ; no egotistic aim would be operative or even necessary. The fact of the matter is that men exist in society and are determined to a large degree by this fact ; biological explanations are not sufficient to describe the nature of man, even psychological ones must be supplemented by sociological principles. As Crocker describes Condorcet's resolution of this problem :

The basic laws of behavior are not moral ; they remain consistent with the analysis of human motivation and behavior. They are self-interest ... and the opinions or pressures of the social group. But they eventuate in moral laws.

Convention and opinion derive their weight from our desire for approval, prestige, admiration, fame, and ultimately, for self-approval. We have the deep need of considering ourselves in the light in which we wish to appear to others[130].

There were some *philosophes,* notably Diderot and Rousseau, who did not find this a satisfactory solution. D'Alembert seems to have been working towards a new kind of psychological principle to explain why men sometimes acted in ways which appeared to contradict their own self-interest. On the one hand, d'Alembert reiterated the basic need which one man feels for the society of another, but he also raised the possibility of a totally new motivational principle, the necessity of suffering. Grimsley has analyzed this principle which d'Alembert outlined only briefly but never developed :

What, therefore, is the real *natural* basis of moral sacrifice ? It is worth noting that in his informal discussions of this topic he makes little use of the facile thesis of ' enlightened self-interest ', but seeks an alternative psychological basis for moral principles. He believed this to lie in the ' necessity of suffering ' which he put forward as one of the essential factors of the human condition[131].

One can imagine how the pleasure-loving eighteenth century would have reacted to such a notion ! Enlightened self-interest was much more comprehensible and indeed acceptable to the eighteenth century, which, for the most part, was not ready to consider the darker side of man's nature. Both Diderot and Rousseau responded in extremely different ways to this problem and gave solutions which opened up new approaches to the whole problem.

Chapter IV

ROUSSEAU

Dualism

As with most eighteenth century writers, Rousseau did not approach the problem of the self in what would today be called a logical, philosophical fashion. However he did make one serious attempt to come to grips with most of the epistemological and ontological problems involved ; this occurs, of course, in the *Profession de foi du vicaire savoyard*. It is interesting to note that even in this case, the arguments are not fundamental to the thesis which is at the base of the *Profession,* the establishment of a natural religion based on subjective and sentimental reasons. In his masterly discussion of the genesis and development of the different sections of this text, Masson points out that the first draft differed from the final text principally in its lack of philosophical argumentation : " Point de discussions subtiles, et d'une philosophie technique. Les dissertations qu'il a insérées plus tard sur la sensation, le jugement, la substance, la matière et le mouvement sont encore absentes[1]." Not only that, but Rousseau refused to go back over this argumentation at any later period of his life, referring to the fact that he had done it once thoroughly and that he intended to hold to his earlier conclusions[2].

For the most part Rousseau's attitude to philosophical questions corresponds to that of Julie in her last letter to St. Preux before her fatal accident : " Voulons-nous pénétrer dans ces abîmes de la métaphysique qui n'ont ni fond ni rive, et perdre à disputer sur l'essence divine ce tems si court qui nous est donné pour l'honorer ? Nous ignorons ce qu'elle est, mais nous savons qu'elle est, que cela nous suffise " (O. C., Pléiade, II, 699). The nature of man is, however, somewhat more accessible than that of God, and Rousseau treats it in several different ways in a number of works written for the most part during his active period at Montmorency. These include the first two books of *Emile,* the so-called *Lettres morales* of 1758, and the *Lettre à M. de Beaumont* of 1762, written as a defense of *Emile.* In the latter work, Rousseau complains that all his critics have overlooked the first part of the *Profession :* " la première, qui est la plus grande, la plus importante, la plus remplie de vérités frappantes et neuves, est destinée à combattre le moderne matérialisme, à établir l'existence de Dieu et la religion naturelle avec toute la force dont l'auteur est capable[3]. "

In the *Profession* Rousseau's point of departure in this philosophical inquiry is the very fact of existence : " J'existe, et j'ai des sens par lesquels je suis affecté " (O. C., Hachette, II, 240). This is a subtle reversal of the Cartesian logic in which an activity of the self points to the existence of that self. Rousseau does not even follow the by then normal pattern established by the French sensationalist school, the *sentio, ergo sum,* which comes from Lockean epistemology. Rousseau's first certainty is that a personal being to which we attach a first person pronoun, *je,* does in fact exist, and this forms the foundation for the rest of his discussion. He cannot doubt this fact, and so a personal self forms the very basis of his whole theory of knowledge and also of the external world.

This is particularly well shown in metaphorical rather than abstract terms in the one-act play *Pygmalion* also written in 1762. Galathée has hardly begun to stir with her new-found life than she makes a symbolic gesture : " Galathée se touche et dit : Moi " (O. C., Pléiade, II, 1230). Just to make sure that there is no mistake she repeats the gesture and the words : " Galathée se touchant encore : C'est moi." Only after establishing this first and absolutely necessary logical point does she go on to the external world and the existence of other people. Her discovery of Pygmalion, whom she considers to be an extension of herself, is somewhat complicated by their unusual relationship and need not detain us here.

To return to the Vicar we find that he establishes his existence, " la première vérité qui me frappe " (O. C., Hachette, II, 240), by the mere force of stating that it is so. The second part of his statement, " et j'ai des sens par lesquels je suis affecté " leads him into his first area of doubt, a doubt which he is never able to resolve. Since Rousseau was trying to refute the materialistic and sensationalist philosophy which denied the existence of the Cartesian subject to which sensations, ideas, and affections adhere, this doubt revolves around the question whether in fact a self exists apart from its sensations : " Ai-je un sentiment propre de mon existence, ou ne la sens-je que par mes sensations ? Voilà mon premier doute, qu'il m'est, quant à présent, impossible de résoudre. Car étant continuellement affecté de sensations, ou immédiatement, ou par la mémoire, comment puis-je savoir si le sentiment du *moi* est quelque chose hors de ces mêmes sensations, et s'il peut être indépendant d'elles ? " (O. C., Hachette, II, 240). Unfortunately the good Vicar goes no further in this inquiry ; instead he heads off towards another thorny philosophical question, that of the existence of matter as distinct from thought. Very quickly he proves the existence of objects which do not inhere in his own self since he is incapable of willing their existence or their destruction. No real proof has been offered for the first of these logical premises, but

Rousseau will from now on act as if these two principles had in fact been established beyond the question of a doubt. At a later point in his argument the Vicar remarks : " Je sens mon âme, je la connais par le sentiment et par la pensée, je sais qu'elle est, sans savoir quelle est son essence " (O. C., Hachette, II, 254). Rousseau himself, defending his theory in the *Lettre à M. de Beaumont* states : " il est certain que nous avons l'idée de deux substances distinctes : savoir, l'esprit et la matière, ce qui pense et ce qui est étendu " (O. C., Hachette, III, 78).

He will give excuses for not being able to say any more about mind and body, relying primarily on the excuse that man is made up of both matter and mind and that this complicates his knowledge of either of these substances[4]. In addition, Rousseau never really gives up the Lockean psychology of knowledge, according to which everything that man knows he must know through his senses, which are deficient and therefore incapable of giving him real information about mind and matter[5].

Rousseau tries to get at this problem in a variety of ways, using a genetic approach in *Emile,* an analytic approach in the two *Discours* and the *Dialogues,* an historical approach in the *Confessions* and what may be termed an experiential approach in the *Rêveries.* Of all his major works only the *Contrat social* does not add anything of importance to Rousseau's idea of the self, which also includes his concept of his own self and its existence in society. The problem troubles him ; he comes back to it again and again but never really gives a direct logical and philosophical answer to the question of the Vicar.

There can be no doubt that Rousseau subscribed to the Cartesian concept of the self as a unit, a substance to which things happened but which was not in any way changed by these happenings. This dualism, plus the one associated with the mind-body dichotomy, runs through all his works, creating a tension which has led many critics to see therein a real dichotomy, or else to single out only one aspect of his system to the exclusion of the other. We shall not here have to argue whether Rousseau is a true liberal or a representative of authoritarianism, whether he believed in individualism or in egalitarianism, whether his thought is rationalistic or sentimental, but it should be clear that this type of division of Rousseau's thought goes against the fundamental dualism which he assumed as the base on which the universe is founded. There is however another strain, a highly developed monistic tendency, which has often been traced to the influence of Platonism, and which leads Rousseau to posit the ultimate oneness of the universe, in many ways corresponding to the ultimate oneness of the individual[6]. He objected to the pluralistic world of the materialistic philosophers precisely because they could not account for the unitary nature of the self : " Mais s'il est vrai que toute matière sente, où concevrai-je l'unité sensitive ou le moi individuel ? sera-ce dans chaque molécule de matière

ou dans des corps agrégatifs ? " [7]   There is no question in his mind
that individuals exist as such and further that God himself exists as a
single principle which underlies the whole universe [8].   In some way
both these strains must be accounted for, just as both of them found a
place in Rousseau's thought.

There are certain *données* to which Rousseau came back again and
again, especially the famous *sentiment de l'existence* which becomes
almost a refrain in his works. He ignored the grounds on which this
type of analysis had been made, leaving aside, for the most part, the
purely philosophical or objective ones in order to plunge directly into
the very subjective sphere of his own personality and experiences.   He
was not unaware of the pitfalls which lie in the path of self-knowledge,
although he became more and more acquainted with them as he turned
to more and more subjective writings.   By the time of the *Rêveries* he
openly admits these difficulties : " le connois-toi toi-même du Temple
de Delphes n'étoit pas une maxime si facile à suivre que je l'avois cru
dans mes *Confessions* " (O. C., Pléiade, I, 1024), but nonetheless he
continues to speak about his subjective status in an objective manner.   It is
thus in some measure correct to say that one must await the final synthesis
offered by the *Rêveries* to arrive at a true appreciation of Rousseau's
concept of the self, but it is nonetheless instructive to delineate Rousseau's
more objective dicta before discussing the final analysis in the *Cinquième
Promenade* [9].

The *Profession de foi* has been termed mediocre, traditional and commonplace [10], but since it does represent Rousseau's only attempt at
logical discourse in this sphere, it must be examined in more detail.   As
Broome has pointed out, this work can be divided into four main movements : " The first of them is a consideration of our sensory knowledge of
' objects ' ; the second, an account of the causes of objects which are
experienced through the senses and revealed by an intuitive judgment ;
the third is a deduction of the principal truths which matter in the practical
business of living ; and the fourth is the establishment of rules of
conduct [11] ".   Thus Rousseau, through the Vicar, moves away from the realm
of the abstract towards that of concrete moral obligations which need to
be translated into action.   The initial starting point, the substance of the
self as immediately experienced by an individual, can only be envisaged
in action.   The real center of Rousseau's concern lies in moral action,
and it is instructive to note that the Vicar's original question about the
existence of his self is preceded by a series of questions which outline
the main divisions of the work : " Mais qui suis-je ? quel droit ai-je
de juger les choses ? et qu'est-ce qui détermine mes jugements ? " (O.C.,
Hachette, II, 240). The *je* can only be known through its active intervention
in the exterior world, and this is primarily considered to be the moral
world of mankind in society.

The abstraction known as the self is manifested primarily in the faculty of judgment, which is in turn dependent on sensations, but which cannot be completely explained by them. Both Diderot and Rousseau reacted against Helvétius' doctrine that all mental functions can be explained in terms of sensation alone ; they both insisted that some other faculty must be invoked to explain this feature of human mentality. Rousseau's notes on Helvétius have been published [12], but his real answer is given in the first section of the *Profession de foi*. According to the Vicar, a distinction must be drawn between judging and feeling : " Selon moi la faculté distinctive de l'être actif ou intelligent est de pouvoir donner un sens à ce mot *est*. Je cherche en vain dans l'être purement sensitif cette force intelligente qui superpose et puis qui prononce " (O. C., Hachette, II, 241). The mind is not merely a passive receptor but also an active sender ; it is characterized by a faculty which has been variously termed " attention, méditation, réflexion " (O. C., Hachette, II, 242). This faculty has no way of activating itself until it comes into contact with the world through the five senses, but its spontaneous activity is not fundamentally dependent upon them.

Although Rousseau is much too imbued with Lockean psychology to say so overtly, one gets the impression that he believes the senses are more a matter of convenience to the mind than vice versa. An analogy may be drawn with his remarks about the origin of language : " Il paroît encore par les mêmes observations que l'invention de l'art de communiquer nos idées dépend moins des organes qui nous servent à cette communication, que d'une faculté propre à l'homme, qui lui fait employer ses organes à cet usage, et que, si ceux-là lui manquoient, lui en feroit employer d'autres à la même fin " (O. C., Hachette, I, 373). If the speech organs were not developed, man would find something else to use to express his ideas ; in the same way, if the senses were not there, the mind would find some other way to express its spontaneous power of judgment. Be that as it may, mind does not exist apart from body and so the only thing to do is to see how the faculty of judgment, a spontaneous inner activity natural to the mind, is manifested in the world of the senses.

Rousseau's insistence on the absolute spontaneity of the mind in its exercise of judgment leads naturally into a discussion of the will. Man himself must be responsible for his every act, and determinism must be held back and overcome. Thus the inner certainty of the existence of a self-moving and active self serves to uphold the most important tenet of Rousseau's ethic, which in turn serves as the basis for his belief in a divine being, the only completely spontaneous force in the universe : " En un mot, tout mouvement qui n'est pas produit par un autre ne peut venir que d'un acte spontané, volontaire ; les corps inanimés n'agissent que par le mouvement, et il n'y a point de véritables actions sans volonté. Voilà mon premier principe. Je crois donc qu'une volonté meut l'univers et anime la nature " (O. C., Hachette, II, 244).

At this stage Rousseau realizes that it will be necessary to establish some sort of continuity in his conception of the self. So far he has established it as an existing entity which makes itself known through spontaneous reactions to external stimuli. But no principle of unity has as yet been discerned. At a later date Rousseau will appeal to *le sentiment de l'existence* as a kind of undertone to all man's actions ; whether a person actually happens to be paying attention to it at that moment or not, it is still there if he were to stop and allow it to become conscious. In the *Profession de foi* Rousseau is making a valiant effort to handle these problems in an objective way, and so his next step must correspond to the one used by other thinkers of the time, particularly Condillac and Helvétius. The role of memory was central to any discussion of the mind and its principles of organization. Poulet has succinctly noted the two diverging interpretations commonly appealed to in the eighteenth century : " Dans l'optique du 18ᵉ siècle, la mémoire, c'est, ou bien—comme le disait Condillac—de la sensation réveillée, de la sensation prolongée, ou bien c'est un réveil des anciens sentiments [13]." Neither of these positions suited Rousseau, who wanted neither to submerge the past in the present nor the present in the past. His need was to effect a fusion of the two, which would in turn lead on to the future.

Significantly enough, the Vicar turns to memory as the unifying factor during a discussion of the immortality of the soul. He is unable to determine whether the soul is or is not immortal, but he insists that the only kind of immortality which makes any sense at all is one in which the soul would remember what it had accomplished during its mortal life : " Ce que je sais bien, c'est que l'identité du *moi* ne se prolonge que par la mémoire, et que, pour être le même en effet, il faut que je me souvienne d'avoir été. Or je ne saurais me rappeler, après ma mort, ce que j'ai été durant ma vie, que je ne me rappelle aussi ce que j'ai senti, par conséquent ce que j'ai fait " (O. C., Hachette, II, 254-55). This survival of individual personal identity justifies the whole course of Providence, and also brings out clearly the fundamental dualism of Rousseau's concept of man. In this world he is limited by his body to be no more than a mind which is dependent upon sensory data, but after death, which implies the destruction of the body, but not of the mind, the individual self really comes into its own : " J'aspire au moment où, délivré des entraves du corps, je serai *moi* sans contradiction, sans partage, et n'aurai besoin que de moi pour être heureux " (O. C., Hachette, II, 265). Eighteenth century Catholic theology involved a belief in the complete efficacy of God's glory as the sole object worthy of contemplation in the afterlife, but this would require a negation of the value of the activities of man in this life. Again we see Rousseau combining two attitudes to produce a complex synthesis which he expounds but does not justify.

The problem of personal survival is handled in an imaginative way in the *Nouvelle Héloïse* during the prolonged death scene which closes the novel. Julie argues just this point with the pastor, insisting on the fact that she will remember her earthly existence and especially " des gens qui m'y ont été chers " (O. C., Pléiade, II, 729), and she closes this discussion with the playful reminder that she will soon be in a better position than the pastor to judge of such matters! Obviously no one could argue with such a statement, and the pastor suddenly withdraws to allow the close members of the Clarens family to occupy the center of the stage for the rest of the scene. Clearly this represents Rousseau's point of view ; in his personal copy he added a marginal note which states : " S'il ne se souvient plus d'être le même il ne l'est plus. On voit par là que ceux qui disent qu'à la mort d'un homme son âme se résout dans la grande âme du monde ne disent rien qui ait du sens " (O. C., Pléiade, II, 1807). The idea of the annihilation of the *moi* by no matter what marvellous apotheosis is anathema to Rousseau who felt his very being threatened by the mere thought of such an occurrence.

In following Rousseau's discussion of the self in the *Profession de foi* it has become more and more clear that he really was not able to mold his beliefs into anything approaching a logical or rational system. At every important step he appeals to a type of certainty which is not objectively justifiable. Some modern philosophers would therefore deny the validity of any of Rousseau's statements, since, according to them, only that which can be proved can be conceded to have any degree of certainty. But Rousseau's value does not lie in his ability, or inability, to support his beliefs in a logical fashion ; he would not subscribe to the position that what cannot be proved is not worth talking about. Quite the contrary, Rousseau would insist on the importance of those beliefs which are of a primitive nature, inherent in the structure of the human being, made up of both body and mind or soul. These beliefs need to be brought out of their incoherent and largely unconscious state and articulated as fully as possible so that men may react more effectively to the many pressures and tensions which otherwise might overwhelm them. Rousseau starts this search with a return to the " primitive " in man, either to the savage or to the child, both of which must be considered to be generically basic to the complex being which is Rousseau's main consideration.

Savage and child

In examining man in society, Rousseau tries to see which features can be attributed to the artificial bonds imposed upon him by group living and which traits are on the contrary "primitive". Modern critics generally agree that when Rousseau discusses the savage in the *Deuxième Discours* he is not presenting a fully worked out anthropological system ; there is great doubt whether Rousseau thought this type of social structure ever actually existed or whether he is merely positing what he considered to be necessary as a base for his searing criticism of eighteenth century society, especially that of Paris. It is more likely that he inclined to the latter position : what is primitive in man is that which can be found in every man in no matter what society, as distinguished from those characteristics which are a product of that society alone.

This represents an attempt to disengage the essence of man, what the eighteenth century called " natural man," from his environment, and it implies a belief in the continued existence of natural man beneath societal man. Much of what Rousseau says about natural man is therefore based on the fact that he is opposing two concepts to explain the phenomenon of modern man. To use twentieth century terms, modern man is presented as being completely outer-directed, primitive man as inner-directed ; all the actions of modern man are based on comparisons he makes between himself and others, and especially on what others think of him. The term Rousseau uses is *amour-propre*, which he contrasts to *amour de soi*, a totally self-sufficient principle which never directs behavior according to the judgments of others but only according to those of the individual involved. This contrast is developed at some length in Note XV of the *Deuxième Discours* in which Rousseau stresses the individualistic, almost solipsistic state of natural man :

> dans nôtre état primitif, dans le véritable état de nature, l'Amour propre n'éxiste pas ; Car chaque homme en particulier se regardant lui-même comme le seul Spectateur qui l'observe, comme le seul être dans l'univers qui prenne intérèt à lui, comme le seul juge de son propre mérite, il n'est pas possible qu'un sentiment qui prend sa source dans des comparaisons qu'il n'est pas à portée de faire, puisse germer dans son âme (O. C., Pléiade, III, 219).

Not only is this creature isolated physically from his fellow men, but he is also isolated from himself in terms of time. He lives entirely in the present, making no plans for the future and taking no heed of the past. As Starobinski has pointed out in his notes to the *Deuxième Discours*, this portrait of primitive man is very close to Buffon's description of animality in the *Discours sur la nature des animaux*, but to Rousseau there are already discernible certain characteristics which distinguish man from the other animals, namely free-will and the possibility of perfecting himself.

The fact that the savage is characterized almost entirely in negative terms—no imagination, no concept of the future, neither good nor bad, happy or unhappy, not active, not reasonable—shows clearly that he exists primarily in logical opposition to social man. There are some positive aspects, mainly based on the fact that the savage is a purely sentient being, motivated by nothing more complicated than self-conservation. And even this goal is not hard to achieve, since Rousseau saw primitive man as a strong, self-sufficient being whose needs are so small as to be easily satisfied. He is, however, aware of himself as a unit : " Son ame, que rien n'agite, se livre au seul sentiment de son existence actuelle " (O. C., Pléiade, III, 144). This does not imply any real consciousness of himself as existing apart from others or even as apart from the outside world ; everything appears to him to be immediately related to himself through his senses. As Burgelin puts it :

> A l'état de nature, il est simple, caractérisé par sa parfaite unité : l'âme adhère au corps et ce bloc sans fissure exclut la conscience, qui suppose toujours un certain écart en face de soi, un détachement. D'autre part, il constitue une monade qui reflète un univers sans le distinguer de soi. Comme il ignore le rapport, hors de lui il n'y a rien, il s'étend sur tout[14].

In many ways this ideal is the one which is basic to all Rousseau's future work : the desire to recapture the marvellously passive, completely transparent state of being enjoyed by primitive man. But, as he himself remarked, " la nature humaine ne retrograde pas " (O. C., Pléiade, I, 935), and, not only that, primitive man himself was unable to remain in his privileged position. Actually this is a considerable simplification, because Rousseau never completely clarified whether this state represents the ideal of human possibilities or not. In comparison with the tormented state of modern man, the quiet tranquillity of primitive man does seem to be attractive, but there are passages in which Rousseau notes that primitive man was very little more than a brutish animal, whose stupidity was so profound that it is little short of miraculous that he was ever able to create languages (O. C., Pléiade, III, 151).

And yet Rousseau realizes that there must be some explanation of the development from the primitive to the modern condition of man, and, characteristically, he wavers between two divergent explanations. In the first place he has already distinguished primitive man from the animals by virtue of his free-will and the fact that he is aware of being able to make these choices himself. These may be termed natural explanations of man's development, inherent in the structure of the body and mind, which exist for the most part only potentially in primitive man. This potentiality is termed by Rousseau the gift of perfectibility ; in other words, there exists in primitive man more than one might expect solely on the basis of an analysis of his behavior. What activates this potential ? The well-known explanation of a " concours fortuit de plusieurs causes étrangeres " (O. C., Pléiade, III, 162) seems to beg the question to a certain degree. It would seem that the two must be considered as intimate parts of one another. The spontaneous drive of the will can only be manifested under the right conditions, but the conditions are of no use to the other species which are not endowed with this potential. From the standpoint of ethics this is a

happy blend of free-will and determinism; from the standpoint of the
concept of the self, it again shows how Rousseau is committed to the
idea of the thing in itself, underlying all human behavior, but only coming
into its own through a process of experience.

This important theory is brought out more clearly in *Emile*, in which
Rousseau applied to the evolution of individual man the concepts worked
out for the species. If Rousseau's first method was that of examining man
in society, his second approach to the definition of a human being is
through the analysis of an individual and the growth of a single personality. Instead of describing the various stages on the road to societal man,
Rousseau concentrates on the idealized and, in many ways, abstract portrait of the various states on the way to individuality. It is interesting to
note that the further one goes in *Emile*, the more individualized and
concrete does Emile himself become. This fits in extremely well with
Rousseau's ideas but also shows that we are dealing with an author of
high imaginative power who is not long content to remain in the realm
of the purely abstract. Since we shall be mainly concerned with the first
two books of *Emile*, it would be possible to get the incorrect impression
that Rousseau is much more abstract in this work than he actually is.

Emile is dominated by the eighteenth century interpretation of
Locke's psychology, according to which the mind at birth represents a
tabula rasa. All thoughts and feelings are generated through the senses
by means of sensations; the child has no innate ideas which can serve
as points of comparison. He is a completely passive being entirely
dependent on the effects produced upon him by the outside world. Of
course Locke had posited an inner faculty of reflection which was capable
of combining these sensations, but this faculty had been completely denied
by his French disciples, Condillac and Helvétius. To Rousseau, however,
even the return to Locke's faculty of reflection was not sufficient to
account for the growth of the child from a passive receptor to an active
judger and actor.

Rousseau's portrait of the *infans* in Book I of *Emile* corresponds to
the ideas of Condillac, in that the baby is, so to speak, a blank at birth,
in fact Rousseau compares him to a mechanical being (O. C., Hachette, II,
29). All infants are immediately assailed by various sensations caused
by the exterior world and react by movements and noises to this new
situation. The discussion of the custom of binding babies is instructive in
this regard, since Rousseau condemns it precisely because it limits the
possible reactions open to infants. If they are deprived of the opportunity
of thrashing around, in an uncoordinated way of course, then they will
have recourse to the only other avenue open to them, that is to crying
(O. C., Hachette, II, 10-11). Whether this is true or not (and modern
infant psychology has cast much doubt on this idea), need not concern us
here; what does concern us is Rousseau's concept of the most primitive

stage imaginable, that of the newborn baby. He is considerably troubled by the problem of this totally negative and passive entity which is assailed by a host of sensations over which it has absolutely no control. Even more disturbing is the necessity of considering the question of whether the infant has the power to distinguish between the realm of the subjective and the objective. Two possible explanations are available : first, that the infant is a totally solipsistic being who must learn to distinguish from his own feelings which are internally generated those sensations which are dependent upon objective realities ; second, that the infant has absolutely no concept of individuality, that this is what he must learn to distinguish from those sensations which are externally generated. Rousseau inclines towards the latter solution, as would most eighteenth century sensationalists, and, incidentally, most twentieth century psychologists. However Rousseau needs the idea of the self as an active being in order to explain the future development of the individual.

As he did in the *Deuxième Discours,* Rousseau resorts to the concept of a potential force, although it is not explicitly stated as such in *Emile.* Two passages will serve to bring this out (italics added) :

> Nous naissons sensibles, et, dès notre naissance, nous sommes affectés de diverses manières par les objets qui nous environnent. *Sitôt que nous avons pour ainsi dire la conscience de nos sensations,* nous sommes disposés à rechercher ou à fuir les objets qui les produisent, d'abord, selon qu'elles nous sont agréables ou déplaisantes, puis selon la convenance ou disconvenance que nous trouvons entre nous et ces objets, et enfin, selon les jugemens que nous en portons sur l'idée de bonheur ou de perfection que la raison nous donne (O. C., Hachette, II, 5-6).

> Nous naissons capables d'apprendre, mais ne sachant rien, ne connoissant rien. *L'âme, enchaînée dans des organes imparfaits et demi-formés, n'a pas même le sentiment de sa propre existence.* Les mouvements, les cris de l'enfant qui vient de naître, sont des effets purement mécaniques, dépourvus de connoissance et de volonté (O. C., Hachette, II, 29).

In both of these passages, the infant is represented as limited by a lack of consciousness, first of his sensations, and second of himself. But it is clear from the second passage that something does exist within the infant which is capable of serving as a receptor of sensations and at the appropriate moment as the focus of judgment. This entity corresponds to the Cartesian concept of the substance of the soul, but in Rousseau's scheme it must await the development of the body in order to manifest its own particular qualities.

Right after the second passage quoted above, Rousseau takes up the well-known metaphor of the statue coming suddenly to life, characterizing it as a newborn being who has at birth all the physical force and stature of an adult : " cet homme-enfant seroit un parfait imbécile, un automate, une statue immobile et presque insensible " but this robot-type person will have one idea which distinguishes him sharply from the newborn baby : " il n'existeroit que dans le commun *sensorium* ; il n'auroit qu'une seule idée, savoir celle du *moi*, à laquelle il rapporteroit toutes ses sensations " (O. C., Hachette, II, 30). Even with no experience whatsoever, the newborn adult would have knowledge of his self. So this idea of the self is of such a basic nature that it is only because of the baby's lack of physical development, and not his lack of experience, that he is unable to experience it. Whereas the baby must learn to distinguish his own inner being from the exterior world, this newborn man must reverse the process. He starts from the premise that he is the center of the universe and gradually learns that there exist things over which he has no control. But the first step must be the consciousness of the self as a unit, and this is precisely what Rousseau denies to the infant.

At the end of Book I, the baby suddenly comes into his own ; almost simultaneously he learns to speak, feed himself and walk, and as far as Rousseau is concerned this represents " la première époque de sa vie " (O. C., Hachette, II, 43). Up to this point, the baby is really less than an animal, and certainly less than the natural man envisaged in the *Deuxième Discours*, who is distinguished by his very active *sentiment de l'existence*. Only with the flowering of this feeling does anything resembling a human being come into existence : " C'est à ce second degré que commence proprement la vie de l'individu, c'est alors qu'il prend la conscience de lui-même. La mémoire étend le sentiment de l'identité sur tous les momens de son existence ; il devient véritablement un, le même, et par conséquent déjà capable de bonheur ou de misère " (O. C., Hachette, II, 45). With this sense of identity, the young child is now ready to progress through a series of experiences to become a fully active man. We may note in passing that the appeal to memory occurs at exactly the same point in the development of the individual as it did in the more abstract epistemology of the *Profession de foi*. But without the previous existence of the self, memory would serve no useful purpose. It cannot create the self ; it can only give to it a sense of its continuity.

As with the natural man the young child is characterized by a state of natural indifference to his surroundings. Since a child grows up to be a man regardless of the restraints placed upon him, there must be some inner force which explains this change. In the *Deuxième Discours* Rousseau had recourse to both environmental and psychological factors to explain the development of modern man from natural man : " un concours fortuit de plusieurs causes étrangères " and " la faculté de perfectibilité " (O. C., Pléiade, III, 162). In Book I of *Emile* Rousseau points to the existence of a *principe actif* which explains the frenzied activity pattern of babies and young children and notes that in an older person this force is on the decline, which explains the progressively more tranquil movements of the old man (O. C., Hachette, I, 36). As the child moves towards adolescence and eventually towards adult maturity, this *principe actif* is transferred from the purely physical to the mental : " A l'activité du corps qui cherche à se développer, succède l'activité de l'esprit qui cherche à s'instruire. D'abord les enfans ne sont que remuans, ensuite ils sont curieux " (O. C., Hachette, II, 137). It is at this point that the tutor finds it necessary to arrange scenes in which Emile will discover for himself certain important principles about the governing of human behavior. Again we note the combination of an innate proclivity which needs a certain environmental condition in order to manifest itself.

The duality of Rousseau's approach is also noticeable in the double standard of ideals which he sets up for childhood. In the first place he idealizes an active life, one in which all possible use is made of all the faculties of man : " Vivre ce n'est pas respirer, c'est agir, c'est faire usage de nos organes, de nos sens, de nos facultés, de toutes les parties de nous-mêmes qui nous donnent le sentiment de notre existence " (O. C., Hachette, II, 9). But he also idealizes a state of equilibrium, especially in Book II. The very young child is presented as living in what corresponds to the Golden Age. His desires are matched by his abilities, producing an era of repose for the self : " En quoi donc consiste la sagesse humaine ou la route du vrai bonheur ? ... c'est à diminuer l'excès des désirs sur les facultés, et à mettre en égalité parfaite la puissance et la volonté. C'est alors seulement que toutes les forces étant en action, l'âme cependant restera paisible, et que l'homme se trouvera bien ordonné " (O.C., Hachette, II, 47). The young child lacks imagination and is not therefore troubled by unfulfillable dreams. He feels at home in the universe precisely because he is content to remain in a very limited sphere in which he hardly needs to think at all[15].

This dichotomy of ideals based on a unified concept of the self will continue to be apparent, in fact will become more marked as we turn from Rousseau's objective theoretical works to his subjective and empirical ones. As Gossman succinctly points out, what Rousseau has to say about man in general is based upon his own experience : " Rousseau's formal sociological reflexions on man and society are accompanied, enriched and in an important sense completed by a concrete personal experience of alienation, isolation and disharmony. The autobiographical works can in fact be thought of as presenting in the form of an existential self-analysis that which in the political and sociological works is the object of an abstract and theoretical analysis[16]. "

Self-concept

Having considered Rousseau's philosophic concept of the self as an agent which has a determining influence upon the behavior pattern of the individual, we now turn to the other meaning usually associated with the word : " the self as the individual who is known to himself [17]. " In a paradoxical way this self-concept is considered by modern psychologists as being in some ways *more* objective than the self as subject or agent, which is usually termed " ego " in contemporary discussions. And yet it is obvious from the following definition that the self-as-object is dependent upon subjective interpretation : " it denotes the person's attitudes, feelings, perceptions, and evaluations of himself as an object. In this sense, the self is what a person thinks of himself [18]." Certainly in the case of Rousseau the subjective aspect overrides the objective one ; his self-concept does not correspond to objective criteria, and he is conscious of this discrepancy. Even as early as the *Lettres morales* (1758), he notes : " Nous ne voyons ni l'âme d'autri [sic], parce qu'elle se cache, ni la nôtre, parce que nous n'avons point de miroir intellectuel [19]." And yet he went on to write the *Confessions*, the *Dialogues*, and the *Rêveries*, all of which involve the creation of a self-portrait as a central theme.

The opening paragraphs of the *Confessions* proclaim triumphantly that Jean-Jacques Rousseau has accomplished what no other writer has ever even tried to do and what no other writer will ever be able to accomplish, to wit, the complete, true-to-life self-portrait. The positive element is so strong that Rousseau appeals to God himself as the final arbiter ; the all-seeing, all-knowing Deity would not be able to discern any falsehoods in Rousseau's account of his life : " j'ai dévoilé mon intérieur tel que tu l'as vu toi-même " (O. C., Pléiade, I, 5). This absolute confidence in his accomplishment is a necessary note at the beginning of the *Confessions*, since Rousseau must persuade his reader that no possibility of error or doubt exists and that this is a definitive self-portrait.

His oratorical and persuasive style carries the reader into the body of the text and sustains this suspension of doubt well into the body of the second book, at which point Rousseau as author, not narrator-hero, inserts a short paragraph which reiterates the fact that he is giving a complete self-portrait. But a note of doubt creeps in at this point since there are some readers who would be only too glad to find grey areas which lend themselves to criticism (O. C., Pléiade, I, 59-60). The same argument is repeated in the famous passage which closes the fourth book : " Je voudrais pouvoir en quelque façon rendre mon âme transparente aux yeux du lecteur " (O. C., Pléiade, I, 175). It is the reader who must form for himself the portrait of Rousseau based on the numerous details of events and feelings which are furnished by the author. And yet one wonders just how to interpret this instruction, especially in view of the fact that Rousseau's tone changes rapidly from expository to accusatory when he states that, if the reader does not emerge from this process with a picture which corresponds to the one Rousseau has of himself, then the fault must lie with the reader and not with the author : " s'il se trompe alors, toute l'erreur sera de son fait." Obviously the desire for clarity and transparency exists only if the window functions like a mirror.

The introduction to the *Confessions* in the Neuchâtel manuscript gives a rather different point of view. Here Rousseau portrays himself as much less sure of his results and also of his, or indeed of anyone's ability to create a life-like self-portrait. What emerges tends to be an idealized self-portrait, what one would like to be rather than what one actually is : " Nul ne peut écrire la vie d'un homme que lui-même. Sa manière d'être intérieure, sa véritable vie n'est connue que de lui ; mais en l'écrivant il la déguise ; sous le nom de sa vie, il fait son apologie ; il se montre comme il veut être vu, mais point du tout comme il est " (O. C., Pléiade, II, 1149). Unfortunately Rousseau does not go on to the obvious conclusion that his book must suffer from the same defect ; on the contrary, he attacks Montaigne and Cardan but does not come back to himself except to note that his position in society puts him in a privileged position, since he has access to sources of information which remain closed to other auto-biographers (O. C., Pléiade, I, 1150).

Of course the most privileged position of all stems from the fact that he is describing his own inner sensations and sentiments. In some ways Rousseau seems to be saying that it would be absolutely impossible for him to be mistaken in his self-concept, since he is the only one who has access to the means of forming such a concept. But the discrepancy between his own self-concept and the image of himself generally accepted by his contemporaries was too wide for Rousseau to rest easy in this assumption. The two portraits must be made to coincide for him to be satisfied with himself. It is a fact that no self-concept is completely uncontaminated by the views of others ; in fact some psychologists believe that it is only because other people react to a person as an object that that person learns to think of himself as such[20]. Most of the drive which Rousseau experienced in the formation of his series of self-portraits was generated by his reaction against being treated as an object by others.

The warmth and intimacy which Rousseau associates with his experience of his own unique identity is lacking when the self-concept is objectified, either by others or by himself. Many critics have confronted this problem. For instance, Ricatte refers to the old adage that you cannot go to the window to see yourself pass by and uses this example to explain the remarkable isolation of Rousseau in the *Rêveries*. According to Ricatte, most people are able to identify with the rest of the world sufficiently to be able to see themselves through the eyes of others, but " Rousseau ne peut devenir les autres, il ne peut se diviser intérieurement ainsi, et c'est la vraie raison de sa solitude[21]." Muntéano's thesis of a *moi permanent* and a *moi agent*, developed into the concept of a principle of *contradiction dialectique* of the whole of Being itself, postulates a basic duality not only in Rousseau's self-concept but in his very existence[22].

Grimsley advances the ingenious idea that the ever-present persecutors who haunted Rousseau's mind " symbolize not only the unrelieved hostility of the outside world, but that element in his own personality which, though partly dissociated from the rest and ignored by him for what it truly was, still formed part of his personal existence, whether he was willing to acknowledge it or not [23]." This critic also points out that the very act of writing permits Rousseau to achieve identification with both subject and object. Rousseau's self-portrait is that of his ideal self, in some ways his alter-ego : " the unique other with whom he can remain in personal contact [24]." To close this list of discrepant opinions, Grosclaude puts his finger on an anxiety factor which cannot be overlooked : " cette perpé-tuelle hantise d'un moi dont il craint toujours qu'il lui échappe [25]."

When such eminent critics disagree to this extent it is worthwhile to make yet another attempt to determine just how Rousseau saw himself as an object worth describing and how his supposedly objective self-portrait is riddled with contradictions in view of Rousseau's very real fears about the congruence of his own self.

The first area of alarm, as far as Rousseau was concerned, is that of reconciling the individual " I " with a steadily deteriorating society. Twentieth century jargon refers to this phenomenon as alienation, although the word in its modern usage would not really fit Rousseau's position since he always assumed that the universe was governed according to some principle of order. His problem was to fit himself into this system, and to that end he had to recreate society in such a way that his integration with it would become possible.

His politico-sociological works are all critical of the major institutions of eighteenth century France, and in his more personal works he portrays himself as a victim of the injustice and hypocrisy inherent therein. It is his contention that modern society reinforces inequality and injustice by making *amour-propre* the basis of social behavior : " Il falut pour son avantage se montrer autre que ce qu'on étoit en effet. Etre et paroître devinrent deux choses tout à fait différentes, et de cette distinction sortirent le faste imposant, la ruse trompeuse, et tous les vices qui en sont le cortége " (O. C., Pléiade, III, 174). His regulations for improving society require a radical restructuring of man's place therein ; so radical indeed that he has recourse to such terms as *dénaturer, transformer, altérer,* and *mutiler* to describe what must be done to man himself in order to create a viable society [26].

Whether he likes it or not, modern man lives in society and must continue to do so ; the tension created from this inevitability is reflected in the anguish portrayed in Rousseau's autobiographical works, especially the *Dialogues*. If society itself is based on a set of completely false values, how can any one individual hope to find therein a basis on which to construct a united and congruent self ? And yet no one can completely dissociate himself from society ; even in the *Rêveries,* which Rousseau claims he wrote only for his own delectation, the urgency of communicating with the rest of the world is strongly felt, especially in those passages where Rousseau bitterly regrets the isolation of his current condition. If he were given a free choice, this would not be the account of the activities of *un promeneur solitaire* but rather the joyous recounting of a life lived among friends and loved ones[27]. His final isolation has been forced upon him, and he is making the best of a bad situation in turning to himself as his only source of consolation.

This sense of divorce between the individual and society is brought out early in the *Confessions.* As Starobinski has pointed out, it is the incident of the comb at the Lambercier's that Rousseau develops in such a way as to make concrete his belief that society is founded on a series of appearances and that the forthright, innocent, and transparent child learns this fact the hard way :

> Cette révélation du mensonge de l'apparence est subie à la façon d'une blessure. Rousseau découvre le paraître en victime du paraître. A l'instant où il aperçoit les limites de sa subjectivité, elle lui est imposée comme *subjectivité calomniée.* Les autres le méconnaissent : le moi souffre son apparence comme un déni de justice qui lui serait infligé par ceux dont il voulait être aimé... Avant qu'il ne s'éprouve distant du monde, le *moi* a subi l'expérience de sa distance par rapport aux autres[28].

The concept of transparency, developed by both Starobinski and Grimsley, involves not only the possibility of total communication with others but also of total unity of the self. If the one is threatened, so is the other. This dichotomy is especially marked in the *Dialogues ;* in the *Deuxième Dialogue* the character Rousseau, commenting on the condition in which he had found Jean-Jacques, makes the following judgment : " Notre plus douce existence est relative et collective, et notre vrai *moi* n'est pas tout entier en nous. Enfin telle est la constitution de l'homme en cette vie qu'on n'y parvient jamais à bien jouir de soi sans le concours d'autrui " (O. C., Pléiade, I, 813). It would seem, therefore, that an affirmative answer must be given to the desperate question formulated in the *Histoire du précédent écrit :* " Si les hommes veulent me voir autre que je ne suis, que m'importe ? L'essence de mon être est-elle dans leurs regards ? " (O. C., Pléiade, I, 985).

Perhaps there is a hint of a solution in these two passages. It may very well be that we are dealing with a philosophical dichotomy between existence and essence, between becoming and being, between Kant's phenomenological and transcendental self. On the one hand what one is, is what one does ; on the other hand, what one is, is what one is. In other words, what happens to a person in the course of his life has no real effect upon his inner being, but only on his way of life. Unfortunately it is only through the evolving process of life itself that one has any access to this stable center. It would be useless to enumerate the number of times that Rousseau advises his reader to " rentrer en soi," " se circonscrire en soi," to center down into an area of tranquillity which is only accessible to someone who has experienced the hurly-burly of the world, survived it, and withdrawn from it.

The unfinished continuation of *Emile* graphically portrays this ideal young man, wedded to the nearly perfect young lady, rapidly losing all sense of his own self through dissipation of his energies in Parisian society : " je ne me laissois pas le temps de rentrer en moi, crainte de ne m'y plus retrouver " (O. C., Hachette, III, 4). Soon after being struck dumb by the news that Sophie has been unfaithful to him, Emile has a moment of clarity in which he realizes that his essential being has in no way been affected by this infidelity : "Quel mal ai-je reçu dans ma personne ? quel crime ai-je commis ? qu'ai-je perdu de moi ?[29] " Emile goes on to devise a new way of life based on the rather amazing assumption that each moment represents a new beginning and that, therefore, the past has no relevance in the present or future : " Je me disois qu'en effet nous ne faisons jamais que commencer, et qu'il n'y a point d'autre liaison dans notre existence qu'une succession de momens présens, dont le premier est toujours celui qui est en acte " (O. C., Hachette, III, 18). Again we see the dichotomy between the changing world of existence and the semi-eternal world of being. Nothing that happens can really alter Emile's inner self, but everything he does represents a new beginning, the creation of a new self. A person's self-concept varies according to time, place, and the influence of other people, but the inner self transcends these limitations.

The fact that Emile symbolizes these two concepts is brought out by the development of the story in this first and only complete letter of *Les Solitaires*. Immediately after discovering that the past has no meaning in the present, Emile makes the decision to take his son away from Sophie, the now unworthy mother. This choice is made in a rational, deliberate manner fully consistent with his new principles according to which the past is eliminated by the present. As soon as Sophie succeeds in tracing Emile, she appears at the shop where he is working, and all his noble decisions are forgotten. The past is still an effective, operative force which makes Emile realize that it would be unnatural to take a small child from its mother. However, in order to nullify the influence of the past on his own conduct, Emile decides to leave France in order not to risk a possible reconciliation with his erring wife. At this point he pontificates as follows : " Le sage vit au jour la journée, et trouve tous ses devoirs quotidiens autour de lui. Ne tentons rien au delà de nos forces, et ne nous portons point en avant de notre existence. Mes devoirs d'aujour-

d'hui sont ma seule tâche, ceux de demain ne sont pas encore venus "
(O. C., Hachette, III, 22). In his turbulent future career Emile will cling
to this morality, never looking beyond the needs and duties of the
present day.

The novel is, of course, unfinished, but Rousseau told a friend how
it was to end. Emile and Sophie are to be reunited in love and marriage ;
even in the first letter we get a premonition of this future blissful state.
Emile notes that his family, in contradiction to his orders, took the child
away from Sophie and that it eventually died. However this has had the
unexpectedly fortunate result of reuniting Emile and Sophie :

> Si ma famille eût suivi mes intentions, Sophie eût élevé cet enfant,
> et peut-être vivroit-il encore : mais peut-être aussi dès lors Sophie étoit-
> elle morte pour moi ; consolée dans cette chère moitié de moi-même,
> elle n'eût plus songé à rejoindre l'autre, et j'aurois perdu les plus beaux
> jours de ma vie. Que de douleurs devoient nous faire expier nos fautes
> avant que notre réunion nous les fît oublier ! (O. C., Hachette, III, 21).

Is it too far-fetched to interpret this as the eventual working out of
Emile's true inner state, his self, which involves a happy conjugal union
with a faithful and loving wife, and that all the rest of the numerous
adventures which he was to undergo, including capture by pirates, slavery
under various masters, and shipwreck on a desert island, symbolize his
passage through existence ? The two conditions occur together, and
existence is often not a happy experience, but if one can live as *le sage*
in the maelstrom of life itself, one can expect to reach that haven of
tranquility in which total transparency of being is at last experienced.
It is also interesting to note that in the final outcome of *Les Solitaires*, not
only is a loving couple reunited in complete and total faith in one another,
but there is formed on this desert island a small society made up of two
such unusual couples. The analogy with the society of Clarens is too close
not to be deliberate.

In *La Nouvelle Héloïse* Saint-Preux makes a somewhat similar
distinction between his real being and his situation in life : " Sans toi,
Beauté fatale ! je n'aurois jamais senti ce contraste insupportable de gran-
deur au fond de mon ame et de bassesse dans ma fortune " (O. C.,
Pléiade, II, 89). And speaking of himself in the *Lettres morales*, Rousseau
comments on the contrast to be found between the same two terms :
" Dans toutes les situations, je me suis toujours senti affecté de deux
maniéres différentes et quelquefois contraires, l'une venant de l'état de
ma fortune et l'autre de celui de mon âme ... je sentois pour ainsi dire en
moi le contre poids de ma destinée[30]." *Fortune* and *âme* : the first
forever in a state of flux, constantly changing and developing, progressing
in a way which the individual cannot really control ; the other a steady

state, always the same no matter what the circumstances, usually much better than its observable counterpart.

However there are times when this distinction between stable inner being and mutable outer existence is not clearly drawn by Rousseau. Indeed there are times when he questions the very unity of his inner self ; he seems to shudder at the thought that perhaps there is no real coherent structure to his self. This tendency towards dissociation of personality is quite marked, but even more noticeable is the striving towards unity. The theme is basic to the whole of the *Confessions* and is stated most candidly in the Neuchâtel introduction : " mais il faut faire ces aveux ou me déguiser ; car si je tais quelque chose on ne me connoitra sur rien, tant tout se tient, tant tout est un dans mon caractére, et tant ce bisarre et singulier assemblage a besoin de toutes les circonstances de ma vie pour être bien dévoilé " (O. C., Pléiade, I, 1153).

There are numerous places in which Rousseau makes the same charge about his personality, about how difficult it is to discover any principle of unity in his very diverse aspects. He does this jokingly in *Le Persifleur :* " Rien n'est si dissemblable à moi que moi-même " (O. C., Pléiade, I, 1108), and with much more gravity in the *Deuxième Dialogue* : " Il est actif, ardent, laborieux, infatigable ; il est indolent, paresseux, sans vigueur " (O. C., Pléiade, I, 817). The first few books of the *Confessions* are filled with incidents which Rousseau ascribes to " folie romanesque," " délire," " égaremens du cœur," " extravagance," all terms which, in addition to emphasizing the fact that these actions are not really charac- teristic of his personality, also serve to justify and excuse these very actions, since the inner self has no control over them and so cannot be held responsible for them.

La Nouvelle Héloïse is again a good source for examples, worked out in an artistically unified way, of the difficulties encountered in being true to one's inner self especially during the period of youth. Saint-Preux voices his problem in an early letter to Julie : " Je ne suis plus à moi, je l'avoue, mon ame aliénée est toute en toi " (O. C., Pléiade, II, 101). It is possible to read this remark in the tradition of Platonic love, but, as Bernard Guyon points out in his note to this passage, it is also possible to read this as " l'anéantissement de la raison par le désir sensuel... Com- ment être un parfait amant et demeurer maître de soi, ne pas être ' un autre ' ? " (O. C., Pléiade, II, 1402). Julie is certainly conscious of this difficulty, and most of the second half of the novel is devoted to a picture of what can be done when such a remarkable person does remain true to her inner being. The miraculous conversion of Julie during the wedding ceremony is presented in exactly these terms. She undergoes a revolution in her way of thinking and feeling, and she ascribes this to the interference of Providence : " Je le vois, je le sens ; la main secourable qui m'a conduite à travers les ténebres est celle qui leve à mes yeux le voile de

l'erreur et me rend à moi malgré moi-même " (O. C., Pléiade, II, 356).
Her renaissance is just that, a return to something which represents her
inner being rather than her exterior behavior pattern.

One cannot, however, overlook the fact that at the end of the novel
Julie is reprieved from slipping back into her unsatisfactory behavior
pattern with Saint-Preux only by her untimely death. In many ways it
is a very timely death, as she acknowledges herself. Without this second
interference of Providence, she might have found herself worse off than
before her marriage. Some critics have interpreted her death as a form of
suicide, in view of the fact that she welcomes its arrival with such genuine
enthusiasm. It is also possible to regard it as the only possible point at
which the line of development represented by the outward manifestations
of personality can ever really meet the unchanging point of inner stability.
And there is no doubt that her death, coming at just this point, resolves a
dilemma which Rousseau found himself unable to handle. The two
manifestations of self are indeed unreconcilable in this life, at least
for Julie.

Shortly before the accident Julie wrote a long letter to Saint-Preux
analyzing her state of mind and being, and dwelling at some length on her
growing predilection for prayerful ecstasy. What has led her to this is a
certain discontent she feels about her all too happy state : " Je ne vois
par tout que sujets de contentement, et je ne suis pas contente. Une
langueur secrette s'insinue au fond de mon cœur ; je le sens vuide et gonflé,
comme vous disiez autrefois du votre ; l'attachement que j'ai pour tout ce
qui m'est cher ne suffit pas pour l'occuper, il lui reste une force inutile
dont il ne sait que faire. Cette peine est bizarre, j'en conviens ; mais elle
n'est pas moins réelle. Mon ami, je suis trop heureuse ; le bonheur
m'ennuye " (O. C., Pléiade, II, 694). Perhaps her discontent can be traced
to the fact that for a number of years she had been living from the very
center of her being, which means that no change of activity had really been
going on in her personality. This is not a normal position for a living
being, and so she feels pressed into trying to find some other way of
developing herself. Grimsley has analyzed this discontent as " the frus-
tration of the desire for the absolute[31]." In my opinion it is rather the
overwhelming stifling of the relative by the absolute. Julie has given
herself up to her inner state of being which allows of no dynamic development in her personality. Her excursion into mysticism is bound to be a
failure since she expresses such severe doubts about its efficacy ; she uses
the same terminology Rousseau applies to his uncontrollable aberrancies
in the early books of the *Confessions* : " Lequel est le plus heureux dès
ce monde, du sage avec sa raison, ou du dévot dans son délire ? Qu'ai-je
besoin de penser, d'imaginer, dans un moment où toutes mes facultés sont
aliénées ? L'ivresse a ses plaisirs, disiez-vous ! Eh bien, ce délire en est
une." (O. C., Pléiade, II, 695).

No one can live happily without experiencing change, and yet it is change which represents a threat to the unity of the self. During the course of a lifetime everyone has the opportunity of becoming conscious of these two great forces, but no one can reconcile them until the moment of death, which must, of necessity, remain a mystery for those left in life. Most people live almost entirely in the transitory world of becoming without really being aware of their condition. When they do realize the precariousness of their position, they tend to panic and try to withdraw from the world. This does not lead to any better solution, although the conscious pursuit of the second is far better than the unconscious pursuit of the first, which is what most people indulge in. A person cannot freeze his development at any given point, without forfeiting a large part of what makes life worth living. Death is the true immobility, after which the personality, which is primarily dependent on change, becomes fused with the inner self, which transcends all mutability. Before death, however, some people can experience in fleeting glances the fusion of these two contradictory states during certain privileged moments. These are analyzed at some length by Rousseau, especially in the *Cinquième promenade* of the *Rêveries*, and we will now turn to this aspect of the self in which Rousseau truly does effect a unification of seemingly contradictory principles.

Le Sentiment de l'existence

As we have already seen, Rousseau's whole epistemology and psychology of man is based on the assumption of the self as a given unit which is absolutely primitive in man. As early as the *Discours sur l'inégalité*, he had noted this fact : " Le premier sentiment de l'homme fut celui de son existence, son premier soin celui de sa conservation " (O. C., Pléiade, III, 164). But in some ways this does not go quite far enough, because even without any feeling of self-awareness, Rousseau assumes the existence of the self. In the totally unthinking infant no such feeling exists, and yet the self is certainly present, even though it is as yet inaccessible to consciousness. Much of the *Rêveries* is concerned with the problem of how to bring to consciousness this underlying being which normally is merely the essential base of all our activity and not really accessible to feeling or consciousness, especially since it is, in some way, anterior to them both. Once made conscious, the self can then be described and integrated into an individual's mode of life.

Both Burgelin and Starobinski have noted this ambiguity in Rousseau's thought : the necessity of combining a certain immediacy of self with a reflective process of feeling or thought. Starobinski stresses the combination of the two : " Il y a une connaissance intuitive, qui est présence immédiate à soi-même, et qui se constitue tout entière dans un acte unique du sentiment[32]." On the other hand, Burgelin brings out the paradoxical side : " Le seul fait absolument constitutif ne peut être que la simple conscience d'exister, qui ne comporte aucune limitation. Cette adhésion immédiate et totale à soi n'implique rien, ni connaissance, ni même effort " and " la conscience d'exister est réflexive, non immédiate[33]. " The problem is further complicated by the fact that we are of necessity dealing with the account rendered at some later time of such an experience. Rousseau himself admits that " rêverie " recalled is better, more heightened and profound than the actual experience (O. C., Pléiade, III, 1049).

At the risk of being too analytical in an area where synthesis is obviously most useful, let us enumerate the various levels with which we are dealing :

1. the basic reality of the self
2. the feeling of self-awareness
3. the consciousness of existence
4. the recalling of this feeling and consciousness and the recording of it.

The first level is not accessible to analysis ; it just exists as the basic substratum of the whole of man's existence. While the self has only the normal channels of communication open to it, those of feeling and consciousness, it exists at a deeper level, and the problem is to penetrate this level by these rather inadequate means and then to express it in terms of language which automatically deforms it. The self does not need to be felt or thought or expressed in order to have being, but it is only through these means that it becomes accessible to the individual. Furthermore the individual feels an inner urge which drives him on to objectify this experience. Both Emile and Saint-Preux openly express their fear of losing their very being in the hectic life of Parisian society, and Rousseau himself often expresses the same feeling. In the *Cinquième Promenade* he describes himself as anxious to find " un état où l'ame trouve une assiete assez solide pour s'y reposer tout entiére et rassembler là tout son être " (O. C., Pléiade, I, 1046), a state of being in which the individual is aware of " rien d'extérieur à soi, de rien sinon de soi-même et de sa propre existence " (O. C., Pléiade, I, 1047).

In this last quotation, it is clear that a distinction is made between the self and its existence. It is only through the ever-changing facets of existence that one can approach the unchanging self, but this does not mean that the two are equivalent to each other. On the contrary, the fact that one has to go through the channels of feeling and consciousness is a limitation on the absolute perfection of the inner self, as is clearly seen in the continuation of the last quotation : " tant que cet état dure on se suffit à soi-même comme Dieu ".

The clearest description of such a state occurs in the *Cinquième Promenade*, but earlier texts also approach this problem, especially the *Lettres morales,* in which Rousseau gives instruction to Mme d'Houdetot on how to live properly, and the *Lettres à Malesherbes*, in which he describes his earlier experiences of *rêverie*. In all these works the central admonition is to " rassembler son être," " se replier sur elle-même," " circonscrire notre âme." However these texts are easily matched by another series in which Rousseau stresses the expansive nature of the soul. Julie's description of the meeting of souls in the *salle d'Apollon* contains this description of the perfect life : " je ne vois rien qui n'étende mon être, et rien qui le divise ; il est dans tout ce qui m'environne, il n'en reste aucune portion loin de moi " (O. C., Pléiade, II, 689). The same vocabulary occurs in the unfinished continuation of *Emile :* " vous m'apprîtes... à étendre pour ainsi dire le moi humain sur toute l'humanité " (O. C., Hachette, III, 2), and significantly enough in the *Sixième Promenade* : " enfin je m'aime trop moi-même pour pouvoir haïr qui que ce soit. Ce seroit resserrer, comprimer mon existence, et je voudrois plustot l'étendre sur tout l'univers " (O. C., Pléiade, I, 1056).

The two conditions must be closely related to each other, not only in temporal sequence but also in their very mode of being. Only through concentration on self can one reach the possibility of true expansion of self. The kind of expansive effusiveness which Rousseau depicts as characteristic of the adolescent is so diffuse and uncentered that it often leads into irreality. At the beginning of Book II of the *Confessions* Jean-Jacques is shown as completely sure of himself : " en me montrant j'allois occuper de moi l'univers " (O. C., Pléiade, I, 45), but the actual events of his life show that this type of certainty is not founded on a realistic basis. The irony of the following remark which occurs in the very next paragraph is clearly directed at the adolescent dream of glory : " En attendant ce modeste avenir, j'errai quelques jours autour de la Ville " (O. C., Pléiade, I, 46). However this is not the only occasion in the early books of the *Confessions* in which Rousseau describes the young man's sense of filling the whole universe. In Book IV the lovely description of a night spent out-of-doors portrays the young Jean-Jacques as accomplishing to some degree this desire : " Je me promenois dans une sorte d'extase livrant mes sens et mon cœur à la joüissance de tout cela " (O. C., Pléiade, I, 169). And yet this state of *extase*, which is also analyzed in the *Lettres à Malesherbes,* is subtly different from the *rêverie* experienced at the Ile St-Pierre. The sense of expansion is much more marked than the need for retraction, and the reader gets a feeling of a certain amount of effort being expended in order to reach this state of being, which does not result in the total fusion of subject and object, absolute and relative, eternal and fugitive which is so well expressed in the *Cinquième Promenade.*

It is almost as if Rousseau had been searching for this means of transcending his personal experience, and that he did not realize that he had found the way of doing so until it was almost too late. The most poignant note of the *Rêveries* lies in the fact that they describe past experiences, ones which Rousseau now feels to be beyond his powers. The best he can do now is to look back and recreate in perfect narrative prose those individual experiences which in retrospect serve as the unifying force of his life. But, if we look at the texts which were composed earlier in his life and which in one case at least overlap the particular experiences described in the *Cinquième Promenade,* the whole issue is much less clear. *La Nouvelle Héloïse* is again a fruitful source, especially since Rousseau can be more objective in his handling of the material. In the well-known letter on the Valais, Saint-Preux notes how the mountain scenery leads him into great and sublime meditations, which lift man out of his normal place so that his soul takes on some of the " inaltérable pureté " of the surroundings (O. C., Pléiade, II, 78). This is seen as a sort of cleansing experience in which sensations, sentiments and even the self are left behind and abolished. But something is missing in this all-too-ethereal realm, the warm and sweet world of mankind itself : " J'aurois passé tout le temps de mon voyage dans le seul enchantement du paysage, si je n'en eusse éprouvé un plus doux encore dans le commerce des habitans " (O. C., Pléiade, II, 79). This rather frigid and sterile type of meditation is not a satisfactory substitute for life itself ; true *rêverie* will combine purity and warmth.

The *Lettres à Malesherbes* analyze a slightly more effective type of solitary meditation. The immediate motive is found in a certain feeling of loss : " Je trouvois en moi un vuide inexplicable que rien n'auroit pu remplir." But this is soon superceded by a systematic elevation of Rousseau's thoughts, feelings, and sensations towards the overwhelming sphere of the universe as a whole, in which he feels completely enveloped. And yet the outcome of the " etourdissante extase " is not an immediate consciousness of self as expressed in the whole but rather a division of subject and object which forces Rousseau to cry out : " O grand être ! ô grand être " (O. C., Pléiade, I, 1141).

The same result is experienced in the *rêveries* of the Ile St-Pierre as reported in Book XII of the *Confessions :*

> Souvent laissant aller mon bateau à la merci de l'air et de l'eau je me livrois à des rêveries sans objet et qui pour être stupides n'en étoient pas moins douces. Je m'écriois parfois avec attendrissement : ô nature, ô ma mère, me voici sous ta seule garde ; il n'y a point ici d'homme adroit et fourbe qui s'interpose entre toi et moi (O. C., Pléiade, I, 643-44).

This particular instance is an extremely clear case of what Rousseau has not as yet managed to accomplish. In the first place, he is still very much aware of his position in the world, of his *fortune*. While there may be no other people between him and the whole of the universe, there still remains the fact that he sees himself as separate from it, to the degree of being able to address an exhortation to it. Nothing of the sort is possible in the *Cinquième Promenade* where no distinction exists between the individual consciousness and the whole of experience.

In the *Deuxième Dialogue* Rousseau makes an analysis of the state of *rêverie* which is Jean-Jacques' way of escaping from reality. This type of *rêverie* is based on imagination and is compared to that of the Orientals. But this kind of imaginative ecstasy is too passive for Jean-Jacques, who feels a need of relaxation. He turns away from the inner-seeking state of repose to the exterior world, which offers an ever-changing scene : " pour peu que l'impression ne soit pas tout à fait nulle, le mouvement léger dont elle nous agite suffit pour nous préserver d'un engourdissement léthargique et nourrir en nous le plaisir d'exister sans donner de l'exercice à nos facultés " (O. C., Pléiade, I, 816). It is obvious that what he fears is a state of absolute rest, *engourdissement léthargique,* the slowing down of change to a point which approaches total deprivation of life itself. Total immobility is to be avoided at all costs ; the only vision of death which appeals to Rousseau is one in which the individual self survives and continues to live fully and to enjoy itself. He is unsure of how to imagine this state of being, since, in life itself, man is always limited by his body and his senses, but he envisions it as a state of pure joy, " une jouissance positive " (O. C., Pléiade, I, 1169).

Without a doubt the *rêverie* of the *Cinquième Promenade* is presented as a state in which Rousseau has realized his ambition of attaining a condition of pure and unadulterated joy, a state in which the whole of the universe including his own self has reached a stage of perfection which permits him to enter into the deepest recesses of being itself without having to give up existence as such. The description of this state is accompanied by such adjectives as *délicieux, heureux, précieux, doux,* all of which show how desirable it is. And yet Rousseau closes this section on the rather contradictory note of " une rêverie abstraite et monotone " to which in retrospect he is able to add " des images charmantes qui la vivifient " (O. C., Pléiade, I, 1049). There is obviously a certain danger of suffocation involved in allowing *rêverie* to occupy too large a space in one's life. However, in permitting himself to re-live these privileged moments, Rousseau can compensate for their passivity and control their content.

In his analysis of what took place on the Ile St-Pierre Rousseau emphasizes the place therein of various movements, both interior and exterior. The central paragraph in which he renders the rocking motion of the lake's waters has been admirably analyzed stylistically by Osmont[34], but it is worth noting that what the motion of the water does is to com-

pensate for the immobility of Rousseau's inner state : " son bruit conti-
nu... suppléoient aux mouvemens internes que la rêverie éteignoit en moi "
(O. C., Pléiade, I, 1045). His inner being is close to extinction at that
moment, but he is saved from total immobility by the effect on the senses
of the gentle lapping of the waves. This in turn permits Rousseau to
become conscious of his own existence, that part of his being which is
also always in a state of development. However the exterior motion
which has its immediate effect upon the senses of sight and sound must
never become too frenetic, because this runs the alternate risk of recalling
the self back into the sphere of experience and its attendant unhappiness :
" Si le mouvement est inégal ou trop fort, il réveille ; en nous rappellant
aux objets environnans, il détruit le charme de la rêverie, et nous arrache
d'au dedans de nous pour nous remettre à l'instant sous le joug de la
fortune et des hommes et nous rendre au sentiment de nos malheurs "
(O. C., Pléiade, I, 1047). Here again we can see the distinction made
between an individual's inner being and his outer experience, the distinction made in the *Confessions* and *La Nouvelle Héloïse* in terms of *âme*
and *fortune*.

What Rousseau has reached in the *Cinquième Promenade* is a state
of almost perfect equilibrium between the two terms of his being and
his existence : the inner self is able to manifest itself through the very
feeling of existence which in turn is able to penetrate to the very center
of being. A final quotation should serve to bring this out : " Le mouvement qui ne vient pas du dehors se fait alors au dedans de nous. Le
repos est moindre, il est vrai, mais il est aussi plus agréable quand de
légéres et douces idées sans agiter le fond de l'ame ne font pour ainsi dire
qu'en effleurer la surface " (O. C., Pléiade, I, 1048). Total repose is not
a desirable condition and must be avoided at all costs. This may be
accomplished by one of two methods : either an external motion which
occupies the senses and keeps one's soul from solidifying into an immobile
state or an internal surge of imaginative power which accomplishes the
same goal.

In this analysis we have opposed the two terms of being and existence
within the individual. There is, however, the further question of subject
and object and of their relationship. In many of his descriptions,
Rousseau stresses the fact that he ceases to feel himself as a separate
unit, that he actually becomes one with the universe : " Je sens des
extases, des ravissemens inexprimables à me fondre pour ainsi dire dans
le systême des êtres, à m'identifier avec la nature entière " (O. C.,
Pléiade, I, 1065-66). This corresponds to the experiences analyzed in the
Lettres à Malesherbes and the *Confessions*, but now there is no drawing
back of the individual consciousness. In the face of the majesty of nature
Rousseau allows himself to be entirely identified with it. This loss of
self is not characteristic of the *rêverie* in the *Cinquième Promenade*, which,

on the contrary, emphasizes the absolute self-sufficiency of this privileged state. It would be convenient if Rousseau had clearly distinguished between these two states; he often uses *extase* to describe the pantheistic loss of self in the universe, but he also resorts to the word *rêverie*. In the *Cinquième Promenade*, however, he confines his vocabulary to the word *rêverie* and does not stress the expansive movement of his soul[35].

In its purest form *rêverie* accomplishes that unification of self with experience which has troubled Rousseau for so long. In the first place there is no objectification of the self into a self-concept; other people are completely eliminated from this closed world and yet it does not exclude a certain degree of mobility which is a necessary feature of life itself. Only in these privileged moments does the individual really get a feeling of his absolute value, of what Grimsley terms his "absolute personal unity[36]." The basic unit of the self is permitted to shine through the feeling of existence, and the individual becomes aware of this fundamental stability of his being but in a way that almost approaches unconsciousness.

At the time of the *rêverie* itself, Rousseau stresses the fact that he is in an almost totally unreflective state, a state in which only his senses are occupied. It is not until he comes out of this trance-like state that he becomes conscious of what has been transpiring, and, as we have already noted, it is not until the time of the composition of the *Cinquième Promenade* that he is able to grasp the marvellous privilege which has been granted to him. Partly this may be due to nostalgia, since he no longer finds himself capable of reaching the same condition except through a conscious effort of remembering and of heightening that memory. Partly it may be wishful thinking, the creation of that ideal state which Rousseau sees as the only possible solution of his particular problem. It is somewhat doubtful that in reality two such opposite states could ever merge and appear as a single unified whole; Rousseau certainly was aware of this difficulty but also felt the necessity of finding such a solution. In so doing he may very well have taken an actual experience and endowed it with meaning which it did not have at the time of its happening. This is really beside the point, for what counts here is the expression of this experience; whether the experience took place or not has no bearing on the validity of the solution offered. The quiet, passive center of being, which exists at a pre-conscious stage of human development, and which continues to underlie all future experience, is rendered cognizable if not exactly conscious in this interpretation.

The eighteenth century as a whole may have had intimations of the existence of a strata of human experience which lies beyond the realm of consciousness, but unless it could in some way be brought into the sphere of the cognizable, this area had to be excluded from all considerations of the psychology of man. That which exists beyond these limits

was considered to be quite strictly unthinkable and therefore unmention-
able. No greater tribute can be paid Rousseau than to point out that
he was one of the few who saw this problem clearly and who made some
attempt to come to grips with it in other than simplistic terms. For the
most part, the sensationalist empiricism of the time refused any validity
whatsoever to any experience which lay outside these rather narrow limits.
Rousseau's success lies in the degree to which he was to stretch these
limits to the utmost, really beyond the breaking point, in order to admit
a series of experiences which were almost of necessity pre-conscious. His
analysis of early childhood in *Emile*, abstract though it may be, is another
attempt in the same direction. The description of his own early experiences in the *Confessions* approaches the same problem, although he is
forced to admit that his memories do not really antedate his consciousness
of self (O. C., Pléiade, I, 8 [37]).

The clearest expression of such a pre-conscious state occurs in Rousseau's description in the *Deuxième Promenade* of his recovering consciousness after being knocked down by a dog. His whole approach is con-
ditioned by what he sees ; nothing else exists at that moment. Even his
own individuality has disappeared as has the conception of time. The
sight of his own blood flowing from his wounds is as indifferent to him
as the sight of a brook would be. During that instant of time there
exists for him no distinction whatsoever between subject and object,
because the subject has entirely disappeared, or rather has not as yet
been delineated. This corresponds closely to the condition of the infant,
who must learn to separate his own self out of the myriad sense impressions
which assail him. Poulet has assimilated this pre-conscious state to the
tabula rasa of Locke : " l'être... est en train d'émerger d'une sorte de
torpeur, d'une sorte de nullité qui porte sur lui-même et sur son antécé-
dent. C'est quelqu'un qui est en train de naître à sa propre existence
mais qui se trouve entièrement ouvert du côté de la sensation[38]." This
corresponds in certain details to the experience of *rêverie*, which is also
characterized by the complete abolition of the sense of time and an almost
total reduction of the means of cognition to sense impressions.

In his description of his return to consciousness, Rousseau also
stresses the desirability of such a condition. He speaks of it as " un
moment délicieux " and goes on to say : " Je sentois dans tout mon être un
calme ravissant auquel chaque fois que je me le rappelle je ne trouve
rien de comparable dans toute l'activité des plaisirs connus " (O. C.,
Pléiade, I, 1005). The inner self, which normally seems to operate as a
closed system, is permitted to extend its being, to embrace everything with
which it comes into contact through the senses. It is only the abrupt
shock of the return to consciousness of self as distinct from the exterior
world which imposes limits upon what is basically an unbounded and
all-filling entity. True happiness for Rousseau lies in the possibility of

giving this inner being a chance to express itself in terms of existence. Mauzi has noted that this return to consciousness is qualified by a number of negative characteristics, notably the suppression of the exterior world as such and of the feeling of both space and time, but also of any type of emotion which could serve to distinguish the subjective from the objective world : " Dans cette âme vide, qui s'ignore elle-même, s'installe une extase tranquille, une euphorie liée à la seule conscience d'exister[39]."

Another way of looking at the new synthesis which Rousseau has effected in the *Cinquième Promenade* in particular but also in his description of his accident at Menilmontant is to consider the composition of this primitive inner being, the *âme*. The French sensationalists, notably Condillac and Helvétius, had reduced this entity to a closed and passive system of receptivity. The " soul " could not be really changed by the impinging upon it of the outside world through sense impressions. It remained separate, wholly independent of the rest of the world in a kind of timeless, spaceless sphere which was so remote from reality that the inner self was no longer felt to be an adequate explanation of man's psychology. The active nature of the mind was explained by resorting to the passions, ultimately dependent upon the sensations of pleasure and pain which accompany the sense data.

This analysis did not satisfy Rousseau, but his critical remarks in his own copy of *De l'esprit* do not offer an adequate solution to this question. That the very basic nature of man is that of an active and expansive being, is not clearly brought out until the *Rêveries*. Here at last Rousseau reaches an original synthesis of two formerly exclusive concepts, the totally passive and closed self with the vitally active and open-ended personality, what we have termed being and existence. He significantly concentrates on terms of motion to describe this unusual experience, but he also has recourse to expression of time, which is seen as another dimension of this new view of mankind.

Almost all the critics who have commented on the *Rêveries* have noted the fact that Rousseau discovers therein a new level of time, which he terms *le présent* and which seems to have no limitations whatsoever. Up to this point Rousseau had seen time in much the same way as did other eighteenth century writers, either as the endlessly moving succession of exterior and objective facts or as the absolute immobility of eternity. Both of these concepts, according to Rousseau, are antithetical to man, the first because it " threatens the unity of personality and shakes the stability of being[40]," the second because it transcends entirely the individual experience, denying to it any validity whatsoever[41]. Rousseau portrays himself as an individual who is driven, in the words of Grimsley, " to the quest for a sort of absolute, timeless fulfilment of the self in terms of values which transcend the vagaries of finite existence and yet preserve its concrete immediacy[42]. " The open, active self cannot become manifest in the world of ordinary time, which is marked by the constant succession of past, present and future, forever merging into one another. Nor can it exhibit its truly dynamic properties in the timeless void of neo-Platonic eternity. In the *Deuxième Promenade,* the self does manage to make its appearance in *le moment présent* which is described at greater length in the *Cinquième Promenade* : " sans avoir besoin de rappeler le passé ni d'enjamber sur l'avenir ; où le tems ne soit rien pour elle [l'âme], où le présent dure toujours sans neanmoins marquer sa durée et sans aucune trace de succession " (O. C., Pléiade, I, 1046). This concept of time is clearly a third type which can only be described in negative terms.

Just as the new type of motion was described as neither too much nor too little, this new concept of time is neither a succession nor a secession of moments. The quiet, gentle flow of space and time, which characterizes the inner self, has neither the deadening immobility of death nor the frenetic mobility of life. *Le sentiment de l'existence* points in a third direction, but this basic mode of being is not truly analyzable in logical terms since it exists prior to experience and yet is not separable from it. An individual becomes conscious of the existence of his inner self only in extremely rare, privileged moments and even then seldom realizes its true significance. The search for identity, for unity of self, is terminated only by the acknowledgement of the futility of this search if pursued in analytic and logical terms. What is cognizable is not sufficient to describe the human condition ; beyond and beneath these limits exist the only true grounds of self-fulfillment and self-satisfaction. The individual must become aware of the existence and also of the nature of the inner self before he can hope to find any basis of happiness.

Rousseau has clearly reached a new concept of personality, one which ingeniously combines the simple Cartesian sense of self-identification with the post-Lockean empirical development of the self. His concern with these two concepts is clearly visible in all his works but it is not until *Les Rêveries* that he manages to capture the very elusive pre-conscious state which permits these two varieties of self to manifest themselves, not as contradictions but rather as complements of one another. Neither of them do or can exist by themselves but it is only in the privileged moment of *rêverie* that any human being is able to perceive their relationship as he experiences his own inner being.

The fact that Rousseau does not prove the existence of a unitary self but rather discloses it in a work that is as far as possible from a logically reasoned proof is indicative of the general movement of ideas during the eighteenth century. The tremendous faith in reason which characterized earlier writers is no longer endemic toward the end of the period. Diderot's approach is very different from that of Rousseau but they are united in this one aspect. Neither of them felt that the light of pure reason was sufficient to explain all there is to know about man.

Logical analysis breaks down in the face of the enormous complexity of a human being. Rousseau's appeal to his own personal experience of a very special emotional state will have parallels in Diderot, although the latter reaches quite a different conclusion about the nature of the self.

Chapter V

DIDEROT

The Developing Self

In passing from Rousseau to Diderot, we go from one kind of world to another. Many words and expressions are common to the two writers, but more often than not, Diderot means something quite different from what Rousseau does in his use of such terms as *le sentiment de l'existence* and *l'unicité du moi*. Some of the difference in their approach may have its origin in the fact that whereas Diderot was as conscious as Rousseau of the difficulty of finding a congruent self to which all his various moods and tempers might be related, this condition did not disturb him. On the contrary, Diderot appears to take great delight in his own rather checkered personality ; he reveals the fact that he was very much like the other inhabitants of Langres whose personalities are compared to weathercocks constantly changing their direction[1]. He knew that he himself was of the same nature and, despite efforts to control his sensibility, he remained this way all his life. At no point does this infinite variety of selves cause real depression in Diderot ; he was capable of taking what life offered and enjoying it to the hilt. Rousseau, on the other hand, was always searching for a principle of identity which would mold his multiple character traits into a single unified personality on which both he and his friends could rely. Of course there were moments of doubt for Diderot too, but, on the whole, he responded to these concerns with the same ebullient and energetic acceptance which he gave to just about any problem or task which confronted him. The fact that this was his own self which was at stake did not make the issue any more productive of anxiety than the general questions of moral determinism for instance.

We shall not find, therefore, the prolonged and profound analysis of self which finally led Rousseau to his matchless fusing of being and existence in the experience of *rêverie*. Diderot will speak of *rêverie*, and it is clear that he was able to analyze himself introspectively but, according to him, the results of such an analysis must then be related to the whole condition of mankind rather than to that of a single individual. Rousseau's last introspective study of himself may be taken as an example for all men, but he is quite clear that he is describing something which happened to him personally and which other people may or may not be able to imitate. This last point is not central to Rousseau's thought; in the latter part of his life his thought and writings were dominated by his fascination with his own personality and its problems, and the solutions which he was striving to find to them.

Diderot's accusations against " le solitaire " can easily be assumed to be directed against Rousseau whether indeed they were so intended. To Diderot, all thought and expression thereof should fall within the general definition which he gives of philosophy in one of his last works, the *Essai sur les règnes de Claude et de Néron* : " Quel est l'objet de la philosophie ? c'est de lier les hommes par un commerce d'idées, et par l'exercice d'une bienfaisance mutuelle[2]." Any self-analysis which speaks only to one particular individual is not worthy of this title ; and we should not forget that Diderot accepted the nickname *le Philosophe*. In the same essay he notes that, whereas Seneca might have been tempted to withdraw to " la vie retirée," he chose to stay in the center of activity because that was " plus utile et plus honorable " (A.-T., III, 322-23). Diderot obviously feels that this was the wiser choice.

Such a stand, which represents a fairly stable point of view for Diderot, since it occurs early in his career in the article " Philosophe " and then at intervals through all his other works, does not mean that a philosopher should not attempt introspective self-analysis. On the contrary, knowledge of self, conducted and used in the right way, is a very valuable contribution to philosophy, for, as he notes in the *Eléments de physiologie :* " Ce que nous connaissons le moins, c'est nous. L'objet, l'impression, la représentation, l'attention " (A.-T., IX, 346). But Diderot's development was from the outer world to the inner one ; he settled his philosophy of science, so to speak, before turning to his philosophy of man. As I. W. Alexander notes in his excellent article on Diderot's philosophy of consciousness : " The evolution of Diderot's materialism indeed corresponds to the development of a thought which, starting from the objective data of perception from which it distinguishes itself with difficulty, unveils slowly its inner core—the reality of the self-conscious and reflective self[3]." We shall follow the same path in an attempt to arrive at a synthesis of Diderot's thought on the subject of the self, that inner unity which each and every person carries with him at the very center of his personality and which is constantly in a state of development.

It really took the shock of the posthumous publication of Helvétius, *De l'homme* (1772) to force Diderot into a close look at the make-up of an individual man. Up to that point he had considered man as a part of a much larger whole, an important part but still not to be considered in isolation from the rest of the material universe. Very early in his career Diderot had accepted a purely materialistic position : nothing exists except matter which is organized in various ways. What distinguishes his materialism from that of many others is that Diderot introduced a principle of activity into the elementary particles themselves. In the *Rêve de d'Alembert* he posits the existence of *sensibilité* in each and every atom of matter. This kind of energy is present in an inert and only potential form in the things we term inanimate. As one goes up the ladder of being, this internal force becomes actualized and manifests itself as *sensibilité active*. In other words, the whole universe is made up of particles of matter each of them possessing an internal principle of change which means that everything is in a continual state of flux.

The problem arises of how to distinguish any individual unit from this mass of free-flowing matter. The solution is again in terms of *sensibilité* combined with a principle of organization : the formation of units of sensible molecules depends on the law of continuity. Instead of one molecule remaining juxtaposed to another, it actually fuses into others and so forms a new and different aggregate : " vous ne supposez que de la contiguïté où il y a continuité... Comme une goutte de mercure se fond dans une autre goutte de mercure, une molécule sensible et vivante se fond dans une molécule sensible et vivante[4]." Another example is that of a swarm of bees which would become a single animal if, instead of contiguity, there were continuity amongst them all (*O. phil.*, Garnier, 293). Once such an entity has come into being it no longer functions as a mere grouping of sensible molecules ; a principle of organization takes over which determines the reactions of the newly created unit. Thus, in an animal, all the organs cooperate and partake in the life of that single animal ; they are not independent of each other.

The question of human identity is more complicated because of the problem of self-consciousness. In the *Rêve* Mlle de l'Espinasse suggests a solution through the fact that touching oneself is an entirely different experience from touching something which does not form part of your body. Dr. Bordeu points out that this distinction is not made by the hand or by the part of the body touched by the hand, but that it is made in the head. When questioned about which part of the head makes these decisions, M[lle] de l'Espinasse quickly turns to an analogy, the well-known one of the spider and its web. Bordeu is delighted with her comparison and notes that there is one particular area of the brain which serves as a unifying center for the whole of human experience. If this area is damaged the whole human body is affected (*O. phil.*, Garnier, 315). Physiologically this is an acceptable resolution of the problem of individual identity, but it leads to rather thorny philosophical problems.

The fact of the matter is that the final outcome of the law of continuity plus a center of consciousness in each individual is a kind of idealism. If all phenomena are represented to some degree within any one individual consciousness, on what principle can one distinguish one of these centers of sensibility from another ? This is not so much the idealism of Berkeley as the pantheism of Spinoza, and Diderot's only response in the *Rêve* is the rather weak remark of Bordeu : " c'est qu'entre Saturne et vous il n'y a que des corps contigus, au lieu qu'il y faudrait de la continuité " (*O. phil.*, Garnier, 316). As Vernière points out in his footnote, Diderot falls back on the Newtonian doctrine of the void. Both Descartes and Spinoza had proceeded on the assumption that there could be no empty space in the universe, that everything was ultimately connected to everything else. Newton had shown that this was not so, and Diderot is attempting to use this physical principle to establish personal identity. As he goes on to note in the *Rêve*, the mind which could take in all that impinged upon it would be the mind of God himself since it would be truly omniscient (*O. phil.*, Garnier, 316). So from a purely physical basis, individuality is posited on two principles, the law of continuity for the individual himself and the law of contiguity for the rest of the universe. Within a purely physical frame of reference such a distinction might be satisfactory, but even in the *Rêve* there is an indication that this definition does not answer the problem of individual self-consciousness. At one point Bordeu and Mlle de 'Espinasse are talking about sleep and dreams, and he asks her what kind of a dream is totally impossible ; her response, " c'est qu'on est un autre " is not explicable within the framework of this materialistic system (*O. phil.*, Garnier, 362).

This strong feeling of personnal identity had been identified very early by Diderot. In the *Lettre sur les aveugles* he remarks that we would have great difficulty in remembering what we look like for the following reason : " Nous n'étudions les visages que pour reconnaître les personnes ; et si nous ne retenons pas la nôtre, c'est que nous ne serons jamais exposé à nous prendre pour un autre, ni un autre pour nous." (*O. phil.*, Garnier, 88). What is it that makes us so familiar to ourselves although we are incapable of describing ourselves ?

Before trying to answer this question, let us note that the same problem arises if we follow Diderot's epistemological reasoning rather than his physical arguments. At numerous times and places Diderot complains that no one has yet given a logical proof of the existence of anything but a single mind. He often refers to Berkeley as the only irrefutable philosopher, and he repeats this charge in the *Essai sur les règnes de Claude et de Néron* : " l'évêque de Cloyne a dit : ' Soit que je monte au haut des montagnes, soit que je descende dans les vallées, ce n'est jamais que moi que j'aperçois ; donc il est possible qu'il n'existe que moi... ' Et Berkeley attend encore une réponse. Lier l'existence réelle de son propre corps avec la sensation, n'est point une chose facile " (A.-T., III, 257-8). In a way the problem here is just the opposite from the one posed by Diderot's physical principles. According to the physical theory there is no way to distinguish the individual from the whole flux of matter in motion ; according to the epistemological theory there is no way to distinguish external objects from the ever changing perceptions which occupy the mind.

Either of these theories leads to a denial of the principle of personal identity, a conclusion that Diderot was not willing to accept. He was not keenly apprehensive of the personal consequences of such a position, as was Rousseau. At times one gets the impression that Diderot would keenly have enjoyed identifying himself with the whole universe, witness his effusive remarks to the absent Falconet : "Mon ami, ne rétrécissons pas notre existence ; ne circonscrivons point la sphère de nos jouissances. Regardez y bien ; tout se passe en nous. Nous sommes où nous pensons être... Car après tout, qu'il y ait hors de nous quelque chose ou rien, c'est toujours nous que nous apercevons, et nous n'apercevons jamais que nous. Nous sommes l'univers entier[5]." However he quickly adds a disjoinder to these speculations and is really only interested in proving to himself that thinking of his absent friend is almost as good as having him present in the room.

What is needed to avoid the twin pitfalls of pantheism and solipsism is a principle of distinction, one which would make a clear-cut division between the individual self and the rest of the world, whether the whole be considered as a set of material entities or as a flow of perceptions. Both physical and epistemological approaches are used by Diderot to account for individuality, and we shall start with the first as did Diderot himself.

In reacting against Helvétius' rather simplistic analysis of what makes a man, Diderot realized that the theory that man is merely a more complicated form of organized matter than anything else known to exist in the world is not a satisfactory explanation for the really unique features which characterize him. Helvétius assumed that all men were absolutely equal in their physical structure at birth and that the differences which are so noticeable in character and accomplishments are entirely due to environmental factors. Diderot was willing to concede that education and environment play a large part in the formation of individual personalities, but he was sure that even at birth there are certain distinctive features in each person. Otherwise, as he points out, a good educational system would produce an unlimited number of geniuses, and of course this is just not so. Each person has a slightly different organization which means that no two people are exactly alike. In his comments on François Hemsterhuis' *Lettre sur l'homme et ses rapports,* written at about the same time as his *Réfutation de l'Homme,* Diderot notes the consequences of a society in which all individual members are exactly alike in terms of intelligence, activity, etc. : "Dans une pareille société, il n'y aurait plus de *moi,* il n'y aurait qu'un être ; l'individu ne tarderait pas à s'identifier avec tous les autres. Les autres individus seraient, par rapport à lui, comme autant de membres de lui-même, émancipés. Il croirait exister en eux[6]." It is curious to note how close Diderot came to the principle which modern anthropologists have found to be true in extremely primitive societies.   There seems to be no sense of individual identity amongst members of these tribes who conceive of themselves purely and simply as parts of a larger whole ; only the group has any identity.   This points to a failure in this type of society to permit the formation of an individualized self-concept amongst its members and does not really lead to the conclusion that these people are not in possession of a self-as-agent.   Be that as it may, Diderot wished to deny that such a total lack of individuality was likely to exist, at least in society as he knew it.   For each individual is distinguished in physical terms from his fellow men and most particularly in the way in which his brain is constructed.   While each person may be endowed with approximately the same amount of sensibility and may receive external stimuli in much the same way, what happens to these impulses once they are internalized differs in each and every case. The five senses report to a central organ, the brain, and it is this part of the individual which determines how he actually reacts.   And so five different people in exactly the same situation will have five completely different reactions to it.   Obviously the brain cannot think and decide what to do without the presence of external stimuli, but neither is it true to say that these stimuli alone are responsible for a person's actions.

Diderot denies the distinction between a passive understanding and an active will and insists that all features of human nature are active. Sensations may be received willy-nilly but not assimilated in this way.   In the *Rêve*, he compares the brain in its capacity of store-house of all experience to a clavecin, but one which is capable of playing itself.   The major capacity of the brain is that of memory, but no one, even today, has been able to discern exactly how this is accomplished.   Diderot's analogies are useful, imaginative ways of approaching the problem and they serve to show the direction of his thoughts on this issue.   It was clear to him that no purely physical impression could explain the uncanny ability of the human brain.   In the first place there would have to be too many individual impressions in a very small space ; secondly these impressions would not be linked in the way that memory seems to operate. The association of ideas which characterizes all human thought is not easily reduced to a series of impacts from external forces on a material entity within the head.   In addition one must not overlook the fact that each human being is in a continual process of change :   " Tout s'est fait en nous parce que nous sommes nous, toujours nous, et pas une minute les mêmes. " (A.-T., II, 373).   Therefore any principle of personal identity, whether it be stated in physical or epistemological terms, must accommodate change.   There can be no single unchanging unit to which we can attach the denomination of the self.

In the *Eléments de physiologie* Diderot uses another analogy to describe the organization and functioning of the brain. In this instance he compares the brain to a book made of wax: " Regardez la substance molle du cerveau comme une masse de cire sensible et vivante, mais susceptible de toutes sortes de formes, n'en perdant aucune de celles qu'elle a reçues, et en recevant sans cesse de nouvelles qu'elle garde " (A.-T., IX, 368). It is clear from this example that the brain itself undergoes a continual series of modifications, and yet its very structure determines to a certain degree what these modifications will be and what form they will take. The book that reads itself is at the same time the book that writes itself. The elements which are to be inscribed therein are limited by the external conditions under which this particular organ operates, but the way in which these elements are combined and inscribed in the brain is a function of its own structure. Diderot does not make the comparison himself, but the brain is very like a person writing a book. The author is limited by the number of letters in the alphabet and the words which these letters make up in the language in which he is writing, and yet no two original books are ever exactly the same because the writer controls the central organizing power. Some internal force must be brought to bear upon the external stimuli before they can be assimilated into the mental world of that particular person. In comparison with animals, man has a brain which is stronger than any of the sense organs, and it is this physical characteristic which has enabled him to make so much more progress than any other animal : " La perfectibilité de l'homme naît de la faiblesse de ses sens dont aucun ne prédomine sur l'organe de la raison " (A.-T., III, 304).

The brain is the most important differentiating factor, but we should not overlook the fact that Diderot also realized that individuals differed considerably in their emotive capacities. He ties this *sensibilité* to the diaphragm and at times places almost as much emphasis on this center of emotional reaction as on the brain, the center of intellectual reactions. However even the emotional responses are ultimately under the control of the brain since it serves as the *sensorium commune*, a nerve center which acts as a screen for all sensations and sentiments and also governs the responses to these external and internal stimuli. At times Diderot suggests that the genius is the man who has a less well organized brain or one which is less forceful in its control : " Homme, songe que c'est à la faiblesse de tes organes que tu dois la qualité qui te distingue des animaux... S'il existe dans ton cerceau une fibre plus énergique que les autres, tu n'es plus propre qu'à une chose, tu es un homme de génie : l'animal et l'homme de génie se touchent " (A.-T., III, 304). However, even in this instance it is a peculiar structure of the brain itself which makes this distinction and not the predominance of any one of the sense organs or even of the diaphragm.

The element which gives unity to a disparate series of sense and emotional impressions is not just the brain structure itself; unity implies self-consciousness and the only base on which this can be erected is that of memory itself. There are numerous passages in which Diderot clearly outlines his position that it is memory alone which serves as the basis for the self. In his commentary on Hemsterhuis he notes: " Le *moi* est le résultat de la mémoire qui attache à un individu la suite de ses sensations... Sans la mémoire qui attache à une longue suite d'actions le même individu, l'être, à chaque sensation momentanée, passerait du réveil au sommeil; à peine aurait-il le temps de s'avouer qu'il existe " (241). Thus there is more to the concept of the self than the mere sum of sensations, perceptions and sentiments which accumulate in the brain. When Hemsterhuis tries to prove the existence of a soul on the basis of the fact that it is quite different from its own ideas, Diderot replies that what Hemsterhuis is taking to be the soul is really only *le soi* :

> Hemsterhuis : Elle sent qu'elle est autre que tout ce dont elle a des idées ; qu'elle est autre que tout ce qui est hors d'elle.
> Diderot : Elle sent même qu'elle n'est pas l'âme de son voisin ! Mais ce que vous prenez pour l'âme, c'est le *soi* ![7]

There is a principle of unity which brings all of these stimuli together as soon as the brain, which is the physical source of memory, is mature enough to function properly.

Diderot realizes that very small children do not think in the same way as adults, and, in the *Rêve* he suggests that these early years do not form part of the conscious self : " Songez que, quoique votre naissance ait été liée à votre jeunesse par une suite de sensations ininterrompues, les trois premières années de votre [existence] n'ont jamais été de l'histoire de votre vie " (*O. phil.*, Garnier, 342). The reason for this discontinuity in the sense of one's existence is not so much the fact that a person is not conscious of his very early activities but that the very young child has no means of establishing himself as an independent entity. His mind does not function in the way an adult's does, and he is therefore limited to the present and immediate past. This is not enough to constitute a sense of self, which involves a long sequence of past impressions and some projection into the future. It is in part a lack of the sense of time in human events which limit children in rather the same way as animals, but there is also the fact that young children are incapable of pausing long enough to be conscious of their own existence. This is done almost automatically by normal adults as Diderot notes in the *Lettre sur les sourds et muets :* " il y aura en nous des sensations qui nous échapperont souvent par leur continuité. Telle sera celle de notre existence. L'âme ne s'en aperçoit que par un retour sur elle-même, surtout dans l'état de santé " (A.-T., I, 368).

But the "histoire de ma vie" as constituted by memory once the brain is mature enough to function properly is not all that there is in the self. Diderot notes a great many sensations are recorded in the mind in such a way that they are not accessible to conscious thought. He suggests that everything we have ever seen or known is buried in the depths of our memory without our knowing it, and, if this were true, then certainly all the experiences of early childhood would also be present in an unconscious way in the brain (A.-T., IX, 366-7). They will play their part in determining the sense of the self which the adult carries with him through his life, even though he is incapable of bringing them into the sphere of consciousness. In this suggestion, Diderot joins Rousseau as one of the very few eighteenth century writers who were willing to consider the possibility of a definition of the human mind which includes non- or sub-conscious factors. For instance, he notes that it is foolish to believe that the mind is always thinking (A.-T., IX, 347), but this does not mean that a new individual is created at each moment of thought. On the contrary, memory supplies the link between one conscious state and another, and, since memory is totally dependent on the structure of the brain, it will not be annihilated unless something radical happens to that organ. Diderot speaks of memory as "la propriété du centre, le sens spécifique de l'origine du réseau, comme la vue est la propriété de l'œil" (O. phil., Garnier, 354). No one doubts the seeing ability of the eye after it has been closed for hours during deep sleep, nor should the thinking ability of the brain be impaired by such a gap. Discontinuity in the stream of impressions received by the brain and stored by memory does not mean discontinuity in the self.

It is, therefore, an actual physical entity which gives unity to the varied sensations and emotions which assail a man during his lifetime, and this organ has a directing energy of its own which permits it to shape the various elements which the outer, and inner, world offers to it. The way in which experience is organized depends upon the original structure of this particular organ and also upon the way in which it has assimilated previous experiences. This interpretation dovetails with Diderot's belief in the existence of three kinds of force in the universe: gravitation, la force intime and the action of all the other molecules on an object (O. phil., Garnier, 395). The second one is internalized and can never cease while that particular organization exists, and the combination of the three keeps the whole mass of heterogeneous matter in a state of constant flux.

These physical and biological explanations may seem a little simplistic to twentieth century eyes but when one remembers the state of physics, chemistry and biology in the eighteenth century they are remarkable in their accuracy. In philosophical terms Diderot's perceptions in the area of the concept of the self are also very modern. As early as the Lettre sur les sourds et muets he questioned the privileged access theory in much the same terms as Hume was to do in the *Treatise* :

> plusieurs fois, dans le dessein d'examiner ce qui se passait dans ma tête,
> et de *prendre mon esprit sur le fait,* je me suis jeté dans la méditation
> la plus profonde, me retirant en moi-même avec toute la contention
> dont je suis capable ; mais ces efforts n'ont rien produit. Il m'a semblé
> qu'il faudrait être tout à la fois au dedans et hors de soi ; et faire en
> même temps le rôle d'observateur et celui de la machine observée.
> Mais il en est de l'esprit comme de l'œil ; il ne se voit pas... Un monstre
> à deux têtes, emmanchées sur un même col, nous apprendrait peut-être
> quelque nouvelle. Il faut donc attendre que la nature qui combine tout,
> et qui amène avec les siècles les phénomènes les plus extraordinaires,
> nous donne un *dicéphale* qui se contemple lui-même, et dont une des
> têtes fasse des observations sur l'autre (A.-T., I, 402).

The appeal to a monstrous form of human organization to provide the
needed insight is typical of Diderot's constant recourse to teratology to
find the answer to certain seemingly insoluble problems[8]. But in this
case, the remark must certainly be taken with a grain of salt, for the
likelihood of such a monster occurring is slight and in the meantime the
problem of the self is not one which can be ignored.

In the *Réfutation de l'Homme* Diderot makes a distinction between
passive sensations and active judgment ; without the latter the individual
would not exist as such since he would have no way of distinguishing
himself from the fleeting sense impressions which are continually impinging
upon him. Sensations are not accepted passively by the mind but are put
in their place, so to speak, according to some internal principle of
organization. It is this activity plus memory which constitutes for Diderot
la conscience du soi : "Et d'où naît la conscience ? De la sensibilité et
de la mémoire. C'est la mémoire qui lie les sensations et qui constitue
le *soi*[9]." However when Diderot speaks of memory we have already noted
that he does not mean a kind of mechanical recall of all past experience
but an active force which assimilates the storage of individual sensations
and controls their feedback. Thus each person differs from every other
person not merely because his experiences have differed but also because
the way in which he comprehends these experiences differs.

In this way the self may be considered to be a point in both space
and time. It is in a continual process of change and yet cannot be equated
with the myriad sensations occasioned by outside influences. The *force
intime* must also be taken into account, and it is this principle which
explains the organizing power of the self. The self does not exist as an
entity outside of time, as does Rousseau's for instance ; it is very much
a developing unit but one which is self-controlling because it is oriented
towards the future as well as the past. Ontologically speaking the self
is a unit of both space and time ; in the *Elements de physiologie* Diderot

points out how ridiculous it is to try to separate these two concepts from that of existence itself : " Je ne puis séparer, même par abstraction, la localité et la durée, de l'existence. Ces deux propriétés lui sont donc essentielles " (A.-T., IX, 254). This is a more logical statement of a suggestion outlined in the *Lettre sur les sourds et muets* in which Diderot notes that it is impossible to describe our *état d'âme* since language involves analysis and therefore separates all the individual elements which go to make up a single moment of existence : " Notre âme est un tableau mouvant, d'après lequel nous peignons sans cesse : nous employons bien du temps à le rendre avec fidélité : mais il existe en entier, et tout à la fois " (A.-T., I, 369). The self has both spatial and temporal characteristics, but in a way it transcends them both because, although it is linked to a physical organ, the actual matter of the brain does not constitute the self. This depends upon the brain's ability to be influenced by outside forces, to internalize these forces and to organize them in accordance with its own force. Energy is at the very heart of the self ; it is in movement just as the rest of the universe is, and we find at the center of Diderot's concept of the self not a still quiet pool but a bubbling fountain.

Alexander compares Diderot's concept of consciousness to Leibniz' monad which functions as a *miroir représentatif* :

> Like the monad, the latter is a " miroir représentatif " of the whole universe by virtue of the law of continuity. Like it too, it is " limited not in its relations, but in its knowledge " : it receives the impression of everything, directly or indirectly ; the whole world is gathered up within the field of its perceptions ; but it is not conscious of them all, for, if consciousness is the focal point wherein all are mirrored, it is a narrow focal point that brings only some to the clear light of consciousness, while the others remain at varying degrees of potentiality [10].

This is an excellent definition of *la conscience du soi*, that sense of the self which is the result of quiet concentration upon one's inner being. The self surpasses this sense of the self, just as memory surpasses what one can actually remember. The true self is the sum of all past experiences as reflected within a single mind which is constantly in a process of self-development. Thus the elements which are assimilated into it are fused into its very being and continue to develop in accordance with the pattern established by this organizing force. For this reason one cannot detach oneself from experience and observe the self in action. The very act of observation forms part of the development of the self, and no separation exists between being and existence. The self as observer is automatically and concurrently the self as organizer and mover.

Nor is the composition theory of the self sufficient to account for all its facets, since it also ignores the active nature of the self. No mere summation of the past can possibly do it justice since the self exists as a moving point in time which projects itself into the future as well as reflecting the past. In the *Rêve* the dreaming d'Alembert asks this question : " Qu'est-ce qu'un être ? " and the reply is " la somme d'un certain nombre de tendances " (*O. phil.*, Garnier, 312). No description of the self is adequate which does not take this into consideration ; the definition which was suggested by some of Lelarge de Lignac's remarks is applicable to Diderot : a system of existential events which is controlled and developed by a central source of energy, the mind itself. At no one point can we say that the self has arrived at its fullest development ; as in modern existentialist thought, death is the only experience which can put a term to this internal development.

Just as physical identity is constituted by continuity rather than contiguity, so is personal identity. The disparate series of sense impressions are fused into a single unit, which vastly surpasses the sum of its parts. Each person has in some form or another the memory of everything with which he has ever come into contact. Some of these experiences may be completely sub-conscious, but they are still linked to the conscious mind and play their part in determining the actions of the individual. In the *Eléments de physiologie* Diderot refers to this phenomenon as *la mémoire immense* and notes that it serves as the base for the *loi de continuité d'état* in the living organism :

> Ainsi, la mémoire immense, c'est la liaison de tout ce qu'on a été dans un instant à tout ce qu'on a été dans le moment suivant ; états qui, liés par l'acte, rappelleront à un homme tout ce qu'il a senti toute sa vie.
>
> Or je prétends que tout homme a cette mémoire.
>
> Puis les conclusions seront faciles à tirer.
>
> Loi de continuité d'état, comme il y a loi de continuité de substance.
>
> Loi de continuité d'état propre à l'être sensible, vivant et organisé.
>
> Cette loi de continuité d'état se fortifie par l'acte réitéré, s'affaiblit par le défaut d'exercice, ne se rompt jamais dans l'homme sain ; elle a seulement des sauts, et ces sauts se lient encore par quelques qualités, par le lieu, l'espace, la durée...
>
> La mémoire immense ou totale est un état d'unité complet ; la mémoire partielle, état d'unité incomplet (A.-T., IX, 370).

Two points deserve our attention here ; first the insistence on the active use of memory in the daily round of life. What Diderot terms *l'acte* is the acting out of the inner impulses which give direction to one's life. His inner self is not secluded and passive, but forceful and active. Secondly his mention of *sauts* ties in with his well-known theories about the association of ideas. These seemingly discontinuous states of being are often disconcerting because it is not possible to give a rational explanation for many of them. However they are all linked to the same center of energy by the law of continuity and therefore form part of a single and unified, even if changing, self.

It may be argued that memory and the law of continuity are sufficient to establish identity but not personal identity, that the self of a human being must have other characteristics. To this Diderot would reply that human memory involves self-consciousness. This distinguishes it from that of other animals and enables a person to realize that he is an individual. Diderot makes a very clear distinction between *la conscience du soi* and *la conscience de son existence*. It is this latter which is described in the article "Délicieux" in which Diderot stresses the completely passive character of this experience and the fact that it is totally divorced from all concepts of time : "Il ne lui restoit dans ce moment d'enchantement et de foiblesse, ni mémoire du passé, ni désir de l'avenir, ni inquiétude sur le présent. Le tems avoit cessé de couler pour lui, parce qu'il existoit tout en lui-même ; le sentiment de son bonheur ne s'affoiblissoit qu'avec celui de son existence. ... il en jouissait d'une jouissance tout-à-fait passive, sans y être attaché, sans y réfléchir, sans s'en réjouir, sans s'en féliciter[11]." In this condition, which is one of pure sen-sation, a person is not even conscious of his self ; the self involves active participation in the world, even if this occurs in a nostalgic frame.

The description of *rêverie* in the *Salon de 1767* contrasts vividly with the passive *sentiment de l'existence* of the article "Délicieux." In the later passage Diderot is fully conscious of himself as a unit, and he permits ideas and emotions to well up from within and totally exclude the outside world for a short period of time :

> J'en étais là de ma rêverie, nonchalamment étendu dans un fauteuil, laissant errer mon esprit à son gré, état délicieux où l'âme est honnête sans réflexion, l'esprit juste et délicat sans effort, où l'idée, le sentiment semble naître en nous de lui-même comme d'un sol heureux ; ... le plaisir d'être à moi, le plaisir de me reconnaître aussi bon que je le suis, le plaisir de me voir et de me complaire, le plaisir plus doux encore de m'oublier : où suis-je dans ce moment ? qu'est-ce qui m'environne ? Je ne le sais, je l'ignore. Que me manque-t-il ? Rien. Que désiré-je ? Rien. S'il est un Dieu, c'est ainsi qu'il est, il jouit de lui-même[12].

The state of *rêverie* is soon interrupted by a sudden noise which brings Diderot back to the world of men. What is most important to note in this passage is the insistence upon memory and the sense of self-satisfaction which accompanies these recollections. The moment of forgetfulness follows a concentration upon the inner resources of the self, a centering down upon the whole accumulation of the past and the feeling of control which this engenders. As Alexander remarks : "In the last analysis, self-consciousness is the experience of the self as cause, as wholly responsible for the world which it has re-made 'for itself', which it has mastered and comprehended. Its victory is celebrated in the subsequent ecstasy where the self ' exists wholly in itself ', enjoying a pure sentiment of existence[13]." This is not a fusion of being and existence as expressed by Rousseau when he uses the term *rêverie* ; it is rather the concentrated essence of existence itself, a narrowing down to a single point in the space-time continuum which distills the very essence of the whole life experience of an individual up to that point in time. The self is a unique existential unit ; no two persons can ever have the same essence nor does one person's self ever remain in an absolutely unchanging state of being. It is created as one goes along in life and only posterity will be able to judge the whole self of any individual. But at any moment during the course of a lifetime an individual can experience the joyful ecstasy which comes from a pure state of concentration upon one's inner resources. The inner organizing force together with the external conditions which give it something to act upon constitute the self. The pulsation of energy flows in and out ; both directions are necessary to the constitution of the self and for this reason the experience of *rêverie* is of necessity short and easily interrupted. No state of absolute rest exists in the universe nor is it desirable that it should. A short pause during which only the internal forces are at work is permissible but then the ordinary process of formation and development of the self must continue.

One rather curious consequence of a concept of the self as a unique and ever-changing unit is the fact that if each person were to express himself fully no two people would ever be able to communicate with each other : " si chaque individu pouvait se créer une langue analogue à ce qu'il est, il y aurait autant de langues que d'individus ; un homme ne dirait ni bonjour, ni adieu comme un autre " (A.-T., II, 279). This implies that the origin of language is the creative force of the individual himself as modified by the necessities of group living. Each person controls his own means of expression to some extent, and this is particularly true of the language of the body which is not subject to the same degree of societal control. For this reason gestures and facial expressions are often more indicative of a person's real feelings than what he manages to convey through speech. At the theatre Diderot shocked his fellow spectators by covering up his ears in order to concentrate on the way in which the actors expressed themselves through their bodily movements. Each gesture has to be interpreted by the spectator to tell which emotion is being suggested. In everyday life the inner organizational force governs even such prosaic actions as how one stands and walks ; the artist who re-arranges a model is interfering with this principle[14].

The only way we really know that someone else is suffering pain is through the heart-rending cries and contorted muscular reactions which characterize this condition. In *Jacques le fataliste* Jacques notes that his master has no real idea of what kind of pain is involved in hurting one's knee and so Jacques arranges a little accident in which *le maître* falls off his horse onto his knee. Only then can Jacques be sure that they are both talking about the same kind of experience. Obviously this is not possible in all cases, and so we have recourse to a standardized set of signals which conveys at least part of our own particular experience to others. The only sensation which must be almost exactly the same for all people is that of existence itself : " Je suppose que Dieu donnât subitement à chaque individu une langue de tout point analogue à ses sensations, on ne s'entendrait plus. De l'idiome de Pierre à l'idiome de Jean, il n'y aurait plus un seul synonyme, si ce n'est peut-être les mots *exister, être* et quelques autres qui désignent des qualités si simples, que la définition en est impossible ; et puis toutes les sciences mathématiques " (A.-T., II, 325). The totally abstract and the utterly concrete are here joined as being the only interchangeable aspects of human personalities. But it is important to note that it is only *le sentiment de l'existence* which is treated in this way ; *la conscience du soi* involves individuality and its unique qualities and so can never be adequately conveyed through a series of arbitrary signs.

This paucity of language creates great difficulties for writers who wish to communicate some part of their original view of the universe to the rest of humanity. Obviously the relativism of this world-view works in two ways ; first of all the creative genius has his own special vision of the universe which no one else can possibly hope to grasp in its entirety ; secondly this vision changes as the individual writer or artist matures. At no one point can there be a distilled essence of his view of reality which can be totally comprehended by any other person, who is also in a continual state of flux. However the idea of an inner vision, a special way of organizing the objective data presented to the mind, is central to Diderot's esthetic and ethical ideas to which we will now turn.

Esthetics and Ethics

In the article " Beau " of the *Encyclopédie* published in 1752 and therefore representative of Diderot's early thought in this field, we can already see the consequences of some of his philosophic principles. Although he was very anxious to establish the concept of beauty on a more stable ground than the perception of this quality by the spectator, he already realized that relativism of judgment leads directly to relativism in the realm of taste. Therefore he gives a two-fold definition of the beautiful as being dependent on certain *rapports* which inhere in the object and which must also be perceived as such by the contemplating mind (*O. esth.*, Garnier, 418). But people differ in their ability to take cognizance of these relationships and so the element of variableness is inevitable : " Il n'y a peut-être pas deux hommes sur la terre qui aperçoivent exactement les mêmes rapports dans un même objet, et qui le jugent *beau* au même degré" (*O. esth.*, Garnier, 435). He tries to save some of the impersonal quality which he would like to see attached to this term by declaring that only an idiot would not be so affected in any case at all.

Diderot's later thought does not reflect this urge towards the absolute ; indeed he capitalizes on the relativity of all things in the universe, and this of course must include such concepts as the beautiful. After his experience as an art critic for Grimm's *Correspondance littéraire* Diderot realized that each artist presents his own view of reality and that a great deal of the joy of looking at pictures lies in the new vision which is thus presented to the spectator. Literature is even more personal than the visual arts since the author is not just imitating nature but giving a picture of his own feelings. Boutet de Monvel has noted this distinction quite clearly ; speaking about the painter he notes : " cette vision subjective n'est pas hétérogénéité intime, comme plus haut pour la poésie. Le tableau reste la représentation, en partie personnelle, d'une réalité univer- selle ; la poésie était représentation personnelle d'une réalité elle-même fondamentalement personnelle[15]." The writer is part of his work of necessity since it is he who gives to the standardized vocabulary and sentence structure something of his own, a unique way of arranging words in order to give access to his own inner convictions. The artist, on the other hand, is working with physical materials, canvas and colors, and his own imprint is done at second-hand so to speak. The painter aims at a representation of external reality while the writer concentrates on his own inner life.

In both cases however the result is the same : the writer or artist cannot hope to capture the existential reality of the external world. What he can do is convey to the reader or spectator his own particular and unique way of seeing things. In his art criticism Diderot expresses this in two principal ways. In the first place he speaks of " le soleil du peintre " which is different from the sun which we see in nature[16]. This idea was first broached in a review of a poem by Watelet on *L'Art de peindre* (1760) : " La peinture, pour ainsi dire, a son soleil, qui n'est pas celui de l'univers. ... Chaque artiste ayant ses yeux, et par conséquent sa manière de voir, devrait avoir son coloris " (A.-T., XIII, 25). This rather timid statement is picked up in the *Pensées détachées sur la peinture*, which accompanied the *Salon de 1765*, and again in the *Salon de 1767*. In these instances it is no longer a rather abstract concept which explains why the sun in a picture does not give the same impression as the one up in the sky but Diderot emphasizes the personalized vision of the artist himself : " Eclairez vos objets selon votre soleil, qui n'est pas celui de la nature ; soyez le disciple de l'arc-en-ciel, mais n'en soyez pas l'esclave " (*O. esth.*, Garnier, 771). The artist himself has an active role to play in the process of creating a picture ; he is not confined to a passive role of imitator of nature, on the contrary he must be able to construct a whole universe which has its own laws of harmony paralleling those of external reality but not slavishly imitative of them.

The second way in which Diderot brings out this personalized concept of the role of the artist occurs in his insistence upon the fact that " la belle nature " does not exist per se and that the artist has to create for himself an idea of what he wants to represent before he goes about painting a picture. The painter does not copy directly from life but follows an internalized concept of what he is seeing. The same holds true for the writer : " Est-ce que chaque écrivain n'a pas son style ?—D'accord.— Est-ce que ce style n'est pas une imitation ?—J'en conviens ; mais cette imitation, où en est le modèle ? Dans l'âme, dans l'esprit, dans l'imagi-nation plus ou moins vive, dans le cœur plus ou moins chaud de l'auteur. Il ne faut donc pas confondre un modèle intérieur avec un modèle exté-rieur " (O. esth., Garnier, 838). The interior model is of course dependent upon the exterior one, but at the same time it is a creation of the artist's or writer's mind.

As we have seen, the self for Diderot is not a passive point of receptivity of external stimuli ; it exists as a dynamic center of force which gives a new form to the data which it receives from the outside world. It does not exist apart from the external world but neither is it totally controlled by this world. There is a merging of the objective data into the subjective consciousness, and neither of these facets can or do exist apart from each other. The données are internalized according to a principle of organization unique to that particular person, so it is clear that his vision of the world will differ from that of any other person. It is the artist's special role to externalize this internalized structure in order to permit others to see things as he does. This whole process, the gathering in of data into the human mind, its being put into shape by the mind itself, and then communicated in its re-ordered form, involves numerous circular movements between what has been almost always thought of as two separate ontological realms, mind and matter, the internal and the external. The radical element in Diderot's thought is the result of his fusion of these two areas, not into a single static whole but into a constantly changing and developing system.

Within the whole flux of the universe the creative genius plays a very special part, that of showing to others what one individual's point of view is on any given subject. Communication of ideas and feelings is merely one aspect of the constant communication pattern which is always in progress in the universe. Nothing exists in total isolation and everything is related to everything else through a series of intermediary steps. The true genius will be able to present his vision in a harmonious whole which will have affinities with the harmony of the universe. Esthetics is not either a science of things or a science of personal reactions to things. It is both objective and subjective, absolute and relative, in exactly the same way as the rest of knowledge. Indeed just as we have seen that language is ultimately a creative process working its way to a definite system of symbols, so art as a means of communication partakes of both these aspects. In defining the sublime Diderot notes the creative and the communicative power of art : " le sublime, soit en peinture, soit en poésie, soit en éloquence, ne naît pas toujours de l'exacte description des phénomènes, mais de l'émotion que le génie spectateur en aura éprouvée, de l'art avec lequel il me communiquera le frémissement de son âme, des comparaisons dont il se servira, du choix de ses expressions, de l'harmonie dont il frappera mon oreille, des idées et des sentiments qu'il saura réveiller en moi " (A.-T., II, 330). Art functions like philosophy ; it serves to link men together in order to improve their condition.

Since art reflects the harmony of the universe Diderot can admit the horrible and the terrible into its sphere. The artist must make sure that they are not the only elements however ; he must integrate them into a greater and more harmonious whole. For the most part Diderot tempers his admiration for the terrible with an insistence on certain moral standards : " Soyez terrible, j'y consens ; mais que la terreur que vous m'inspirez soit tempérée par quelque grande idée morale " (O. esth., Garnier, 764). The formulation of these moral standards is also affected by the concept of the self and its unique way of combining the outer and the inner realities.

It is quite clear that the concept of the self as a developing unit which is to a certain degree responsible for itself since it plays a definite part in its own creation has implications for ethical theory[17]. Man is not a totally determined creature at the mercy of heredity and environment ; these are controlling factors but they are governed in their operation by that very principle of organization which we have found to be central to all Diderot's thought. Nothing goes in or out of the mind without being screened by the individual who imposes upon all knowledge some print of his own structure. The brain controls the nervous structure and so all action is ultimately dependent on the mind. Every past experience and all future projections act together in the instant of decision to produce a unique solution to the problem of the moment. The fact that no man exists in total isolation means that his decisions will harmonize with those of others and thus form the basis of a societal ethic. All these items come under the general heading of communication which is the principle at work in all relationships. There can be communication of energy, of thought, of action, of emotions, but each and every interchange is a product of a series of interactions, all of which harmonize in the totality of the existential world. It may seem that the only governing principle in morality is " Each one to himself," and there certainly are some misguided people who act as if this were true. However there could not possibly be such a principle since each and every individual carries within himself a form of the rest of the universe which he has assimilated and which forms part of his own life center.

In his commentary on Hemsterhuis Diderot notes that " ce *moi* veut être heureux. Cette tendance constante est la source éternelle, permanente, de tous ses devoirs, même les plus minutieux[18]." What is not mentioned here is the fact that the *moi* is a product of a combination of sensations, memory, and internal organization which does not allow it to be considered as an entity in and for itself. It forms part of a larger whole and its reactions are also in harmony with those of others. No one can escape from himself, which means that no one can escape from what he has assimilated into himself. As Alexander notes, this forms the limits of moral determinism :

> Diderot as a philosopher leaves us with a final vision of a universe infused in all its parts with energy, a universe where all is effort, not consciously directed in its lower levels, but in man achieving that self-consciousness which enables it to be comprehended. Thereby Diderot's determinism meets with its limits.
>
> In this universe all is organic relation, each level rises above its determining conditions and itself becomes a cause : ... consciousness is seen as always consciousness of the world from which it springs and which in part conditions it, and as the means whereby this world gains an inwardness and is vested with a new degree of subjectivity[19].

The best course of action for an individual is therefore to take cognizance of his own limitations and to work out a way of life consistent with them. This is just about what Jacques does although he insists on attaching the concept of fatalism to all his pronouncements. He confesses to his master that he often tried to become a cynic who valued nothing but only made fun of infirmities and sorrow. Having found that this attitude was not possible for him he has resigned himself to be what he is : " J'y ai renoncé ; j'ai pris le parti d'être comme je suis[20]." He now takes great satisfaction in being himself and in being conscious of this. He may complain about his limitations in the same way as Rameau's nephew, but the reader gets the impression that Jacques is thoroughly enjoying his life while Lui is miserable most of the time. Jacques has a degree of self-awareness which enables him to partake in the general creative process of life itself in a conscious way. He arranges little tricks to play on his master, he dominates others in a friendly way, and his tales open up to him the possibility of re-creating his past and of interpreting it in new and different ways. The joy which is characteristic of the creative process is also seen in a different way in the portrait of the narrator-author. He is not completely independent even in composing a novel, but he can manipulate and combine elements to form an interesting and cohesive whole. The unfinished quality of *Jacques le fataliste* reflects the same aspect of life itself; different endings are possible for similar sets of circumstances although of course only one result will ever be actualized.

What Jacques thinks of himself forms part of the basis on which he makes fundamental decisions about his life. How he and others arrive at such a self-concept and the part it plays in the decision-making process is examined in the next section.

Self-concept

Although we have no truly autobiographical works of Diderot which correspond to the *Confessions* and the *Rêveries* of Rousseau, it is still possible to get a picture of what Diderot thought of himself. This information comes from two distinct sources and represents divergent attitudes for the most part. In his correspondence Diderot reveals himself in what seems to be a totally unselfconscious way. This is especially true of his letters to his mistress, Sophie Volland, and to his best friend, Grimm. However even his more businesslike letters show us more about his character and temperament than we glean from Voltaire's personal correspondence. In some ways one can say that Diderot emerges more clearly from his correspondence than does Rousseau from his autobiographical works, because all Rousseau's writings have a defensive and justificatory tone which makes the reader suspicious of their sincerity. Rousseau is presenting himself in the best light possible even when he is recounting his own evil thoughts and deeds. Diderot on the other hand, appears to be reacting immediately to the given situation and recounting exactly what he thought and felt at the time. Unfortunately this is a conclusion which is neither provable nor refutable, and one must be very cautious in speaking about sincerity, especially when dealing with two such eminently creative authors. Some degree of conscious or unconscious control operates even in the most effusive outpouring of one's heart, and a number of the portraits of himself that Diderot draws for Sophie are obviously constructed so as to elicit her sympathy. At times however he gives ironical self-portraits, ones at which Sophie must have been expected to smile and shake her head; this is particularly true of his description of scenes in which his well-known *sensibilité* comes into play. The reader gets the impression of a distinct contrast between Diderot, the agent in the event, and Diderot, the narrator, looking back on his own actions. Diderot the agent becomes a character in the story as does anyone else.

The other source of information about Diderot's own personality and his view of himself comes in those imaginative works in which he has created new and living characters. This is particularly true of the *Neveu de Rameau* but is characteristic of almost all his works of fiction and even of his philosophic works since he had a predilection for the dialogue form and so created characters even in otherwise didactic works. Diderot externalizes certain of his own personality traits in the characters he creates. He usually divides the discussion between two types of characters, the first active and subject to emotional stress, the second reasonable and objective. That these two types of temperaments were united in Diderot himself is hardly subject to question. His friends knew him as an excitable demonstrative person, but he was also known as *le Philosophe*, both to them and the world at large. Friends and acquaintances appealed to him for judgments on their literary endeavors and on moral disagreements and obviously relied on him to give just criticism in both these areas.

At no point does Diderot claim to have written an authentic self-portrait, and so we are justified in looking through his whole *œuvre* in order to find out what he thought about himself. Two critics have already done a great deal of work in this area and much of what follows owes a lot to their insights[21]. Both Grimsley and Chouillet agree that there exist two easily separable Diderots : the first characterized by *sensibilité* and the second a more judicious observer. Both of them suggest that this represents a split between the actual Diderot and the ideal self-portrait, and there certainly is merit in this description. However the ideal self-portrait may indeed play more of a part in the formation of the self-concept than has been noted in the past.

Diderot's biographers have commented upon the sense of annoyance expressed by Diderot at the way in which his friends were always making use of his talents. They cite the following passage : " Je vous jure que je ne suis nulle part heureux qu'à la condition de jouir de mon âme, d'être moi, moi tout pur... Ces gens-là ne veulent pas que je sois moi : je les planterai tous là et je vivrai dans un trou ; il y a longtemps que le projet me roule à la tête (A.-T., II, 142-43). Obviously Diderot was troubled by the constant requests for copy presented to him by Grimm ; he was also asked to give advice to many less well known writers, witness the story he tells in *Jacques le fataliste* about the poet whom he advised to go to Pondichéry and who reappeared upon the scene years later with the same importuning request for advice (*O. rom.* Garnier, 527-28).

On the other hand, Diderot certainly enjoyed playing the role of mentor and indeed was hardly happy unless he was being asked to give advice and make judgments. The portrait of Hardouin in *Est-il bon ? Est-il méchant ?* has commonly been accepted as a self-portrait, and a more officious busybody could hardly be imagined. But Hardouin enjoys his role and would not be able to step back and isolate himself from all the requests which pour in. Diderot must have been much the same ; as Grimsley observes : " this sense of being exploited by his friends was not a simple one-way relationship... While a part of Diderot certainly rebelled against such treatment, another side derived some satisfaction from the attitude, for he always experienced a compelling—one might almost say compulsive—need to be busy with some enterprise or other[22]."

The idea of Diderot living a solitary life hidden away in a tree-trunk is just not very convincing. It may represent a fleeting wish to get out of the hurly-burly of his life for a while but certainly could not have been sustained by this energetic and gregarious individual. His *moi tout pur* did not exist in splendid isolation but rather depended upon the give-and-take of everyday life to continue to develop. There is no real drive in Diderot's personality towards the absolute sense of rest and repose which gave Rousseau so much pleasure   Diderot admits as much in the *Salon de 1767* when he remarks that the presence of a rather boring abbé is better than solitude :   " Si la compagnie de l'abbé n'était pas tout à fait celle que j'aurois choisie, je m'aimais encore mieux avec lui que seul.   Un plaisir qui n'est que pour moi me touche faiblement et dure peu.   C'est pour moi et mes amis que je lis, que je réfléchis, que j'écris, que je médite, que j'entends, que je regarde, que je sens ; dans leur absence, ma dévotion rapporte tout à eux, je songe sans cesse à leur bonheur[23]. " He needs both the immediate attention of a constant companion with whom he can share his enthusiasms but also a large circle of devoted friends to whom he can communicate his pleasure through word of mouth or in letters.   Here again we come to the concept of communication as the basic one in Diderot's thought ; things that exist in solipsistic glory are not of enough importance to warrant his attention, in fact he obviously doubted that they existed at all.

The contrast with Rousseau is striking ; in the *Rêveries* Rousseau remarks on the fact that he would have preferred to make these walks with someone else, but that other person would have had to be an alter ego of Rousseau himself in order to enter completely into Rousseau's point of view[24].   Another individual consciousness always represented an obstacle to Rousseau since his own self was considered by him to be a self-sufficient entity not affected by the changing modes of existence.   For Diderot everything and everybody is equally important in the formation of his self, since it is not an already delineated unit but one in a constant state of development.   It is better for him to have even an insensitive companion, one who would never really understand what Diderot felt, than to be alone.   Since Rousseau had real fears about the congruence of his inner being, he could never have put up with such a companion ; his friends all had to accept his point of view or be banished.   To Diderot the question of congruence could hardly arise since it is quite clear that any event, thought, or emotion would find its place in the constantly shifting play of forces which constitute the self.   It did not worry Diderot that he was happy on one ocasion and sad on another ; both these states arc perfectly normal and can be assimilated by any healthy person. Therefore, Diderot could afford to acknowledge his basic emotional instability ; as Grimsley remarks, any conflicts which might arise within himself were externalized [25].

This ability to be objective about himself is in marked contrast to Rousseau's pathological inability to see himself as others did. Irony and humor are characteristic only of the first few books of the *Confessions* which recount his childhood and adolescence. As soon as Rousseau starts discussing his current problems, or any of the people who feature therein, he loses his ability to dissociate himself from these problems and ends up castigating those whom he felt had betrayed him. Diderot complains about people often enough in his correspondence, but they never turn into the monsters of perfidy which inhabit Rousseau's later writings. Of course this also implies that Diderot was not able to, or rather did not choose to do the in-depth research into his own personality which is so characteristic of Rousseau. One book on the period has made the distinction in terms of individualism and egoism : " He [Diderot] was, perhaps, the most thorough-going individualist of his age—for Rousseau was an egoist rather than an individualist—and the free expression of his personality was to him an absolute condition of his existence [26]." For an egoist, no one but himself exists or is interesting, for an individualist every person is just as interesting as any other, including himself. For Diderot there was also the fact that his very concept of individuality involved a principle of communication.

In addition to this need to communicate his thoughts and feelings to others, Diderot also felt the necessity of being judged by others. He was very anxious for the esteem of his contemporaries even though he announced in his letters to Falconet that posterity will have to restore the balance. What other people thought him to be had a profound effect on what he thought himself to be, and his own self-esteem depended upon the approbation of others. This leads directly to the other portrait which he gives of himself in his written works, that of a judicious and reasonable *philosophe*. The ideal self-concept, as portrayed in Moi of *Le Neveu de Rameau* and Ariste in *La Promenade du sceptique* and the *Discours sur la poésie dramatique,* is particularly characterized by a sense of detachment and even of superiority. In Moi this latter trait makes him into a less likable person than he might otherwise have been, as Crocker remarks :

son attitude envers Lui est caractérisée par la satisfaction de soi et par la condescendance. Son ego tire un grand contentement de tous les témoignages d'infériorité de Lui. Comme il est aisé de le voir, son sentiment de supériorité vis-à-vis de Lui repose sur deux idées : l'une, la différence de leur rang et de leur rôle dans le monde ; l'autre, la conviction qu'il est, par sa moralité, sur la voie de Seigneur [27].

Nevertheless Moi does represent certain traits towards which Diderot aspired in his own rather checkered personality. Moi is independent and self-sufficient, but he still takes an interest in such odd characters as Lui. He is surprised by Rameau's ability to see through both society and his own failings especially since it appears that Lui will not take advantage of these insights but will continue to live a parasitic existence, the very opposite of the type of life outlined by Moi as the only one worthy of esteem. If the world is condemned to partake in *la pantomime*, then it seems clear to Moi that the philosopher who has nothing and who needs nothing represents the highest estate possible. His glorification of Diogène serves the purpose of delineating the only possible escape from this parasitic existence ; the philosopher does not have to ask favors and can therefore pursue the truth in a totally disinterested way, which is utterly impossible for any individual living in the hectic society of other men. But one may note that Moi himself does not live in this way ; just as Moi represents certain aspects of Diderot's ideal self, so Diogène represents certain aspects of Moi's ideal self. Neither Diderot nor Moi actually live up to their ideal, but the fact that they have such a concept will play its part in determining their own reactions. The ideal self-concept functions as the carrot to the perennial donkey, ever unattainable but always there to spur him on.

Ariste is also an idealized version of Diderot himself, in fact Chouillet suggests that we have here the portrait of the ideal philosopher :

> Diderot se présente à nous, non pas tel qu'il est réellement, mais tel qu'il se flatte d'être, tel que *doit* être un ' philosophe '. ... Ariste est Diderot, mais il est en même temps plus que lui. Il est *le* philosophe, au sens où l'on dit qu'Alceste est *le* Misanthrope. Il est le portrait idéal de Diderot[28].

His way of looking carefully at all sides of a question before making any decision, his curiosity to hear the other side of any problem under discussion, give us the portrait of a man truly dedicated to the search for truth, no matter what the consequences may be to himself. Actually Ariste as a person is not too lifelike, but his air of indifferent objectivity is obviously one which Diderot was anxious to incorporate into his own personality. Only the person who can stand back and observe the foibles of others and of himself can ever hope to arrive at an accurate picture of the universe and of himself. It is impossible to divorce the outer and the inner life, and true self-knowledge is obtainable only in conjunction with knowledge of others and of society as a whole.

In the same way, insight into others is not accessible to anyone who cannot read his own inner being as Diderot remarks in a letter : " Quand on a un peu l'habitude de lire dans son propre cœur, on est bien savant

sur ce qui se passe dans le cœur des autres[29]." Thus insights into others
depend ultimately on knowledge of self just as the self-concept must be
tested against the societal reality. In the *Réfutation de l'Homme* Diderot
makes a rather ambiguous remark which can probably be understood in
this light : " *Il dit* : On ne peut pas avoir été soi et un autre. *Ajoutez* :
Il faudrait donc s'en rapporter un peu à ce qu'un autre nous dit de lui "
(A.-T., II, 362). The opinion of others forms part of that person's opinion
of himself, and so we find that society as a whole plays a fundamental
role in the definition of an individual's self-concept. This is not to deny
the equally important role played by that individual's own idea of his own
actual self and of his ideal self. The ideal self acts as a guide, determining
in some degree the reactions of that person to any situation. What he
knows to be his limitations also acts as a determining factor in his
behavior, as does what he knows other people think of him. Diderot's
self-concept is no more a static tableau of certain stereotyped character
traits than is his concept of the self as agent. Both are constantly
developing and changing as time goes on. Both self and self-concept
incorporate into themselves all three time ranges : the future in terms
of what the individual is striving towards ; the past in terms of the
determining factors which are now part of this entity ; and the present in
terms of an internalized force which activates the individual.

The problem of role-playing has been lightly touched on elsewhere
but needs to be discussed in this connection. It is clear in the *Neveu de
Rameau* that most people in society have no idea of what or who they
are and merely become what society wants them to be. Many people do
this unconsciously, making no attempt whatever to change themselves
in any way. They are perfectly content to play the role of parasite or
master, according to their position, and they refuse to see the underlying
hypocrisy which governs their behavior.

A few unusual individuals, whom Diderot terms *original*, stand out
in sharp contrast. Lui is a perfect example of this kind of person who
goes through the gestures required of him by the society but who does so
with perfect lucidity, realizing the ludicrous nature of what he is doing.
He dares to be what his own basic nature leads him to be, a glutton and an
easy-liver, but he does so openly and knowingly. Mortier notes that what
attracted Diderot to this type of personality was his resolute adherence to
his own concept of himself : " Ce qui séduit Diderot dans l'*original*, c'est
la force de sa personnalité, son caractère tranché, l'affirmation résolue
de son *moi*[30]." This is certainly true, witness Moi's fascination with Lui's
disclosures about his way of life and his thoughts about society and his
place in it. But Lui is not a very strong character since he never manages
to get out of the tight bind of hypocritical behavior patterns which are
imposed upon him by the Bertin-Palissot group. He acts as a catalyst
for Moi, enabling the latter to gain an insight into a group which he would

never otherwise have been able to understand. But the end of the dialogue is ambiguous, and it remains an open question whether Lui will ever manage to break away from this degrading life which he has molded onto his own. It is indeed highly unlikely that Rameau will do anything but go back to Bertin with humble apologies for having spoken out clearly for once in his life.

Moi also plays a role, that of the contented family man, whose domestic peace is conserved at the expense of a certain amount of conscious hypocrisy. This situation parallels Diderot's own relationships with his wife. The role of devoted father came naturally to him, and he enjoyed all the various behavior patterns which it entailed. However it was not possible to ignore the mother of his little girl, and so he subdued his own boisterous nature as much as possible in the confines of his home in order to continue to fulfil the requirements of fatherhood. A certain degree of self-conscious choice is reflected here, and it might be possible to say that this role of family man does not fit into either Diderot's real self or his self-concept. However such a conclusion cannot be justified, since any behavior must be accounted for in terms of the constantly developing self. Bourgeois father and husband are therefore equally as descriptive in speaking of Diderot as materialist philosopher or radical thinker. To the outside eye there may appear to be a discrepancy here, but for Diderot he was all of a piece and no real difficulty arose for him in terms of his concept of himself. Very diverse elements can be accommodated in a self-concept which is not static like that of Rousseau's.

A final note should be added about this concept of role-playing. Psychologists today note that it is through this process that children learn to become individuals; the question of sincerity and hypocrisy really does not arise until the adult is mature enough to have found his own identity, at which point his personality coalesces around certain salient traits which form the central core of his individuality. Certainly Diderot never expressed himself in these terms, but it may be possible to see a suggestion of such a thesis in some of his remarks. This is particularly true of his ideas about the education of children. In the *Neveu de Rameau*, Moi discusses the education of his little girl with Lui who has a boy to bring up; Moi insists upon the fact that a girl must be close to her mother in order to be able to function properly when she grows up (*O. rom.*, Garnier, 419-21). A little boy should model himself on his father, which is exactly what happens when Lui tells the story of how he struts around with money in his pocket so that the child will understand the power of wealth (*O. rom.*, Garnier, 475). When the child observes the parent, he or she is studying certain behavior traits which will be incorporated into his or her own pattern. In time these become second-nature and are totally assimilated into the personality so that one can no longer discuss them in terms of sincerity and hypocrisy, nature and culture.

The conflicts which are raised by the requirements of society working on the totally undeveloped self are fundamental to the process of maturing. The difficulty arises only when the divergence between the two sets of requirements is too great, for Diderot claims that temperament and character are determined to a large degree by the biological structure of the individual : " Je ne sais si le génie se décèle dès l'enfance ; pour le caractère, il n'est pas permis d'en douter. Cependant Helvétius attribue indistinctement la création de l'un et de l'autre à l'éducation et au hasard, à l'exclusion de la nature et de l'organisation (A.-T., II, 291). If this basic natural structure is totally thwarted by society, then the conflict will not be resolved peacefully within the confines of the self but will be externalized and become manifest in the behavior of this individual. For this reason Diderot insists on the necessity of making sure that all laws are compatible with what he thinks are the fundamental realities of human nature. This is discussed at most length in the *Supplément au voyage de Bougainville* in terms of the sex drive which cannot be overlooked in any discussion of mankind. And yet the conclusion that morality and human nature are automatically exclusive does not seem justified. Lester Crocker's remarks on *Le Neveu de Rameau* show the radical conclusions which may be drawn from Diderot's thought in this area :

> Ce qu'il [Lui] représente, n'est-ce pas la nature humaine originelle, dépouillée de cette éducation que donne la culture sociale, que certains écrivains au XVIIIe siècle appelaient " l'artificiel " et qui est considérée ici comme un " masque " ? C'est un naturalisme radical, qui abaisse l'homme au niveau des demandes instinctives de l'égo. ... Mener une vie morale, n'est-ce pas trahir la nature humaine tout court, semble conclure Diderot, dans son portrait de Lui[31].

Certainly it is true that Lui retains a clearer idea of his " natural " self than do most members of society, but he has a concept of himself which is not in accordance with the facts. His ideas of what he is doing with his life are belied by the situation in which he exists, and he is too weak a character to break out of these unsatisfactory and undesirable conditions. His real self is that of a severely limited and restricted personality rather than the free spirit which he thinks he is.

This brings up a final point about the formation of a self-concept ; it cannot ever conform to reality since an individual obviously sees himself in a better light than is the case. *Amour-propre* is a fundamental force in any individual and inevitably forces him to see himself in a slightly different way : " Cratès disait à un jeune homme : Que fais-tu là seul ? Le jeune homme lui répondit : Je m'entretiens avec moi-même. Prends garde, lui répliqua le philosophe, de t'entretenir avec un flatteur " (A.-T., III, 207). But even though one's self-concept may not be true to life it is still a force to be reckoned with in the formation of the self, since it has some effect on one's behavior.

In fact all these factors which we have been discussing must be taken into account in the formation of the self : self-concept, society's requirements, the opinion of others, and role-playing. None of these influences are exclusively determinent in the process of maturing, and life itself is a constant process not a series of arrested points in time. As Diderot remarked in a letter to Voltaire : " Pour se donner l'existence, il faut agir[32]." A constantly developing self in a constantly changing universe— this represents Diderot's considered judgment in this sphere.

CONCLUSION

The conclusions which we will draw from this analysis of the concept of the self in the French Enlightenment will be neither startling nor unexpected. The *Weltanschauung* of the period has been extremely well described by numerous critics, mostly recently in Robert Mauzi's excellent study of *L'idée du bonheur*. The period is one of transition with new forces becoming operative around 1750 and clearly visible by 1770. By this time the old reliance on rationality and absolute standards had given way to a feeling of *inquiétude*. All values and methods came under scrutiny, and the previous resolutions of such age-old questions as the relationship between mind and body, subjectivity and objectivity, relativism and absolutism, time and eternity, man and nature were reassessed in the light of a supposedly infallible epistemology, sensationalism. As Palmer remarks : " Sensationalism was not only a psychology but a metaphysics, and not only a theory of knowledge but a theory of human nature[1]."

Certain writers had already become aware of the limitations of this methodology and questioned the results obtained by strict adherence to its precepts. The reduction of human nature to an automatic response to external stimuli was seen to be unsatisfactory, and certain new approaches were devised. The one which met with most favor was the reliance on emotional tone, on *sensibilité* rather than on sensations which are dependent upon outside elements. Feelings were assumed to be internally generated, and the scorn of the rational seventeenth century towards the passions was replaced by an exaltation of strong emotions. But reason was not abandoned and most characteristic eighteenth century thought combines the rational and the emotional. Such a compromise position produced a certain tension and anxiety which in turn led these thinkers to question just about every value and method hitherto devised. They were not happy with past solutions but for the most part were unable to come up with new ones which offered any better conclusions. In some writers, as Crocker has demonstrated in *An Age of Crisis* and *Nature and Culture*, this led to an incipient form of nihilism, according to which the very search for truth and values was denigrated as being ludicrous and unworthy of serious attention. In other writers, as Mauzi has noted, this led to what he terms " une crise de l'existence " : " C'est au XVIIIᵉ siècle que se constitue l'idée d'une *crise de l'existence*, toujours virtuelle en l'homme, mais le plus souvent masquée par la diversité des actions et des jeux composant l'apparence d'une vie[2]." What distinguishes this anxiety crisis from that of our own times is that no one really doubted the existence of an overall pattern to the universe. The whole of existential matter was assumed to be an ordered unit, although serious doubts were expressed about the possibility of man ever being able to unravel its mysteries.

What troubled the eighteenth century was how man fitted into this scheme ; there seemed to be very little relationship between his internal structure, the world of sensation, ideas and emotions, and external reality, the world of hard things. Cartesian dualism was accepted by almost all authors ; this was one of the philosophical *données* which formed the very basis of all thought. But Descartes' solution to the problem of dualism had been demonstrated to be false, and no one had as yet managed to get out of the quagmire of dualism except through total idealism or complete materialism. No major French thinker of the period was willing to follow Berkeley's principles to their ultimate end in solipsism, but neither were they very happy with what they thought to be Spinoza's solution. These two monistic systems did not have very much rapport with existential reality, and, if there is one area on which almost all eighteenth century authors agreed, it was on the necessity of abandoning systematic thought in favor of an individual, existential approach. A system, such as that of Leibniz', which certainly gave adequate answers to most of the impersonal questions of the age, was not satisfactory because it did nothing at all for the personal feeling of distress which came to dominate the thought of the latter part of the period.

As Mauzi has shown, happiness was one of the *idées fixes* of the Enlightenment, and he defines this pursuit of happiness as " la poursuite d'une impossible unité[3]." The problem of the self was not one of the guiding ideas of the century, but it crops up at almost every turn, especially when the question of the nature of man is considered. Modern concepts of alienation, of identity crises, etc., play a substantial if minor role in the general considerations of the Enlightenment. For the most part authors assumed that human beings are what they seem to be, and their ideas on the subject fall into one of three general categories. One group continued to see in the self an independent entity, one which existed apart from the vicissitudes of daily life. Christian writers made of this essentialistic unit a soul, non-Christian writers called it a self. Rousseau continues this line of thought although he revivifies its content by showing what a wealth of material there was to discover hidden away in the inner depths of the human personality, a sphere which was essentialy a-temporal. In this approach we see the clearest example of one of the themes developed in the nineteenth century, the in-depth exploration of the inner resources of the human being.

A second group, actually a very small one, saw the self as nothing at all, an existential being which is only definable in terms of the past experience of the individual. This composition theory of the self, Hume's " bundle of perceptions," was thought to be the conclusion of Condillac and Helvétius. In true fact, both these authors fall back on a concept of the self as an essential unit, an observer of existence and the changes produced by time. The totally passive and dependent self of sensationalism is not characteristic of any major author, although it was certainly conceived of as a logical possibility by a great many. One of the major problems of this concept is that the self disappears entirely, leaving the individual with no inner resources whatsoever. Mauzi has noted this *mal de vivre* in the case of Maupertuis and comments as follows : " Les symptômes du mal de vivre sont divers : spleen, mélancolie, vapeurs. Tous se rapportent à la conscience d'un manque, d'une insécurité à l'intérieur de l'être. Le néant s'annonce à l'âme par une double expérience : les marécages de l'ennui, et les menaces explicites ou confuses venant du monde[4]." As he points out the very terms *le néant, le vide*, point to the fact that the self was conceived of ontologically as a spatial being : " on prend la conscience pour un *espace*, qu'il faut meubler, orner, remplir, non pour ce qu'elle est véritablement, c'est-à-dire une durée." What was missing in the composition theory of the self was some kind of container which would hold all the disparate elements together. Without such a receptacle the self seemed likely to disintegrate entirely, and absolutely nothing was left to take its place. Most writers shied away from such a radical conclusion and fell back on the concept of a core which never changes and which thereby provides the necessary principle of identity.

The third group, also an extremely small one, saw into a new sphere of ontological existence, that of time rather than of space. At times Rousseau uses the time element, but eventually he incorporates it into the first, a-temporal concept. We have seen how close Lelarge de Lignac came to such an organic definition of the self, and Diderot is, of course, the best representative of this attitude. Diderot consistently refuses to acknowledge the existence of any unchanging unit and posits instead a principle of personal identity which is intimately involved with movement and change. The developing self is both dependent on and contributory to the external world ; its nucleus is not a thing but a center of energy. This internal force enables the developing self to be active, even to be self-creative to a certain degree. This kind of a self also unites within itself the two spheres of subjective and objective reality ; in truth no such opposition exists and a new kind of monism is perceivable.

It would be foolish to claim that Diderot solved the problems which haunted the century; his thoughts on this subject are tentative and exploratory, not definitive. He realized that the explanations of the past, even when re-combined in new and different ways, would not answer the problems of his age. His imaginative analogies enabled him to make suggestions of completely new methods of approach, ones which would be developed by such philosophers as Maine de Biran and more recently Whitehead. The fluid nature of Diderot's thought is reflected in the type of literary form which he adopted for his most successful works, the dialogue. This represents the quest for knowledge in its freest and least structured manner, with all points of view represented. Diderot's is the way of movement, change and flux, whereas Rousseau manages to fuse the temporal with the eternal, and annihilates change as an operative factor in the formation of a human being. Anything which is added to human nature is to Rousseau an artifical adornment, which needs to be discarded in order to permit the individual to thoroughly submerge himself in his own eternal self.

These distinctions are at the base of their very different ideas about human nature and happiness. The thinker who finds identity to be the fundamental principle of human nature will obviously subscribe to a theory of happiness which stresses the concentration of consciousness upon the inner principle of unity present in all men. Rousseau's call to all mankind to follow his example and retreat from society is only natural for such a thinker. Equally normal is Diderot's insistence upon the necessity of staying in society in order to do something about improving the lot of humanity in general. The total concentration upon self preached by Rousseau could not prove satisfactory to an author who found the principle of identity to involve a principle of communication. As we have seen, even Rousseau was affected by this current of opinion, and he dearly longed for what Starobinski terms *la transparence*[6], the possibility of communicating totally with other people. To Rousseau, Diderot could never be a real friend, since Diderot was always interfering in the behavior of others. This expansiveness was natural to Diderot's own personality but also fits in with his concept of the self. Rousseau preferred a more passive type of friendship, one in which two beings could comprehend each other on another plane of existence entirely. Behavior patterns were not important to Rousseau; they had nothing to do with his inner being and so should be ignored by a kindred spirit who has access to his inner being, the only one which counts. Solitary exploration of self is all-important to Rousseau, but only of minor importance to Diderot, who insisted on the sphere of action. The passive self of Rousseau and the active self of Diderot are poles apart ontologically and psychologically although both of them contain germs of future research and thought in this sphere.

Current criticism has almost abolished the concept of the eighteenth century as an Age of Reason, optimistic and convinced of human progress in all spheres. However it would certainly not be correct to swing to the other extreme and assume that since all was not rosy it was of necessity black. As an age of transition the Enlightenment combines both attitudes and thus produces a tension in its thought and creative works which may seem to be ambiguous at times. These writers were striving to break out of the restrictive categories of past thought and found the going very difficult. Those few who succeeded did so at the expense of considerable personal anguish. Whether Rousseau actually derived as much benefit from the experiences of *rêverie* as we would like to make out is quite a moot question. His insight into the totally different methodology which was to prevail after the Revolution came to him in spurts and is really discernible only in his final unfinished work. This may of course represent a new kind of approach to reality, but in order to arrive at this ultimate point Rousseau had to experience much suffering and doubt about both society and himself. He could find no secure niche for himself within the pattern of the universe, and the divorce between the subjective and the objective seemed to be insurmountable. In a study of time in Rousseau and Kant, Mark Temmer makes an important point :

> Rousseau's being is torn in two directions ; we have seen how his attempts at finding oneness oppose each other, how one is not possible without the other, since the first search for unity presupposes a subjective present, independent of past and future, which without the present, are tragic and impossible aspirations. This sense of being torn, this tension, this shifting from one kind of unity to the other, this estrangement in time and flight from space, represent, we believe, the true meaning of pre-romantic sensibility[7].

Tragic despair, the result of the apprehension that indeed no solution will ever be devised for this dilemma certainly afflicted Rousseau at times during his life. It may be hoped that the production of the *Rêveries* alleviated some of this feeling and that Rousseau's glimpse of a solution gave him much comfort.

The case of Diderot also falls in with the above analysis. Instead of devising an escape route, Diderot concentrated his great energies on the confrontation of man and nature as it actually existed in a true-to-life situation. His refusal to ignore the problems of society and of man as a social being brought him to a realization that individuals differ in their basic make-up and that tinkering with the structure of society would not necessarily be the panacea it was too frequently assumed to be. The external world must, of course, be remodeled, but at the same time man's attitude towards the world in which he lives has to be reconstructed. For Diderot glimpsed the new monism of organic wholism according to which neither objective nor subjective values have any validity apart from each other. The central unit of comprehension, the individual consciousness, must grasp not only the concept of its dependence upon external stimuli but also its own internally generated energy, the power of the self to assimilate and order the elements which come to it from the outside world. The gap between mind and body is not so much bridged as eliminated. In Alexander's words : " Te be conscious is to be aware of participating, in and through a sensibility common to the subject and the object, in an ' other ' which transcends the self [8]. " Again one must question whether Diderot himself saw as clearly as we do today the consequences of some of his remarks, especially those made in the *Rêve* and the *Eléments de physiologie*, which he himself realized were highly speculative.

Finally let us not overlook the work which was done by so many other writers of the eighteenth century. It was a probing, questioning age and these thinkers turned the problem of the self inside out in an attempt to arrive at some valid conclusions about its nature. They were the more inclined to do so since such a definition was of fundamental importance in their more prominent considerations, such as ethical determinism, the nature of society and the pursuit of happiness. Their ultimate reliance on the age-old concept of a self existing apart from what happens to the individual invalidated many of their more speculative conclusions. Even Helvétius, who reduced human behavior to the influence of the environment, was tied to a concept of the self which denied his basic premise. Is it any wonder that two of the key words of the latter part of the century are *ennui* and *angoisse* ? Voltaire's retreat into philosophic ignorance accompanied as it was by frenetic action in the social sphere was one possible reaction to such a condition. As long as one could anticipate some social benefit from activity, no one should despair. Another reaction was the concentration on hedonistic pleasures and even the ultimate reversal of all moral values in the theories of Sade.

But these extreme cases are not representative of the commonest attitude of the age, which was one of empirical determination. Neither well-reasoned systems nor destructive nihilism appealed to most thinkers of the age who resolutely ignored the fundamental discrepancies in some of their basic assumptions. They continued to think and write about what interested them and took great delight in arguing over small points with their peers in the active salons in which almost all of them participated. For they were basically gregarious people ; they were intrigued by Rousseau's exaltation of the solitary life and willing to retreat from society in order to experience this new feeling. However they wanted to come back to their wide circle of friends in order to tell the others all about it. A sense of urbanity and cosmopolitanism remained strong even when *sensibilité* took over from reason as the most admired character trait. For the most part the *philosophes* took strong delight in whatever they did or felt, whether it involved a pleasant or a sad experience. They entered into each facet of existence with gusto and derived almost as much pleasure from recounting their experiences afterward as from the events themselves.

Pessimism may seem to be the ultimate conclusion of their inability to find new solutions, but for the most part they continued to do what they could without falling into either sanguine expectation or despair. Looking back from a distance of two centuries it is tempting to delineate what these thinkers should have thought and how they should have acted under these circumstances, but this would not give us a true picture of the age. Human nature has a strong element of determination, and very few people give up in the face of discrepancies. This is no less true today than it was in the eighteenth century. Inconsistencies and ambiguities are part and parcel of human existence, although each and every one of us is tempted to try to reach ultimate conclusions which would resolve all these tensions.

Printed in Switzerland

NOTES

Chapter I

PHILOSOPHICAL CONCEPTS AND DEFINITIONS

1. MARY W. CALKINS, *The Persistent Problems of Philosophy*, 5th ed., New York: Macmillan, 1925.

2. CALVIN S. HALL and GARDNER LINDZEY, *Theories of Personality* (New York: John Wiley, 1957), 408.

3. *Ibid.*

4. JOSEPH NUTTIN, *La Structure de la personnalité* (Paris: PUF, 1965), 19.

5. STEPHEN STRASSER, *The Soul in Metaphysical and Empirical Psychology* (Pittsburgh, Duquesne Univ. Press, 1957), 148.

6. ROBERT R. PALMER, *Catholics and Unbelievers in Eighteenth Century France* (Princeton: Princeton Univ. Press, 1939), 148.

7. GILBERT RYLE, *The Concept of Mind* (London, New York: Hutchinson's Univ. Library, 1949), 14.

8. NORMAN MALCOLM, " Knowledge of Other Minds ", in *Essays in Philosophical Psychology*, ed. Donald F. Gustafson, (New York: Doubleday, 1964), 373.

9. RYLE, *The Concept of Mind*, 165.

10. STRASSER, *The Soul*, 221.

11. GEORGES GUSDORF, *La Découverte de soi* (Paris: PUF, 1948), 313.

12. JEROME SHAFFER, " Persons and their Bodies ", *Philosophical Review*, LXXV (1966), 59-77.

13. STRASSER, *The Soul*, 74.

14. *Ibid.*, 3.

15. GORDON W. ALLPORT, *Pattern and Growth in Personality* (New York: Holt Rinehart and Winston, 1961), 558.

Chapter II

THE PHILOSOPHICAL BACKGROUND OF EIGHTEENTH CENTURY THOUGHT

1. PALMER, *Catholics and Unbelievers*, 151.

2. ETIENNE GILSON ed., RENÉ DESCARTES, *Discours de la méthode*, (Paris: Vrin, 1930), 437.

3. See MAURICE DE WULF, *The System of Thomas Aquinas* (New York: Dover, 1959), especially ch. 10: " Soul and Body. "

4. In some ways, the Scholastic view is close to that of the current phenomenological one, which helps to explain the recent revival of Thomistic philosophy. Strasser speaks with great admiration of the Aristotelian-Thomistic view: " This profound, well-conceived

and balanced view of man's nature was destroyed by a single word of Descartes—his famous Cogito " (STRASSER, *The Soul*, 30).

5. MARCEL RAYMOND, " La Rêverie selon Rousseau et son conditionnement historique," in Comité national pour la commémoration de J.-J. Rousseau, *Jean-Jacques Rousseau et son œuvre* (Paris: Klincksieck, 1964), 1.

6. RENÉ DESCARTES, " Deuxième Méditation," in *Œuvres et lettres*, ed. André Bridoux (Paris: Pléiade, 1952), 275.

7. DESCARTES, *Discours*, ed. Gilson, 293.

8. See NORMAN KEMP SMITH, *New Studies in the Philosophy of Descartes* (London: Macmillan, 1952), 239-241, 284-85, 301 and 306.

9. Hobbes published his *Objections in Cartesii de Prima Philosophia Meditationes* in 1641, and they were reprinted in all the early editions of Descartes' *Méditations*.

10. DESCARTES, *Discours*, 275. St. Augustine had used the first part of this argument long before in *De Civitate Dei*, XI, c. 26: " If I am deceived, I am. For he who is not, cannot be deceived."

11. Rizieri Frondizi in *The Nature of the Self: a Functional Interpretation* (New Haven: Yale Univ. Press, 1953) bases his criticism of the Cartesian concept of the self almost entirely on this one aspect of the problem.

12. SMITH, *New Studies*, 136-7.

13. *Ibid.*, 4.

14. RICHARD A. WATSON, *The Downfall of Cartesianism, 1673-1712* (The Hague: Martinus Nijhoff, 1966), 3.

15. *Ibid.*, 4.

16. *Ibid.*

17. NICOLAS MALEBRANCHE, *Recherche de la vérité*, Book 3, Part 2, ch. 6; in *Œuvres complètes*, (Paris: Vrin, 1958-1966), I, 445.

18. WATSON, *Downfall*, 63.

19. MALEBRANCHE, *Recherche*, Ecl. XI; *Œuvres*, III, 163.

20. ed. Lewis, MALEBRANCHE, *Recherche*, Ecl. 1; *Œuvres*, III, 27.

21. BEATRICE ROME, *The Philosophy of Malebranche* (Chicago: Regnery, 1963), 273.

22. *Ibid*. 264.

23. MALEBRANCHE, *Recherche*, Book 3, Part 2, ch. 7, Sec. 4; *Œuvres*, I, 451.

24. LESTER G. CROCKER, *An Age of Crisis* (Baltimore: Johns Hopkins Univ. Press, 1959), 116.

25. ANITA D. FRITZ, " Berkeley's Self—its origin in Malebranche," *Journal of the History of Ideas*, XV (1954), 557.

26. WILLIAM H. BARBER, *Leibniz in France from Arnauld to Voltaire* (Oxford: Clarendon Press, 1955), x.

27. *Ibid.*, 97-98.

28. GOTTFRIED WILHELM VON LEIBNIZ, *Die philosophischen Schriften*, ed. Gerhardt (Berlin, 1875-90), V, 219, and *New Essays*, tr. A.G. Langley (New York, 1896), 247.

29. LEIBNIZ, ed. Gerhardt, V, 218, and *New Essays*, 245.

30. LEIBNIZ, ed. Gerhardt, V, 391, and *New Essays*, 469.

31. LEIBNIZ, ed. Gerhardt, V, 391, and *New Essays*, 469.

32. LEIBNIZ, ed. Gerhardt, III, 247.

33. LEIBNIZ, ed. Gerhardt, II, 43 (1686).

34. KARL BARTH, *Images du XVIIIe siècle* (Paris; Neuchâtel: Delachaux et Niestlé, 1949), 75.

35. See CALKINS, *Persistent Problems*, 279; STUART HAMPSHIRE, *Spinoza* (London: Faber and Faber, 1956), 22; also the comprehensive work of PAUL VERNIÈRE, *Spinoza et la pensée française*, (Paris: PUF, 1954, 2 vol.).

36. HAMPSHIRE, *Spinoza*, 22.

37. BARUCH SPINOZA, *Spinoza's Ethic*, tr. Andrew Goyle (London: Dent, 1959), Part II, Proposition X, Corollary, p. 44.

38. SPINOZA, *Ethic*, Pt. II, Prop. XXIX, Corollary, p. 62.

39. SPINOZA, *Ethic*, Pt. II, Prop. XLIV, p. 76.

40. SPINOZA, *Ethic*, Pt. II, Prop. XIII, p. 47.

41. WATSON, *Downfall of Cartesianism*, 145.

42. For a discussion of the eclecticism of the *philosophes*, see Peter Gay, *The Enlightenment, an Interpretation* (New York: Knopf, 1966), 160 ff.

43. JOHN LOCKE, *An Essay Concerning Human Understanding*, II, iii, 6, ed. Alexander Campbell Fraser (Oxford: Clarendon, 1894), II, 192.

44. LOCKE, *Essay*, II, xxiii, 15, ed. Fraser, I, 406.

45. *Ibid.*

46. LOCKE, *An Early Draft of Locke's Essay*, ed. R. I. Aaron and J. Gibb (Oxford: Clarendon, 1936), 40.

47. LOCKE, *Essay*, II, i, 4, ed. Fraser, I, 124.

48. LOCKE, *Essay*, IV, iii, 21, ed. Fraser, II, 212.

49. LOCKE, *Essay*, IV, ix, 3, ed. Fraser, II, 305.

50. LOCKE, *Essay*, II, i, 11, ed. Fraser, I, 130.

51. LOCKE, *Essay*, II, xxvii, 7; ed. Fraser, I, 444.

52. LOCKE, *Essay*, II, xxvii, 11; ed. Fraser, I, 448.

53. See L. Bongie, "Hume 'philosophe' and philosopher in eighteenth century France," *French Studies*, XV (1961), 213-27; L. Gossman, "Berkeley, Hume and Maupertuis," *French Studies*, XIV, (1960), 304-24; R. Mertz," Les Amitiés françaises de Hume," *Revue de la littérature comparée*, IX (1929), 644-713.

54. GEORGE BERKELEY, *The Works of George Berkeley*, ed. A.A. Luce and T.E. Jessop (London: Nelson, 1948), I, 125.

55. BERKELEY, *Works*, I, 60 and 72.

56. FRITZ, "Berkeley's Self," 572.

57. BERKELEY, *Works*, III, 301.

58. WATSON, *Downfall of Cartesianism*, 117.

59. BERKELEY, *Works*, III, 304.

60. BERKELEY, *Works*, IV, 358.

61. FRITZ, "Berkeley's Self," 571.

62. DAVID HUME, *My Own Life*, 1776, as quoted in Ernest C. Mossner, "The Continental Reception of Hume's *Treatise*," *Mind*, n.s., LVI (1947), 31.

63. MOSSNER, *op. cit.*, 43.

64. HUME, *A Treatise of Human Nature*, I, iv, 6, ed. A.D. Lindsay (New York: Dutton, 1911), I, 239.

65. A German translation appeared in 1790-92, too late to have any real effect on the French Enlightenment.

66. Schaupp's thesis that Hume's thought had virtually no influence on Condillac is supported by this fact although it disproves the following statement: "Hume's *Treatise of Human Nature* was not translated until 1758, after Condillac's three chief works had been published " (ZORA SCHAUPP, *The Naturalism of Condillac* [Lincoln: Univ. of Nebraska Press, c 1925], 40, n. 37).

67. THOMAS E. JESSOP, *A Bibliography of David Hume and of Scottish Philosophy* (London: Brown, 1938), 25.

68. BERLIN, *The Age of Enlightenment* (Boston: Houghton Mifflin, 1956), 216.

69. CALKINS, *Persistent Problems*, 180.

70. ROBERT F. ANDERSON, *Hume's First Principles* (Lincoln: Univ. of Nebraska Press, c 1966), 81.

71. HUME, *Treatise*, I, iv, 6; Lindsay ed., I, 239.

72. HUME, *Treatise*, I, iv, 6; Lindsay ed., I, 246-7.

73. BERLIN, *Age of Enlightenment*, 240.

74. *Ibid.*, 239.

75. NORMAN KEMP SMITH, *The Philosophy of David Hume* (London: Macmillan, 1941), 73.

76. HUME, *Treatise*, I, iii, 14; Lindsay ed. I, 163.

77. HUME, *Treatise*, I, iv, 6; Lindsay ed. I, 247.

78. HUME, *Treatise*, Appendix; Lindsay ed., II, 319.

79. SMITH, *The Philosophy of David Hume*, 73.

80. HUME, *Treatise*, II, ii, 1; Lindsay ed., II, 51.

81. THOMAS REID, *An Inquiry into the Human Mind*, II, vii, in *The Works of Thomas Reid*, ed. Sir William Hamilton (Edinburgh, 1852), 110.

82. BERLIN, *Age of Enlightenment*, 273.

83. STRASSER, *The Soul*, 35.

84. As quoted in Crocker, *Age of Crisis*, 95.

85. CROCKER, *Age of Crisis*, 192.

Chapter III

THE EIGHTEENTH CENTURY CONCEPT OF THE SELF

1. JACQUES ROGER, compte rendu de Jean Ehrard, *L'Idée de nature en France*, *Revue d'histoire littéraire de la France*, LXVI (1966), 716-17.

2. RAYMOND MORTIER, " A propos du sentiment de l'existence chez Diderot et Rousseau," *Diderot Studies*, VI, 195.

3. DENESLE, *Examen du matérialisme relativement à la morale* (Paris, 1754), I, 228.

4. FONTENELLE, *Connoissance de l'esprit* as quoted in *Heikki Kirkinen, Les Origines de la conception moderne de l'homme machine* (Helsinki, 1960), 181.

5. DENESLE, *Examen*, I, 3.

6. CONDILLAC, *Essai sur l'origine des connoissances humaines*, I, ii, 1; in *Œuvres philosophiques de Condillac*, ed. Georges Le Roy (Paris: PUF, 1947), I, 11.

7. HYACINTHE CORDONNIER SAINT-HYACINTHE, *Recherches philosophiques sur la nécessité de s'assurer par soi-même de la vérité* (London, 1743), 152.

8. *Ibid.*, 151.

9. Abbé FRANÇOIS ILHARAT DE LA CHAMBRE, *Abrégé de philosophie* (Paris, 1754), I, 25.

10. FRANÇOIS QUESNAY, " Evidence," in *Œuvres économiques et philosophiques*, ed. Auguste Oncken (Francfort s/M: Baer, 1888), 782-83.

11. JOHN LOUGH, " The Problem of the Unsigned Articles in the *Encyclopédie*," *Studies on Voltaire and the Eighteenth Century*, XXXII (1965), 350.

12. ANNE ROBERT JACQUES TURGOT, " Existence," *Encyclopédie*, VI, 261, B.

13. See RONALD GRIMSLEY, " Turgot's article 'Existence' in the *Encyclopédie*," in *The French Mind* (Studies in honour of Gustave Rudler), ed. W.G. Moore (Oxford, 1952), 130-33.

14. JEAN LEROND D'ALEMBERT, *Eclaircissemens* in *Mélanges de littérature, d'histoire et de philosophie* (Paris, 1959), V, 18.

15. RONALD GRIMSLEY, *Jean d'Alembert* (Oxford: Clarendon Press, 1963), 233-35.

16. Abbé FRANÇOIS PARA DU PHANJAS, *Les Principes de la saine philosophie* (Paris, 1774), I, 51-52.

17. JEAN HENRI SAMUEL FORMEY, *Mélanges philosophiques* (Leyde, 1754), I, 100.

18. FORMEY, *Mélanges*, I, 101.

19. *Ibid.*, I, 130.

20. Le Père ANTOINE-JOSEPH PERNETY, *Observations sur les maladies de l'âme* (Berlin, 1777), 139-40.

21. PERNETY, *La Connoissance de l'homme moral par celle de l'homme physique* (Berlin, 1776), II, 57-58.

22. CHARLES BONNET, *Essai analytique sur les facultés de l'ame*, in *Œuvres d'histoire naturelle et de philosophie* (Neuchâtel, 1779-83), VI, 342.

23. ANDRÉ-PIERRE LE GUAY DE PRÉMONTVAL, *Vues philosophiques* (Berlin, 1761), II, 162 ff.

24. CLAUDE HELVÉTIUS, *De l'esprit*, ed. Guy Besse (Paris: Editions sociales, 1959), 71.

25. PAUL-HENRY T. d'HOLBACH, *Le Système de la nature*, ed. Yvon Belaval (Hildesheim; Olms, 1966), I, 131.

26. *Ibid.*, I, 196-97.

27. JULIEN OFFRAY DE LA METTRIE, *Traité de l'ame* in *Œuvres philosophiques* (Berlin, 1764), I, 75.

28. VOLTAIRE, *Traité de métaphysique*, in *Œuvres complètes*, ed. Moland (Paris, 1877-85), XXII, 215.

29. VOLTAIRE, *Le Philosophe ignorant*, ed. Moland, XXVI, 75.

30. GEORGES LOUIS LECLERC DE BUFFON, *Œuvres philosophiques*, ed. Jean Piveteau (Paris: PUF, 1954), 332.

31. DENESLE, *Examen*, 233 and 250.

32. ILHARAT DE LA CHAMBRE, *Abrégé*, I, 33.

33. *Ibid.*, I, 65-67.

34. ANTOINE C. RIVAROL, *De l'homme*, (Paris, 1800), 11.

35. PALMER, *Catholics and Unbelievers*, 103.

36. The best source of information about Lelarge de Lignac is F. LE GOFF, *De la philosophie de l'abbé de Lignac* (Paris: Hachette, 1863).

37. Abbé JOSEPH LELARGE DE LIGNAC: *Lettres à un Américain* (Hambourg, 1751), V, 15.

38. LIGNAC, *Elemens de métaphysique*, (Paris, 1753), 23 and 26.

39. LIGNAC, *Le Témoignage du sens intime et de l'expérience* (Auxerre, 1770), I, 39-40.

40. LIGNAC, *Témoignage*, I, 392.

41. LIGNAC, *Témoignage*, I, 103-04.

42. LIGNAC, *Suite des " Lettres à un Américain "* (Hambourg, 1756), 160; and *Elemens*, 103 and 404.

43. LIGNAC, *Examen sérieux et comique des discours sur l'Esprit* (Amsterdam, 1759), II, 337-8.

44. A.F.B. BOUREAU-DESLANDES, *Pygmalion ou la Statue animée* (London, 1741), 38.

45. ETIENNE BONNOT DE CONDILLAC, *La Logique*, II, 8 in *Œuvres*, II, 411.

46. See HERBERT DIECKMANN, " Condillac's Philosophical Works," *Review of Metaphysics*, VII (1953-54), 255-61; Emile Bréhier, *Histoire de la philosophie* (Paris: Alcan, 1934), II, 391; and LE ROY, Introduction to *Œuvres*, I, xxx-xxxi.

47. Raymond Lenoir, *Condillac* (Paris; Alcan, 1924), 129, n. 2.

48. R. Carré, " Sur la sensation condillacienne," *Proceedings of the Tenth International Congress of Philosophy* (Amsterdam, 1949), II, 1156-59.

49. Condillac, *Œuvres*, II, 553.

50. *Ibid.*, I, 238.

51. *Ibid.*, I, 313.

52. *Ibid.*, I, 342.

53. *Ibid.*, III, 143.

54. *Ibid.*, I, 239.

55. Bonnet, *Œuvres*, VI, xvi-xvii.

56. *Ibid.*, VI, 72.

57. *Ibid.*, VI, 3.

58. *Ibid.*, VI, 19.

59. *Ibid.*, VI, 23.

60. *Ibid.*, VI, 59.

61. D'Holbach, *Système*, I, 122.

62. *Ibid.*, II, 487.

63. D'Alembert, *Elemens* in *Mélanges*, IV, 61.

64. *Ibid.*, IV, 50-51 and 57-58.

65. *Encyclopédie*, I, 338, A.

66. Vernière, *Spinoza*, II, 586.

67. Le Père Hyacinthe S. Gerdil, *L'Immatérialité de l'âme démontrée contre Locke* (Turin, 1747), 45.

68. Pierre Bayle, " Leucippe," Note E, in *Dictionnaire Historique et critique*, 3e éd. (Rotterdam, 1720), II, 1702.

69. Buffon, *Œuvres*, 293.

70. *Ibid.*, 294.

71. Bonnet, *Méditations, Œuvres*, VIII, 388.

72. Buffon, *Œuvres*, 293.

73. Palmer, *Catholics and Unbelievers*, 35.

74. Denesle, *Examen*, I, 402.

75. Rivarol, *De l'homme*, 58.

76. Pierre Carlet Chamblain de Marivaux, *La Vie de Marianne*, ed. F. Deloffre (Paris: Garnier, 1963), 129.

77. Lignac, *Suite*, I, 83.

78. Lignac, *Elemens*, 239.

79. Lignac, *Examen*, II, 316.

80. Lignac, *Témoignage*, I, 63.

81. Lignac, *Témoignage*, II, 317-18.

82. Lignac, *Témoignage*, III, 330.

83. Condillac, *Traité des animaux, Œuvres*, I, 342.

84. Helvétius, *De l'homme* (London, 1776), 575.

85. *Ibid.*, 66.

86. Georges Poulet, *Les Métamorphoses du cercle* (Paris: Plon, 1961), ch. IV, " Le Dix-huitième Siècle."

87. Montesquieu, *Mes Pensées*, in *Œuvres complètes*, ed. Roger Caillois (Paris: NRF, 1949), I, 1544.

88. Robert Mauzi, *L'Idée du bonheur dans la littérature et la pensée française au XVIIIᵉ siècle*, 2nd ed., (Paris: Colin, 1965), 134; Montesquieu, *Mes Pensées, Œuvres complètes*, I, 1063 and 1137.

89. Montesquieu, *Mes Pensées, Œuvres complètes*, I, 1065.

90. D'Holbach, *Système*, I, 21, 25 and 96.

91. *Ibid.*, I, 372.

92. *Ibid.*, I, 441-2.

93. Bonnet, *Essai analytique, Œuvres*, VI, 340 and 342.

94. *Ibid.*, VI, 372.

95. *Ibid.*

96. Lignac, *Témoignage*, I, 76.

97. *Mémoires de Trévoux*, mai 1754, p. 1310.

98. Condillac, *Œuvres*, III, 41.

99. Pierre Samuel Dupont de Nemours, *La Philosophie de l'univers*, 3rd ed. (Paris, 1799), 162.

100. Buffon, *Œuvres*, 367.

101. Lignac, *Examen*, II, 366.

102. Bonnet, *Œuvres*, IV, Part I, 139.

103. Buffon, *Œuvres*, 328-29.

104. *Ibid.*, 298.

105. *Ibid.*, 343-44.

106. Bonnet, *Principes philosophiques, Œuvres*, VIII, 193.

107. *Ibid.*, 199.

108. Denesle, *Examen*, I, 384.

109. Rivarol, *De l'homme*, 175-76.

110. *Ibid.*, 121-22.

111. Lignac, *Elemens*, 30.

112. Lignac, *Témoignage*, I, 322.

113. Condillac, *Essai, Œuvres*, I, 46.

114. Pierre Joseph Boudier de Villemert, *L'Andrométrie ou examen philosophique de l'homme*, (Paris, 1753), 149.

115. Pernety, *Connoissance*, I, 38-9.

116. Pierre A.F. Choderlos de Laclos, *Les Liaisons dangereuses*, Lettre LXXXI.

117. Marivaux, *La Vie de Marianne*, 200.

118. Jean François de Saint-Lambert, *Essai sur la vie d'Helvétius*, in *Œuvres philosophiques* (Paris, 1797), V, 235.

119. Henri Peyre, *Literature and Sincerity* (New Haven: Yale Univ. Press, 1963), 62.

120. Montesquieu, *Eloge de la sincérité, Œuvres*, I, 99.

121. Montesquieu, *Mes Pensées, Œuvres*, I, 1008.

122. *Ibid.*, I, 1061.

123. Crocker, *Age of Crisis*, 424, 432-33, 436, 440.

124. Dom Deschamps, *Le Vrai Système*, ed. J. Thomas and F. Venturi (Genève: Droz, 1963), 132.

125. Marivaux, *La Vie de Marianne*, 86.

126. Boudier, *L'Andrométrie*, 46.

127. Condillac, *Traité des sensations*, I, iii, in *Œuvres*, I, 233.

128. CONDILLAC, *Traité des animaux*, II, v, in *Œuvres*, I, 363.

129. HELVÉTIUS, *De l'homme*, 538.

130. CROCKER, *Nature and Culture*, (Baltimore, Johns Hopkins, 1963), 153-54.

131. GRIMSLEY, *Jean d'Alembert*, 267.

Chapter IV

ROUSSEAU

1. PIERRE M. MASSON ed., *La Profession de foi du Vicaire Savoyard*, (Paris: Hachette, 1914), xxxix.

2. " Je me décidai pour toute ma vie sur tous les sentimens qu'il m'importait d'avoir " in *Rêveries, Œuvres complètes* (Paris, Pléiade), III, 1917 and " Depuis lors resté tranquille dans les principes que j'avois adoptés " in *Rêveries* O.C., Pléiade, III, 1018. References to this edition will be given in the text.

3. JEAN-JACQUES ROUSSEAU, *Œuvres complètes* (Paris: Hachette, 1873), III, 108. References to works not yet included in the Pléiade edition will be to this edition.

4. ROUSSEAU, *Lettre à M. de Beaumont*, O.C., Hachette, IIII, 64-65.

5. See the *Lettres morales* in *Correspondance générale*, ed. T. Dufour (Paris: Colin, 1925), III, 357.

6. See in particular CHARLES W. HENDEL, *Jean-Jacques Rousseau, moralist* (London: Oxford Univ. Press, 1934), 2 vols.

7. ROUSSEAU, *Profession de foi*, O.C., Hachette, II, 250, n.1.

8. ROUSSEAU, *Lettre à M. de Beaumont*, O.C., Hachette, III, 78-79.

9. This point of view is upheld by Basil Muntéano in " La Solitude de J.-J. Rousseau," *Annales Jean-Jacques Rousseau*, XXXI (1946-49), 164-65 and by Mark. J. Temmer, *Time in Rousseau and Kant* (Genève: Droz, 1958), 23.

10. PIERRE BURGELIN, *La Philosophie de l'existence de Jean-Jacques Rousseau*, (Paris: PUF, 1952), 7 and 39.

11. J.H. BROOME, *Rousseau, a study of his thought* (London: Arnold, 1963), 116.

12. PIERRE MAURICE MASSON, " Rousseau contre Helvétius," RHL, XVIII (1911), 103-124.

13. Discussion of B. Guyon's paper, " La Mémoire et l'oubli dans *La Nouvelle Héloïse*," *Annales Jean-Jacques Rousseau*, XXXV (1959-62), 65.

14. BURGELIN, *La Philosophie de l'existence*, 251.

15. See BURGELIN, *La Philosophie de l'existence*, 485-488.

16. LIONEL GOSSMAN, " Time and history in Rousseau," SVEC, XXX (1964), 341.

17. HORACE B. ENGLISH and AVA C. ENGLISH, *A Comprehensive Dictionary of Psychological and Psychoanalytical Terms*, (New York: Longmans, Green, 1958).

18. CALVIN S. HALL and GARDNER LINDZEY, *Theories of Personality* (N.Y.: Wiley, 1957), 468.

19. ROUSSEAU, *Correspondance générale*, ed. T. Dufour, III, 354.

20. This is the position of George Herbert Mead, *Mind, Self and Society* (Chicago, 1934). An analysis of Mead's work is given in Hall and Lindzey, *Theories*, 474.

21. ROBERT RICATTE, *Réflexions sur les Rêveries* (Paris: Corti, 1960), 70.

22. BASIL MUNTÉANO, " La Solitude de Jean-Jacques Rousseau," *Annales J.-J. Rousseau*, XXXI (1946-49), 79-168 and " Les Contradictions de J.-J. Rousseau," in Comité national pour la commémoration de J.-J. Rousseau, *Jean-Jacques Rousseau et son œuvre*, (Paris, Klincksieck, 1964), 95-112.

23. RONALD GRISMLEY, *Jean-Jacques Rousseau, a study in self-awareness* (Cardiff: U. of Wales, 1961), 320.

24. *Ibid.*, 280.

25. PIERRE GROSCLAUDE, " Le Moi, l'instant présent et le sentiment de l'existence," *Europe*, no. 391-392 (1961), 55.

26. In *Emile* [O.C., Hachette, I, 15] and *Du Contrat social* [O.C., Pléiade, III, 381].

27. This attitude is particularly noticeable in the opening paragraph of the *Première Promenade* and again in the unfinished *Dixième Promenade*.

28. JEAN STAROBINSKI, *Jean-Jacques Rousseau, la transparence et l'obstacle* (Paris: Plon, 1958), 9.

29. O.C., Hachette, III, 8. This is obviously the passage Rousseau had in mind in the *Histoire du précédent écrit:* " Un passage de l'*Emile* que je me rappelai me fit rentrer en moi-même et m'y fit trouver ce que j'avois cherché vainement au dehors. Quel mal t'a fait ce complot? Que t'a-t-il ôté de toi? Quel membre t'a-t-il mutilé? Quel crime t'a-t-il fait commettre? " [O.C., Pléiade, I, 985].

30. *Correspondance générale*, III, 361.

31. GRIMSLEY, *Jean-Jacques Rousseau*, 148.

32. STAROBINSKI, *Jean-Jacques Rousseau*, 225.

33. BURGELIN, *La Philosophie de l'existence*, 225 and 125.

34. ROBERT OSMONT, " Contribution à l'étude psychologique des *Rêveries d'un promeneur solitaire*," *Annales J.-J. Rousseau*, XXIII (1934), 7-135.

35. This distinction is made by Muntéano, " Solitude," *Annales J.-J. Rousseau*, XXXI (1944-49), 156-58.

36. GRIMSLEY, *Jean-Jacques Rousseau*, 315.

37. Modern bio-chemists are finding evidence which points to the fact that the brain is the storehouse of all experience and that under certain stimuli past experiences can be totally recreated while the individual remains conscious of the present. Thus even those supposedly pre-conscious events can be brought into the sphere of consciousness and utilized by the individual. So far, however, no one has come up with an authentic case of pre-natal recall! A popular account of these developments is given in Isaac Asimov, " Pills to Help Us Remember? " *New York Times Magazine*, Oct. 9, 1966.

38. Discussion of Henri Gouhier, " Ce que le Vicaire doit à Descartes," *Annales J.-J. Rousseau*, XXXV, (1959-62), 158.

39. MAUZI, *L'Idée du bonheur*, 296.

40. GOSSMAN, " Time," SVEC, XXX (1964), 315.

41. TEMMER, *Time*, 8-9.

42. GRIMSLEY, *Jean-Jacques Rousseau*, 278.

Chapter V

DIDEROT

1. DENIS DIDEROT, *Correspondance*, ed. Georges Roth (Paris: Editions de Minuit, 1955), II, 207.

2. DENIS DIDEROT, *Œuvres complètes*, ed. Assézat-Tourneux (Paris: Garnier, 1875-77), III. 210. All future references to this edition will be indicated in the text by A.-T.

3. IAN W. ALEXANDER, " Philosophy of Organism and philosophy of consciousness in Diderot's speculative thought," in Victoria University of Manchester, *Studies in Romance Philology and French Literature presented to John Orr* (Manchester Univ. Press, 1953), 2.

4. DENIS DIDEROT, *Œuvres philosophiques*, ed. Paul Vernière (Paris: Garnier, 1956), 289. All future references to this edition will be indicated in the text by *O. phil.*, Garnier.

5. *Correspondance*, VI, 376.

6. FRANÇOIS HEMSTERHUIS, *Lettre sur l'homme et ses rapports* avec le commentaire inédit de Diderot, ed. Georges May (New Haven: Yale Univ. Press, 1964), 337.

7. Commentary on Hemsterhuis, 131.

8. See the article by GEORGE NORMAN LAIDLAW, " Diderot's Teratology," *Diderot Studies*, IV (1963), 105-29.

9. Commentary on Hemsterhuis, 159.

10. ALEXANDER, " Philosophy of Organism," 13-14.

11. *Encyclopédie*, IV, 784 A.

12. DENIS DIDEROT, *Salons*, ed. Jean Seznec et Jean Adhémar (Oxford: Clarendon, 1957-67), III, 139.

13. ALEXANDER, " Philosophy of Organism," 19.

14. DENIS DIDEROT, *Œuvres esthétiques*, ed. Paul Vernière (Paris: Garnier, 1959), 782. All future references to this edition will be indicated in the text by *O. esth.*, Garnier.

15. A. BOUTET DE MONVEL, " Diderot et la notion du style," RHL, LI (1951), 298.

16. *Salons*, III, 195.

17. Since I have treated Diderot's ethical thought at some length in two articles, I shall not repeat all my arguments. See Jean A. Perkins, " Diderot and La Mettrie," SVEC, X (1959), 49-100 and " Diderot's Concept of Virtue, " SVEC, XXIII (1963), 77-91.

18. Commentary on Hemsterhuis, 243.

19. ALEXANDER, " Philosophy of Organism," 19.

20. DENIS DIDEROT, *Œuvres romanesques*, ed. Henri Benac (Paris: Garnier, 1951), 574. All future references to this edition will be indicated in the text by *O. rom.*, Garnier.

21. See JACQUES CHOUILLET, " Le Mythe d'Ariste ou Diderot en face de lui-même," RHL, LXIV (1964), 565-88, and Ronald Grimsley, " Psychological Aspects of *Le Neveu de Rameau*," MLQ, XVI (1955), 195-209.

22. GRIMSLEY, " Psychological Aspects," 197, n. 5.

23. *Salons*, III, 141.

24. ROUSSEAU, *Rêveries*, O.C., Pléiade, I, 995.

25. GRIMSLEY, " Psychological Aspects," 197.

26. M. B. FINCH and E. ALLISON PEERS, *The Origins of French Romanticism* (New York: Dutton, n.d.), 4.

27. LESTER CROCKER, " *Le Neveu de Rameau*, une expérience morale," CAIEF, no. 13 (1961), 144.

28. CHOUILLET, " Ariste," 571.

29. *Correspondance*, V, 228.

30. ROLAND MORTIER, " L''Original' selon Diderot," *Saggi e ricerche di letteratura francese*, IV (1963), 148.

31. CROCKER, " Le Neveu de Rameau," 150.

32. *Correspondance*, I, 76.

CONCLUSION

1. PALMER, *Catholics and Unbelievers*, 131.

2. ROBERT MAUZI, " Les Maladies de l'âme au XVIIIe siècle," RSH, no. 100 (1960), 459.

3. MAUZI, *L'Idée du bonheur*, 13.

4. *Ibid.*, 23.

5. *Ibid.*, 23.

6. STAROBINSKI, *Jean-Jacques Rousseau, la transparence et l'obstacle*.

7. TEMMER, *Time in Rousseau and Kant*, 60.

8. ALEXANDER, " Philosophy of Organism," 1.

DATE DUE

JAN 02 2006

GAYLORD   PRINTED IN U.S.A.